PROJECT MANAGEMENT

Second Edition

PROJECT MANAGEMENT

Planning and Control

Second Edition

Rory Burke

JOHN WILEY & SONS

Chichester · New York · Brisbane · Toronto · Singapore

Previously published 1990, second edition 1992, by
Management Press, PO Box 2241, Fish Hoek 7975, Cape Town, South Africa

Reprinted with corrections 1993 by John Wiley & Sons Ltd,
Baffins Lane, Chichester,
West Sussex PO19 1UD, England

Reprinted September 1994, April and October 1995, May 1996

Other Wiley Editorial Offices

John Wiley & Sons, Inc., 605 Third Avenue,
New York, NY 10158-0012, USA

Jacaranda Wiley Ltd, 33 Park Road, Milton,
Queensland 4064, Australia

John Wiley & Sons (Canada) Ltd, 22 Worcester Road,
Rexdale, Ontario M9W 1L1, Canada

John Wiley & Sons (SEA) Pte Ltd, 37 Jalan Pemimpin #05-04,
Block B, Union Industrial Building, Singapore 2057

British Library Cataloguing in Publication Data

A catalogue record for this book is available from the British Library
ISBN 0-471-94272-3 (paper)

Bodytext set in Times Roman 11/12pt, headers & footers in Helvetica Bold, subheadings in
Helvetica Bold 11pt, figure captions in Times Roman 11pt Bold.

Printed and bound in Great Britain by Redwood Books, Trowbridge, Wiltshire.

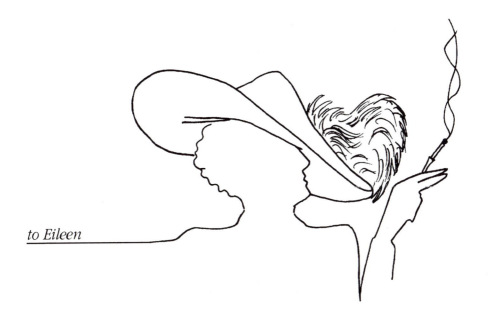

to Eileen

Contents

CONTENTS

CONTENTS

Foreword

I must say I was rather chuffed when Rory asked me to write a foreword to his second edition - then I had second thoughts. I realised that Rory is my cousin and therefore could get me cheaper than Bush, or Major, or even Joan Collins. Also I am a broadcaster by profession - speech comes easily but writing is a chore to me. The odds were moving towards a sneaky opt-out on my part when I was struck by a remarkable coincidence. Now you'll have to pay attention to this.

Rory's father was my first cousin on my mother's side. My father had a first cousin called James who also wrote books - so here I am - the exact fulcrum in the balance between James Joyce and Rory Burke. Such a unique literary position is not granted to many.

Now there are of course differences between the two authors. Rory's work for instance has never been banned. Perhaps if he were to adopt a racier style this accolade might come his way. On a scale of incomprehensibility I would rate Rory somewhere between Ulysses and Finnegan's Wake, but then Project Management is a subject in which I am blissfully innocent. I saw the film of Ulysses before I took up the book and will look forward to seeing the video version of Rory's book - and if there is a part in it for Arnold Schwarzenegger as the Project Manager so much the better.

Even though I have not read this book I most strongly urge you to buy a copy. You see Rory has promised to buy me dinner when the first thousand copied are sold. And I'm getting hungry.

Val Joyce, B.Comm, N.U.I.
Dublin

Preface to the Second Edition

Here is a comprehensive, step-by-step educational guide for the manager who wants to build a successful career in Project Management. As projects grow in size and complexity, the ability to plan and control them becomes an essential Project Management function. The second edition of **Project Management Planning and Control**, introduces the reader to the latest planning and control techniques, through many worked examples and practical exercises. Updated topics include:

*   Work Breakdown Structure
*   Critical Path Method
*   Resource Management
*   Cost Management
*   Earned Value

New topics include:

Scope Management: This chapter uses the Project Management Institute's (PMI) body of knowledge as the framework for development. Scope management is used to not only define the content of the project, but also outline how it will be managed.

Planning for Project Management: Feedback from lecturers requested that this chapter be introduced to expand the content of the book to include; Organisational Structures, Human Factors and Quality Management.

Computerized Project Management: A book on planning and control today would not be complete without a chapter on computer applications. This chapter establishes guidelines for hardware and software selection, together with their subsequent implementation into the information and control system.

Project planning software will certainly help the project manager to plan and control projects, but only if the principles and techniques of project planning are understood. The framework of this text has been designed to give the reader a good understanding of the manual side of these computerized techniques and calculations.

This book is used by many business schools, offering short courses on project management, as their course material. Feedback from such courses helped to develop the structure of this text. Thus, ensuring that the information is presented in a logical sequence and incorporating plenty of worked examples to aid the manager's learning.

Acknowledgements

I have derived considerable benefit and ideas from lecturers, students, consultants and practitioners willing to argue and discuss the commercial applications of project management. Writing this book was a team effort, many people provided support and encouragement, I particularly wish to thank:

Proof reading the content: Gwynne Foster, Chris Naude and Mark Massyn.

Proof reading the grammar and spell checking: Sandra Buchanan, Linda Logan, David and Margaret Whitton, Deirdre Burke and Patrick Burke (family contribution).

Cover design: Ken Green

Sketches: Ingrid Franzsen.

Diagrams: Natalie Van Zyl, Chris Naude and Leslie Willmers.

Dedication: Sandra Buchanan.

Foreword: Particular thanks to my cousin Val Joyce.

Typesetting: Leslie Willmers.

Publishing: Tony Shapiro.

The book was compiled on an IBM Clone, using Wordperfect, Lotus and Harvard Graphics for the draft copy. Final reproduction used CorelDRAW! and Pagemaker.

Rory Burke

Chapter 1

Introduction to
Project Management

Project management is a specialized management technique to plan and control projects under a strong single point of responsibility. The purpose of this chapter is to give the reader a basic outline of the history of project management planning and control techniques and where their application is most effective.

A project is generally deemed successful if it meets pre-determined targets set by the client, performs the job it was intended to do, or solves an identified problem within predetermined time, cost and quality constraints. To meet these targets the project manager uses project management systems to effectively plan and control the project.

Many of the project planning and control techniques currently in use, for example, Critical Path Method (CPM) and Program Evaluation and Review Technique (PERT), were developed to address the needs of large complex capital projects. Since then these applications, which are often client motivated, have become more pervasive.

The purpose of this text is to present the underlying principles and techniques of project planning and control as used in the industrial and commercial environment. The text will clearly outline the conditions under which project planning and control techniques provide a real solution.

1.1 History of Project Management

The history of large projects is often referred back as far as the construction of the Egyptian Pyramids and Great Wall of China. They were certainly large and complex structures, built to high standards, which must have liquidated vast amounts of resources. Unfortunately, there is no documented evidence of any project management systems and the management techniques used can thus only be based on conjecture.

In the text we shall restrict the historical investigation to the more recent developments in project management systems for example the Gantt chart, PERT and CPM.

1.2 The Gantt Chart

The history of project planning techniques can be accurately traced back to World War 1 when an American, Henry Gantt, designed the barchart as a visual aid for planning and controlling his projects. In recognition, planning barcharts are often called after his name. The Handbook of Industrial Engineers 1982, p 11 acknowledges the Gantt chart for significantly reducing the time to build cargo ships during World War 1.

Figure 1 indicates the format of a Gantt barchart, where the top and base are a calendar time-scale in days [1] and the activities [2] are listed on the left. The scheduling of each activity is represented by a horizontal line [3], from the activity's start to finish date. The length of the activity line is proportional to its estimated duration.

Once the project has started the Gantt chart can further be used as a tool for project control. This is achieved by drawing a second line under the planned schedule to indicate activity progress [4]. The relative position of the progress line to the planned line indicates percentage complete and remaining duration, while the relative position between the progress line and Timenow [5] indicates actual progress against planned progress.

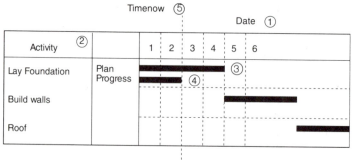

Figure: 1. Gantt chart

The benefits of the Gantt chart can be clearly seen, not only are the calculations simple but it combines all the above information on one page.

1.3 Network Diagrams

For a project plan to be effective it must equally address the parameters of activity time and network logic. As projects became larger and more complex, the Gantt chart was found to be lacking as a planning and control tool because it could not indicate the logical relationships between activities. This logical relationship is required to model the effect schedule variance will have down stream in the project.

In the 1950's feedback from industry and commerce indicated that project cost and time overruns were all too common. It was suggested at the time that the project estimates were on the optimistic side in order to gain work. However, a more important reason emerged which indicated that the planning and control techniques, available to manage large complex projects, were inadequate.

With these short comings in mind, network planning techniques were developed by Flagle, the US Navy and Remington Rand Univac. Flagle wrote a paper in 1956 on "Probability based tolerances in forecasting and planning". Although it was not published in the Journal of Industrial Engineers until April 1961, it was in a sense the forerunner of the US Navy's Program Evaluation and Review Technique (PERT). Both PERT and Remington Rand Univac's Critical Path Method (CPM) used a similar network format, where the activities are presented in boxes and the sequence of the activities from left to right show the logic of the project.

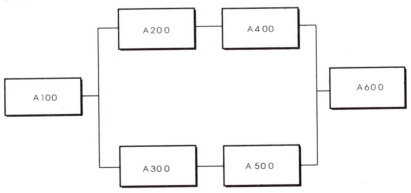

Figure: 2. Network Diagram

1.4 Activity Durations

The main difference between PERT and CPM was how they addressed activity time durations. The accuracy of an activity's time estimate usually depends on the information available from previous projects. If an activity has been performed before, its duration should be accurately predicted. However, activities with a new scope of work, which are difficult to measure or dependent on other uncertain variables, may have a range of possible time durations.

CPM uses a deterministic approach, which suits a project whose time durations can be accurately predicted, e.g. a construction project. PERT on the other hand uses a probabilistic approach, which suits a project whose time durations may vary over a range of possibilities, e.g. a research project.

1.5 Program Evaluation and Review Technique (PERT)

The US Navy set up a development team with the Lockheed Aircraft Corporation, and a management consultant Booz Allen & Hamilton, to design PERT as an integrated planning and control system to manage their Polaris Submarine project.

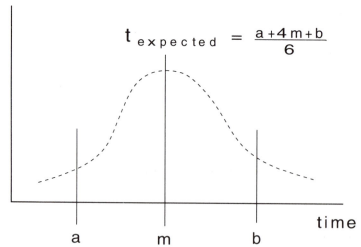

$$t_{expected} = \frac{a + 4m + b}{6}$$

Figure: 3. PERT Three Time Probabilistic Analysis

The PERT technique was developed to apply a statistical treatment to the possible range of activity time durations. A three time probabilistic model was developed, using pessimistic, optimistic and most likely time durations. The three times were imposed on a normal distribution to calculate the activity's expected time.

The success of the Polaris Submarine project helped to establish PERT in the 1960's as a planning tool within many large corporations. There were, however, a number of basic problems which reduced PERT's effectiveness and eventually led to its fall from popularity. These included:

* Statistical analysis was not generally understood by project managers.

* Computer technology limitations; batch card input, and systems were not interactive and had a slow response.

PERT is currently enjoying a renaissance as a tool to address risk management. The software package Cobra, for example, uses the PERT technique to process cost data as a front end to Open Plan's CPM structure.

AND WHAT AM I SUPPOSE TO REMEMBER?

1.6 Critical Path Method (CPM)

The Critical Path Method (CPM) was developed in 1957 by Remington Rand Univac as a management tool to improve the planning and control of a construction project to build a processing plant for the Du Pont Corporation.

CPM was initially set-up to address the time cost trade-off dilemma often presented to project managers, where there is a complex relationship between project time to complete and cost to complete. CPM enables the planner to model the effect various project time cycles have on direct and indirect costs. Shortening the project duration will reduce indirect costs, but may increase the direct costs. This technique is often called project crashing or acceleration, see the project validating chapter.

The initial growth of CPM in the industrial market was slow, this was partially due to the lack of project management education and CPM training offered at the time by the universities and colleges.

Also, as with the PERT application, the computer hardware and software facilities were limited compared with the personal computer of today. Further, the systems were not interactive, they required a batch card input through a hands-off data processing department, which often led to an inherently slow response.

The early differences between CPM and PERT have largely disappeared and it is now common to use the two terms interchangeably as a generic name to include the whole planning and control process.

1.7 ADM or PDM that is the Question

There are two basic networking techniques called:

*   Arrow Diagram Method (ADM), also called
    Network-On-Arrow, See figure 4.

*   Precedence Diagram Method (PDM), See figure 2.

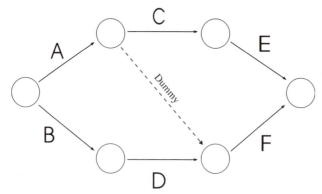

Figure: 4. Arrow Diagram Method (ADM)

The basic difference between the two network diagrams is that with ADM the activity information is written on the arrow or relational link, while in PDM the activity information is positioned in the node or box. After carrying out the activity calculations, both methods will produce exactly the same result.

There are many practitioners who swear by their preference whether it be ADM or PDM. To be fair, both techniques have their benefits, listed here without prejudice are a few of them:

For ADM: The activity (i, j) identification indicates the preceding and succeeding activities, when walking through a large network this can be very useful. However, it does mean when an activity is inserted its neighbouring activities numbers will change. Whereas with PDM inserting an activity only requires the logical links to be modified.

For PDM: PDM offers a number of logical relationships between the activities, such as Start-to-Start, Finish-to-Finish and lag. This over comes the ADM need for dummy activities, see figure 4. The PDM also offers a professional presentation with a more structured format than ADM.

Noting the market trends PDM has now established itself as the most popular planning technique, especially since the recently introduced project management software have adopted PDM as their standard. The techniques of PDM will be developed in the CPM chapter.

1.8 Project Management Software

Today, powerful but inexpensive project management software is readily available for the personal computer. This availability has essentially moved project management computing away from the data processing department to the desk of the project manager. This represents a major shift in the management of information.

Whilst project planning software will certainly help the project manager to plan and control projects, its application will only be effective if the techniques and principles of project planning are clearly understood. The framework of this text has been designed to give the reader a practical outline of the calculations and algorithms used by the planning software.

Although the project planning software can offer a wide range of facilities it cannot make on-the-job management decisions. It will, however, speed up the processing of large amounts of data, which should give the project manager more time to concentrate on managing the project.

1.9 Definition of a Project

In order to define project management we first need to explain what is understood by the term **project**. Any of the following examples may be considered to be a project:

* The transition period during which a change occurs.

* Designing and constructing a house.

* Designing and testing a new prototype (car).

* The launch of a new product.

* Implementing a new system, which could be an information and control system, or a new organizational structure.

* Improving productivity within a target period.

* Management audit.

Other features of a project include:-

*   A life cycle.

*   A start and finish date.

*   A budget.

*   Activities that are essentially unique and non-repetitive.

*   Consumption of resources, which may be from different departments
        and need co-ordinating.

*   A single point of responsibility.

*   Team roles and relationships that are subject to change and need to be
        developed, defined and established.

Having identified some of the main components of a project, we can now define
a project as:

> **A group of activities that have to be performed in a logical
> sequence to meet preset objectives outlined by the client.**

1.10 Definition of Project Management

The definition of project management may be simply stated as:

> **Making the project happen.**

To put project management into perspective consider this brief description of
project management with two other common types of management.

Project Management   The product is sub-divided into work packages, ie.
                          fabrication, repairs, maintenance and jobbing.

Production Management   The product moves along a production line in
                          batches, ie. car production.

Process Management   The product flows along a process line ie. chemical
                          plant processing petrol from crude oil.

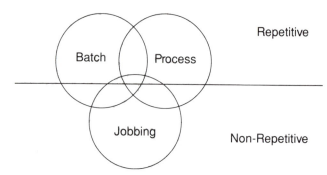

Figure: 5. Indicates three different types of management

The figure shows how the three basic management types inter-link. Consider the manufacture of a steel ship. This has all the characteristics of a project, requiring project management but it would also require production and process management.

Sections of the hull could be manufactured using production management techniques. Instead of identifying every bracket and steel plate as an activity, they would be grouped together into batches. It is obviously more efficient to set-up a production line to manufacture a 100 brackets than to make each one individually.

Process management would be used in the paint shop where steel sections, grit and paint flow through a machine to produce the steel plates ready for fabrication. Similarly both production and process lines would use project management techniques for the initial setup, repairs and maintenance.

The need for project management techniques has grown out of the management of complex projects, where project management systems are required to plan and keep control of the project. The **complexity** of the project may be caused by:

* The speed of the project (fast tracking), giving rise to multi-faceted decision-making within a dynamic environment.

* The number of different departments and sub-contractors that need co-ordinating.

* The limited availability of key resources.

* The high level of innovation.

* More sophisticated communications.

* High volumes of data (Information overload).

Project management may also be defined as a way of developing structure into a complex situation, where the independent variables of time, cost, resources and human behaviour come together. Effective planning and control of projects requires a panoramic view, logical thinking, a feel for detail, good communication skills and a commitment to meet the challenge to make it happen.

1.11 The Project Life Cycle

A project passes through a number of distinct phases or stages, from project conception, through project execution to project completion. These phases are known collectively as the ''Project Life Cycle''.

The project life cycle is presented as a line graph with the level of effort (usually measured in manhours) plotted against time, see figure 6. The typical life cycle profile shows the level of effort starting from a low base, building-up slowly to a peak then declining to completion and termination.

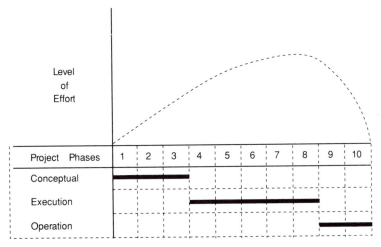

Figure: 6. Project Life Cycle

There are, however, many variations on the theme of project phases, influenced by the project's scope of work. The project phases selected in the examples here are arbitrary and serve only to illustrate the technique for different types of projects. The main features to look for are the key issues, key activities, limiting factors, decisions and hold points in each phase.

The project life cycle is conveniently represented by a barchart which clearly indicates the duration of each phase and its overlap (if any) with the other phases.

1.11.1 Project Life Cycle: House Project

The construction of a house provides a project many of us have personally experienced. Consider here the following simple sub-division into four phases.

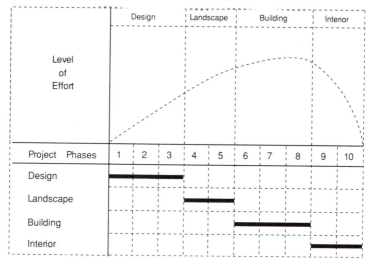

Figure: 7. Project Life Cycle, House Project.

The level of effort follows the typical life cycle profile by increasing to a maximum during the building phase before declining during the interior phase.

1.11.2 Project Life Cycle: Computer Installation

With the improved cost effectiveness of computer facilities most companies will experience a computer installation project sooner or later.

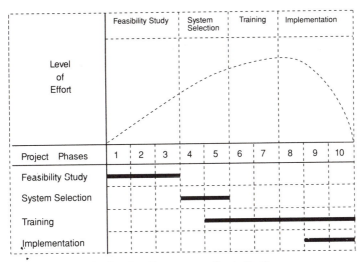

Figure: 8. Project Life Cycle, Computer Installation.

Note here the training phase overlaps with both system selection and the implementation phase.

1.11.3 Project Life Cycle: Engineering Project

An engineering type project is a popular example to illustrate the project phases.

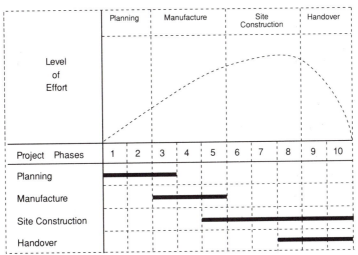

Figure: 9. Project Life Cycle, Engineering Project.

Note here that all the phases overlap which could indicate a fast tracking situation.

1.11.4 Project Life Cycle: Nuclear Power Station Project

This project may well span 50 years with the people involved in the initial phases being retired long before the final phase.

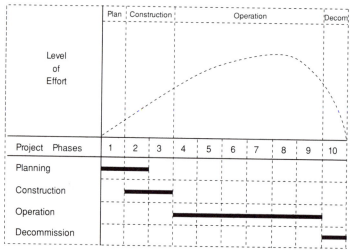

Figure: 10. Project Life Cycle, Nuclear Power Station

The interesting point here is that the environmental constraints will have changed significantly over the fifty years between the design phase and the decommissioning phase.

1.12 Management by Objectives (MBO)

The Management by Objectives (MBO) technique assigns responsibility for the completion of achievable objectives. These objectives will be defined by the project manager as part of the planning and control system. The monitoring of these objectives can be effectively controlled using **management by results**.

An objective within the project management sphere may be defined in terms of the three main parameters: time, cost and quality.

* Time with respect to project start and finish dates.

* Cost with respect to cash flow and the project budget.

* Quality with respect to pre-defined standards and specifications laid down by the client or classification society.

The overall objective is to complete the project within the time, cost and quality constraints set by the client. To achieve this the project manager must sub-divide the client's scope of work into a list of project activities with associated objectives.

The objectives associated with these activities can now be clearly identified and communicated to the responsible parties. The use of graphics (barcharts, networks) will greatly assist the dissemination process.

The triangle of forces is often used to graphically outline the trade-off between the main parameters of time, cost and quality, where:

Time: If the emphasis is on time, the completion date will be the dominant factor. For example, the refurbishment of a hotel would be time influenced if it had to meet the holiday season.

On a fixed price project the client will focus his attention on the contractors performance against a declared schedule.

Cost: When cost is the main consideration, contracts are awarded to the lowest bidder.

If the contractor trades cost in preference to schedule at the beginning of the project, this preference could be later reversed when time penalties rear their ugly head.

Quality: In high technology projects quality requirements often have priority over time and cost.

The quality requirement is usually defined in the contract and therefore not negotiable without a scope change.

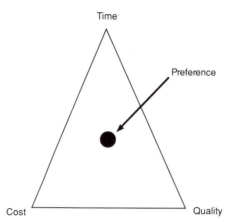

Figure: 11. The Triangle of Objectives

This simple model does not consider any external influences which could impose further constraints on the project e.g. Government laws and regulations, or the increasing influence of the environmentalist and the green lobby.

1.13 Management by Exception (MBE)

To supplement the Management by Objectives approach there is another management technique called Management by Exception (MBE). The Management by Exception technique focuses the manager's attention on the activities that have gone off course and need to be controlled to ensure the activities will meet their objectives.

The MBE technique uses a filter to select the non-conforming activities. When projects have a 100 or more activities the project manager cannot effectively monitor all of them.

MBE addresses this problem by enabling the project manager to set the threshold limits for the exception reports. This could be, for example, the critical activities and any other activities that are running late, over budget or not meeting the required specification.

1.14 The Legal Aspects of CPM

The critical path, besides offering a planning and control tool, can also impose a legal time framework for the project. The critical path defines the series of activities that determine the duration of the project. Should any of the critical activities be delayed this will extend the completion date of the project. Project delays invariably result in financial implications to both the client and the contractor:

* If the client is responsible for delaying critical activities then the contractor should be legally entitled to an extension of time and compensation.

* If the contractor is late completing the project due to poor workmanship and ineffective management, then the client should be entitled to impose financial penalties as stipulated in the contract.

Delays to activities on the critical path usually result in claims. Hence it is of great importance for both the client and contractor to agree on the critical activities at the outset of the project.

1.15 Benefits of a Project Planning and Control System

One of the main responsibilities of the project manager is to plan, track and control the project to meet preset objectives. To do this effectively the project manager requires accurate and timely information. This information should be supplied by the project's planning and control system, which outlines the scope of work and measures performance against the original plan.

Companies sometimes resist using project planning and control techniques because of the additional management cost. However, it should be appreciated that lack of information could be even more expensive if it leads to poor management decisions. Listed below are some of the main advantages associated with a fully integrated project planning and control system:

* **Estimating**: The performance of the current project will form the estimating data base for future projects. If this data is not collected by the planning and control system it may be lost forever.

* **CPM**: Critical Path Method (CPM) forces the managers to think about planning in a structured manner, the critical activities give a guide to the level of detail. The CPM presentation offers a tool for discussion with the other managers.

* **Quality vs Quantity**: Too much data but insufficient information may be generated on a regular basis if the reports are not structured and summarised. CPM and MBE can be used to provide focused information.

* **Project / Corporate System Integration**: The planning and control system can provide the link between the project and corporate reporting systems. Without this link double processing may be necessary to satisfy the information needs of both systems.

* **Response Time**: Timely response on project performance is essential for effective project control. The planning and control system can adjust the feedback to address the needs of the project. However, the corporate systems like the accounts department are set in a monthly reporting cycle where feedback on invoices, for example, may be 4 to 6 weeks behind Timenow.

* **Reporting Interfaces**: The planning and control system's data base can be structured around the Work Breakdown Structure (WBS) for project reporting and around the Organization Breakdown Structure (OBS) for corporate reporting. Without this integrated system the two reporting requirements would have to be processed separately.

* **Trends**: Projects are best controlled by monitoring the progress trends of time, cost and performance. This information may not be available to the project manager if the trend parameters are derived from a number of functional sources.

* **Data Capture**: If the project progress reporting is based on information supplied by the functional departments, the project manager cannot control the accuracy of this information. The problem here is that it may only become obvious that the reporting is inaccurate towards the end of the project, when it could be too late to bring the project back on course to meet its objectives.

* **Responsibility**: If the project manager is to be held as the single point of responsibility his authority should be commensurate with this position. Therefore when the project manager accepts this responsibility, he needs authority over the supply of project information.

* **Cost of Mistakes**: To implement a fully integrated project management system will certainly increase the project office budget. However, without an effective planning and control system the cost of mistakes due to lack of adequate control, may be even higher.

* **Procedures**: The planning and control system enables the project manager to develop procedures and work instructions tailored to the specific needs of the project.

* **Client**: The project manager is the project's single point of responsibility and the company's representative to the client. When holding meetings with the client the planning and control system will provide information about every aspect of the project.

The above points outline the benefits of an independent project management planning and control system to give the project manager the best opportunity to effectively plan, monitor and control the project. Unfortunately it is not always possible to substantiate these benefits financially as many of them like good customer service are intangible.

1.16 Summary

In this chapter we have discussed the history of project management techniques, from the first planning and control systems developed by Henry Gantt, to the more recent development in planning software techniques using PERT and CPM.

A project was defined as a group of activities that have to be performed in a logical sequence to meet preset objectives set by the client. While project management was defined as a way of making this happen, the difference between project management and the other forms of management was also discussed.

The project life cycle approach indicated how the phases of a project can be graphically presented for different types of projects. Management by Objectives and Management by Exception were introduced as two useful management techniques to establish objectives and make them happen.

The legal aspects of the critical path were introduced as a framework for monitoring progress and making claims. Finally the benefits of a planning and control system were outlined as a checklist to support the argument for its implementation.

Chapter 2

Project Selection

This chapter on project selection will outline a framework for evaluating and ranking prospective projects using numeric and non-numeric methods.

The selection of the right project for future investment is crucial for the long-term survival of the company. The selection of the wrong project may well precipitate project failure, some of the well known failures include Rolls Royce's development of the RB111 carbon fibre turbine blades which put the company into liquidation and the Anglo-French Concorde which cost the sponsoring tax payers billions.

Project selection is ultimately the responsibility of senior management, who's decision should be based informative data. This chapter will outline a number of selection methods to prepare numeric and non-numeric models.

These selection models will enable management to:

* Ensure the project will meet company goals and objectives.

* Rank mutually exclusive projects.

Although project selection from an investment point of view is usually based solely on financial considerations this chapter will develop a number of non-numeric and scoring models to offer a wider portfolio of project selection techniques.

Where two or more projects are given an equal ranking by the investment appraisal techniques, sensitivity analysis should be employed as a further selection criteria to determine each project's response to given situations.

The selection appraisal techniques outlined in this chapter will be appropriate for considering any of the following type of projects:

* In the construction environment investment appraisal is often used by clients to determine whether they should go for a new building or refurbish an old one.

* The selection between two or more machines for a production line, each with different costs, production rates, maintenance and life span.

* A company may wish to invest in the organization's information system, which could affect not only the organization structure, but also data processing and human factors. The pay-off for all these different types of investment might be increased sales, increased productivity or greater efficiency and effectiveness.

* A road freight company selecting trucks and trailers.

* A construction company deciding which project to bid on.

* A hospital selecting the best mix of facilities to offer.

* A university selecting new courses and deciding what technology to offer.

* A company deciding which production repair, maintenance or up-grade to authorize.

While the project manager often enters the scene after the project has been selected or even started, in many situations the project manager is the person who has lobbied for selection.

Project selection is obviously influenced by the state of the economy, during a down turn it may be argued that most companies will take on any work that keeps them going in the short term.

2.1 Model Selection

There are two basic types of project selection models used to represent a project's structure, namely numeric and non-numeric. A numeric model is usually financially based and quantifies the project in terms of either percentage return on investment, or time to repay the investment. While non-numeric models on the other hand look at a much wider picture of the project considering items from market share to environmental issues.

The main purpose of these models is to aid decision-making. They are not an end in themselves, as they cannot make decisions on their own. The limitations of a model should be appreciated, because models are only a prediction of what could happen and are as accurate as the data they are based on.

When choosing a selection model, **Souder** suggests a number of points to consider. The key words were; realism, capability, ease of use, flexibility and low cost. But most importantly the model must evaluate projects by how well they meet company goals and objectives.

The first step then is to determine a framework for quantifying company goals and objectives. The following sub-headings indicate the type of questions to ask:

* Will the project maximize profits ?

* Will the project maintain market share, increase market share or consolidate market position ?

* Will the project enable the company to enter new markets ?

* Will the project maximise the utilisation of the workforce?

* Will the project maximise the utilisation of plant and equipment ?

* Will the project improve the company image ?

* Is the project's risk and uncertainty acceptable ?

* Is the project's scope consistent with company expertise ?

This list can be developed further by weighting the evaluation items. The weighting indicates the value of the contribution to the company's goals and objectives. With a numeric value for each project, the projects can be ranked in line with their contribution to the success of the organization.

The relationship between a project's expected results and the company's goals, needs to be understood. In general the kind of information required may be quantified under the following headings as developed by **Meredith** p.38:

* Production
* Marketing
* Financial
* Personnel
* Administration

Consider a project to introduce a new computerised information and control system to replace an existing manual system. For this exercise the system is intended for both in-house and consultancy service.

Production considerations:

1. Method of implementation.
2. Time to be up and running.
3. Period of disruption.
4. Learning curve, time until the product is saleable.
5. Amount of double processing and waste.
6. Cost of power requirements.
7. Interfacing equipment required.
8. Safety of system.
9. Other applications of system.
10. Extent of outside consultants required.

Marketing considerations:

1. Number of potential users.
2. Market share of output.
3. Time to achieve proposed market share.
4. Impact on current system.
5. Ability to control quality of information.
6. Customer acceptance.
7. Estimated life of new system.
8. Spin-offs.
9. Enhanced image of company.
10. Extent of possible new markets.

Financial considerations:

1. Cost of system design.
2. Impact on company cash flow.
3. Payback period.
4. Borrowing requirement.
5. Time to break-even.
6. Size of investment required.
7. Cost of implementation and training.
8. Cost of maintenance and upgrading.
9. Cost of mistakes.
10. Level of financial risk.

Personnel considerations:

1. Skills requirements.
2. Availability of required skills.
3. Training requirements.
4. Employment requirements.
5. Level of resistance to change from current workforce.
6. Impact on working conditions.
7. Ergonomics, health and safety considerations.
8. Effect on internal communication.
9. Effect on job descriptions.
10. Effect on work unions.

Administration and other considerations:

1. Compliance with national and international standards.
2. Reaction from shareholders.
3. Cost of maintenance contract.
4. Disaster recovery planning.
5. Cost of upgrading system to keep pace with new technology.
6. Vulnerability of using a single supplier.
7. Customer service.
8. Effect of centralised data bases.
9. Extent of computer literacy.
10. Legal considerations.

This list is by no means complete, you will notice that each heading has been conveniently sub-divided into ten items, there could be more ! The main **advantage** of this type of list is that it considers a wide range of factors which greatly helps to present a fuller picture of the project.

The main **disadvantage** of the list approach is that all items are viewed with equal importance, others are:

*   Unknown level of error.
*   Different level of effect and importance.
*   Different level of risk and uncertainty.
*   Frequency of occurrence not known.
*   Threshold of rejection not quantified.
*   The list is incomplete.
*   The list may contain redundant items.
*   Some items are intangible and therefore difficult to quantify.

Although the limitations seem to outnumber the benefits, the most important feature is that the check list asks questions which encourage the managers to think about a wide range of possible problems.

2.2 Non-Numeric Models

Four non-numeric models have been selected for discussion.

The MD's pet project: The MD's pet project is essentially a senior management instruction emanating from a casual comment at a meeting or discussion. This informal comment will start an investigation into the feasibility of the MD's idea.

The repair and maintenance project: Repair and maintenance projects are required to keep the production line operational. This project may be to repair a road, roof or building, the replacement of machinery, plant or system. In each case the selection criteria can be quantified on the basis of cash flow. Is the profit from the production line greater than the cost of the project ? Where possible this type of project should be funded from the maintenance budget.

Improve competitiveness and marketability: For companies to continue competing in a free market they must have an ongoing programme for investing in new technology. If your company does not invest your competitors might. New technology may be quantified as anything that makes your product more competitive. This is usually achieved through automation, integrated systems or new machinery. Where possible this type of project should be funded from a development budget.

Product expansion: An expansion project may be to expand or change a production line or product. Management may have sensed a gap in the market and increase production or modify the product to fill it. Where possible this type of project should be funded from the production or capital assets budget.

Within a large company the financing of an investment may simply depend on budget allocation. If the department feels there are sufficient funds within its budget it may go ahead without senior management approval.

2.3 Numeric Models

The numeric selection models presented here may be sub-divided into financial and scoring types. The financial are:

*   Payback period.
*   Return on investment.
*   Net Present Value (NPV).
*   Internal Rate of Return (IRR).

Companies tend to prefer financial models and often select solely on profitability. This may not be as drastic as it sounds because subconsciously one is considering a wider scope of selection criteria anyway.

In an investment appraisal only the incremental income and expenses attributed directly to the project under consideration should be included. Costs that have already been incurred should be ignored as they are irrelevant to decisions effecting future projects.

It should be noted that all the appraisal techniques discussed in this chapter have a limiting factor, they are based on a forecasted cash flow.

2.4 Payback Period

The payback period is the time taken to gain a financial return equal to the original investment. The time period is usually expressed in years and months.

Consider **example 1**, a company wishes to buy a new machine for a four year project. This example will be used extensively in this chapter. The manager has to choose between machine A or machine B, so it is a mutually exclusive situation. Although both machines have the same initial cost ($35000) their cash flows perform differently over the four year period.

To calculate the payback period, simply work out how long it will take to recover the initial outlay.

Year	Machine A Cash flow	Machine B Cash flow
0	($35000)	($35000)
1	20000	10000
2	15000 <<	10000
3	10000	15000<<
4	10000	20000
Payback period	2 years	3 years

Machine A will recover its outlay one year sooner than machine B. Where project's are ranked by the shortest payback period, machine A is selected in preference to machine B.

The **advantages** of the payback method are:-

* It is simple and easy to use.

* It uses readily available accounting data to determine cash flows.

* It reduces the project's exposure to risk and uncertainty by selecting the project that has the shortest payback period.

* The uncertainty of future cash flows is reduced.

* It is an appropriate technique to evaluate high technology projects where the technology is changing quickly and the project could run the risk of being left holding out of date stock.

* For fashion projects where the market demand tends to change seasonally.

* Faster payback has a favourable short-term effect on earnings per share.

* The payback period quantifies the selection criteria in terms the decision-makers are familiar with.

The **disadvantages** of the payback period are:-

* It does not consider the time value of money. Payback period is indifferent to the timing of the cash flows. The project with high early repayments (cash outflow) would be ranked equally with a project which had late repayments if their payback periods were the same (figure 1).

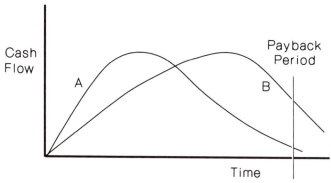

Figure: 1. Payback period

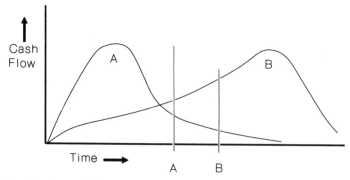

Figure: 2. Payback period

* It does not look at the total project. What happens to the cash flow after the payback period is not considered. A project that built up slowly to give excellent returns would be rejected in favour of a project with lower early returns if the payback period was shorter (figure 2).

* It is not a suitable technique to evaluate long term projects where the effects of differential inflation and interest rates could significantly change the results.

⅄ The figures are based on project cash flow only. All other financial data are ignored.

* Although payback period would reduce the duration of risk, it does not quantify the risk exposure.

The payback period is the most widely used technique, even if this use is only an initial filter for project selection. Its main strength is that it is simple and quick (can be worked out on the back of a cigarette packet).

2.5 Return on Investment

Another popular investment appraisal technique which does look at the whole project is return on investment (ROI). This method first calculates the average annual profit, which is simply the project outlay deducted from the total gains, divided by the number of years the investment will run. The profit is then converted into a percentage of the total outlay using the following equations.

Average Annual Profit $= \dfrac{\text{(Total gains) - (Outlay)}}{\text{Number of years}}$

Return on investment $= \dfrac{\text{Average Annual Profit}}{\text{Original investment}} \times \dfrac{100}{1}$

Using **example 1** calculate the return on investment.

Year	Cash flow Machine A	Cash flow Machine B
	($35000)	($35000)
1	20000	10000
2	15000	10000
3	10000	15000
4	10000	20000
Total gains	55000	55000

Profit $\quad = \dfrac{\$20000}{4yrs} = \$5000$ per year (same for both machines)

Return on investment $\quad = \dfrac{\$5000}{\$35000} \times \dfrac{100}{1} = 14\%$

The **return on investment** method has the advantage of also being a simple technique like payback period, but further, it considers the cash flow over the whole project. The out come of the investment is expressed as a profit and percentage return on investment, both parameters readily understood by management.

The main criticism of **return on investment** is that it averages out the profit over successive years. An investment with high initial profits would be ranked equally with a project with high late profits if the average profit was the same. Clearly the project with high initial profits should take preference.

This point was shown in the above example, where, although machine A and machine B had different cash flows, their profit and return on investment came out the same. To address this short coming of both return on investment and payback period, the time value of money must be considered using a discounted cash flow technique. This is particularly desirable where interest rates and inflation are high.

2.6 Discounted Cash Flow

The discounted cash flow (DCF) technique takes into consideration the time value of money, for example, a $100 today will **not** have the same worth or buying power as a $100 this time next year. Our subjective preference to $100 now is quite rational because we have seen the cost of goods rise with inflation. There are two basic DCF techniques which can model this effect, **net present value** (NPV) and **internal rate of return** (IRR).

These discounting techniques enable the project manager to compare two projects with different investment and cash flow profiles. There is, however, one major problem with DCF, besides being dependent on the accurate forecast of the cash flows, it also requires an accurate prediction of the interest rates.

2.7 Net Present Value (NPV)

To assist the understanding of NPV let us first look at compound interest which is commonly used in our bank accounts. If we invest $100 at 20% interest, after one year it will be worth $120 and after two years compounded it will be worth $144. Now NPV is the reverse of compound interest.

If you are offered $120 one year from now and the inflation / interest rate was 20%, working backwards its value in todays terms will be $100. This is called the present value, and when the cash flows over a number of years are combined in this manner the total figure is called the net present value (NPV). This calculation is best setup in a tabular form using the following headings.

Cash flow Timing (years)	Discount Factor	Project Cash flow	Present Value
0	----	----	----
1	----	----	----
2	----	----	----
3	----	----	----

Where the cash flow timing is expressed in years from the start date of the project, the inflation effect is assumed to act at the end of the year or beginning of the second year, therefore all cash flows in the first year are at present value.

The project cash flow   = income - expenditure.

Present value   = discount factor x cash flow.

The discount factor is derived from the reciprocal of the compound interest formula.

Discount factor $= \dfrac{1}{(1 + k)^n}$

where   k   is the forecast interest rate.

n   is the number of years from start date.

^   means raised to the power of.

The discount factor is usually read from a table, see table of discounting factors (below). Using the formula above calculate a few of the discount factors to satisfy yourself of their origin. You can then forget the calculation and work straight from the tables.

Table of discounting factors

		Interest Rates						
Years	10%	11%	12%	13%	14%	15%	16%	17%
1	.9091	.9009	.8929	.8850	.8772	.8696	.8621	.8547
2	.8264	.8116	.7972	.7831	.7695	.7561	.7432	.7305
3	.7513	.7312	.7118	.6930	.6750	.6575	.6407	.6244
4	.6830	.6587	.6355	.6133	.5921	.5718	.5523	.5337
5	.6209	.5935	.5674	.5428	.5194	.4972	.4761	.4561

		Interest Rates						
Years	18%	19%	20%	21%	22%	23%	24%	25%
1	.8475	.8403	.8333	.8264	.8197	.8130	.8065	.8000
2	.7182	.7062	.6944	.6830	.6719	.6610	.6504	.6400
3	.6086	.5934	.5787	.5645	.5507	.5374	.5245	.5120
4	.5158	.4987	.4823	.4665	.4514	.4369	.4230	.4096
5	.4371	.4190	.4019	.3855	.3700	.3552	.3411	.3277

The NPV is a measure of the value or worth added to the company by carrying out the project. If the NPV is positive the project merits further consideration. When ranking the projects, preference is given to the highest NPV.

Consider **example 1** again (page 27), this time using NPV. Assume the discounting factor is 20%, set up the NPV format. The steps are as follows:

*   Insert the cash flows.
*   Transfer the discounting factors from the table.
*   Calculate present value, multiplying cash flow by discount factor.
*   Aggregate the present values to give the NPV.

Machine A

(1) Year	(2) Cash flow	(3) Discount factor 20%	(2) x (3) Present value
0	($35000)	1.0000	($35000)
1	20000	0.8333	16666
2	15000	0.6944	10416
3	10000	0.5787	5878
4	10000	0.4823	4823
Net Present Value			2783

Machine B

Year	Cash flow	Discount factor 20%	Present value
0	($35000)	1.0000	($35000)
1	10000	0.8333	8333
2	10000	0.6944	6944
3	15000	0.5787	8681
4	20000	0.4823	9646
Net Present Value			(1396)

The NPV for machine A is $2783 and for machine B is ($1396). NPV analysis would select machine A in preference to machine B because it has a higher NPV.

Machine B would be rejected in any case because it has a negative NPV. A negative NPV indicates the company would lose money by carrying out this project. The **advantages** of using NPV are:-

* It introduces the time value of money.

* It expresses all future cash flows in today's values. This enables direct comparisons.

* It allows for inflation and escalation.

* It looks at the whole project from start to finish.

* It can simulate project what-if analysis using different values.

* It can gives a more accurate profit and loss forecast than non DCF calculations.

The **disadvantages** are:-

* Its accuracy is limited by the accuracy of the predicted future cash flows and interest rates.

* It uses a fixed interest rate over the duration of the project. The technique can, however, accommodate varying interest rates, this will be explained later in this chapter.

* It is biased towards short run projects.

* It does not include non financial data like the marketability of the product.

Although NPV quantifies the profit this is expressed in absolute terms. Managers tend to prefer profitability expressed as a percentage. This can be addressed by using another DCF method called internal rate of return.

2.8 Internal Rate of Return (IRR)

The internal rate of return is also called **DCF yield** or **DCF return on investment**. The IRR is the value of the discount factor when the NPV is zero. The IRR is calculated by either a trial and error method or plotting NPV against IRR. It is assumed that the costs are committed at the beginning of the year and these are the only costs during the year. Consider again **example 1** where our selection is between machine A or machine B. Looking at machine A first, to reduce the NPV increase the discounting factor in small steps until NPV goes negative.

Machine A (Discount Factor 22%)

Year	Cash flow	Discount factor 22%	Present value
0	($35000)	1.0000	($35000)
1	20000	0.8197	16394
2	15000	0.6719	10079
3	10000	0.5507	5507
4	10000	0.4514	4514
NPV			1494

Machine A (DF 24%) NPV still positive increase DF by another 2%.

Year	Cash flow	Discount factor 24%	Present value
0	($35000)	1.0000	($35000)
1	20000	0.8065	16130
2	15000	0.6504	9756
3	10000	0.5245	5245
4	10000	0.4230	4230
NPV			361

Machine A (DF 25%) NPV still positive increase DF by a further 1%.

Year	Cash flow	Discount factor 25%	Present value
0	($35000)	1.0000	($35000)
1	20000	0.8000	16000
2	15000	0.6400	9600
3	10000	0.5120	5120
4	10000	0.4096	4096
NPV			(184)

As the discount factor increases the NPV is reducing. The NPV goes negative between 24% and 25%, therefore the IRR is between 24% and 25%. For machine B the NPV is already negative, so decrease the discounting factor until NPV goes positive.

Machine B (DF 18%)

Year	Cash flow	Discount factor 18%	Present value
0	($35000)	1.0000	($35000)
1	10000	0.8475	8475
2	10000	0.7182	7182
3	15000	0.6086	9129
4	20000	0.5158	10316
NPV			102

Machine B (DF 19%) NPV now positive therefore increase DF 1%.

Year	Cash flow	Discount factor 19%	Present value
0	($35000)	1.0000	($35000)
1	10000	0.8403	8403
2	10000	0.7062	7062
3	15000	0.5934	8901
4	20000	0.4987	9974
NPV			(660)

The IRR must lie between 18% and 19%. These values can now be presented in a tabular or graphic form.

Interest rate	Machine A NPV	Machine B NPV
18%	----	102
19%	----	(660)
20%	2783	(1396)
21%	----	----
22%	1494	----
23%	----	----
24%	361	----
25%	(184)	----

Exercise: Complete the table of NPV against interest rate for machine A and machine B, then plot NPV against interest rate to see where the lines cross.

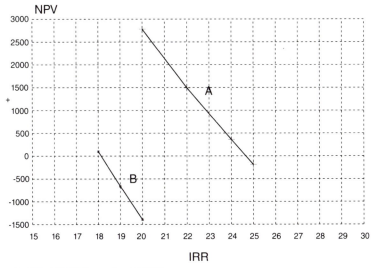

Figure: 3. Plot NPV against IRR

The IRR analysis is a measure of the return on investment, therefore, select the project with the highest IRR. This allows the manager to compare IRR with the current interest rates.

One of the limitations with IRR is that it uses the same interest rate throughout the project, therefore as the project's duration extends this limitation will become more significant. This problem can be addressed, however, using a modified version of the DCF method which will be outlined in the next section.

2.9 Net Present Value Using Variable Interest Rates

In the DCF examples the discounting factor was kept constant for the duration of the project. This unfortunately is not always a true reflection of the world markets which are quite volatile, interest rates can vary considerable over a two to three year period.

Consider the following example which starts with $100, compound forward using different interest rates, then discount backwards using the same interest rates.

Year	Cash Flow	Interest Rate	Compund Interest	Discount Factor Yearly	Total Discount Factor	Present Value
1	100	10%	110	0.9091	0.9091	100
2		20%	132	0.8333	0.7576	100
3		15%	152	0.8696	0.6588	100

Step 1:   The cash flow for the first year is $100.

Step 2:   The forecast annual interest rates are 10%, 20% and 15% respectively.

Step 3:   Using these annual interest rates the compound interest for the three years will be $100, $132 and $152 respectively.

Step 4:   The annual discounting factor is taken straight from the discounting factor tables. Enter year 1 and the interest rate in each case.

Step 5:   The total discount factor for the second year is the total for year 1 (.9091) times the annual discounting factor for year 2 (.8333), giving 0.7576. (This is the most complicated step, the rest is easy).

Step 6: The present value is the total discount factor times the compound interest value, for example, in year 3, the total discount factor is (.6588) times the compound interest value ($152), giving, $100. This is what you would expect, each year should be discounted to $100.

Which DCF Method Should We Use ?: The text has outlined five financial selection acceptance models, there are many more. If you are not already totally confused, which method or methods should be employed ?

If the cash flow data can be set up on a Lotus type spreadsheet there is no reason why one should not use all the methods outlined. Certainly **payback period** should be used as an initial filter, then two more calculations will give **IRR**.

For the DCF methods accountants suggest NPV should be used in preference to IRR, because NPV allows the user to vary the interest rate over the years whereas IRR employs one rate for all the cash flows.

NPV is a measure of profitability depending on the ingredients of a particular transaction, whereas IRR is dependent upon the opportunity cost of capital which is a standard of profitability established in the capital markets.

In the absence of capital rationing, all projects which have an IRR above the opportunity cost should be taken and so should all projects which have a positive NPV. Whichever test is employed, the same decision should be reached.

However, where capital shortages exist, the two approaches may indeed give conflicting results. In this situation NPV must be employed because the fundamental objective of financial analysis is not to measure profitability but to maximize the present value of the company's investment portfolio.

2.10 Scoring Models

The numeric models discussed so far all have a common limitation, they only look at the financial element of the project. In an attempt to broaden the selection criteria a scoring model called the factor model which uses multiple criteria to evaluate the project will be introduced.

The Factor Model simply lists a number of desirable factors on a project selection proforma along with columns for Selected and Not Selected. The development of the list should certainly have senior management input and approval. The following list shows a development of a rating sheet from **Meredith** p.46.

	Select	Do not Select
1. Profit > 20%	x	
2. Enter new market		x
3. Increase market share	x	
4. No new equipment required		x
5. Use equipment not being utilised	x	
6. No increase in energy requirements	x	
7. No new technical expertise required	x	
8. Use unutilised workforce	x	
9. Manage with existing personnel		x
10. No outside consultants required		x
11. No impact on workforce safety	x	
12. No impact on environmental issues		x
13. Payback period < 2 years	x	
14. Consistent with current business	x	
15. Offer good customer service	x	
Total	10	5

A weighted column can be added to increase the score of important factors while reducing the scoring of the less important. The weighted column is calculated by first scoring each factor, then dividing each factor by the total score. The total of the weighted column should always summate to one.

The factors can be weighted simply 1 to 5 to indicate; 1 "very poor", 2 "poor", 3 "fair", 4 "good" and 5 "very good". Three, seven and ten point scales can also be used.

Scoring model **advantages** are:

*   Uses multiple selection criteria to widen the range of evaluation.

*   Simple structure, therefore easy to use.

*   The selection factors are structured by senior management. This implies that they reflect the company goals and objectives.

*   Easy to change factors.

*   Weighted scoring reflects the factor's differential importance.

*   They are not biased towards short run projects favoured by financial models.

*   Very low weightings can be removed from the list as they have little to no influence. This will reduce the number of questions.

*   The weighted model can also be used as a flag to improve projects by identifying the variance between the factor score and the maximum possible score.

Scoring models **disadvantages** are:

*   If the factors are not weighted they will all assume equal importance.

*   A simple model may encourage the development of long lists which could introduce trivial factors and therefore waste management time.

2.11 Cost Break-Even Analysis

The cost break-even analysis should not be confused with the cost-benefit analysis which follows in the next section. The separation of costs into **fixed** and **variable** will be discussed in the project estimating chapter. This section on cost break-even analysis will outline how fixed and variable costs change with production.

Example: A company makes a product which sells for $15. The variable cost per unit is $5, this covers labour and material, leaving $10 per unit as a contribution towards fixed costs. The fixed costs total $75000 per annum, this covers all the overhead costs. The break-even point is reached when the contribution equals the fixed costs.

Break-even point $=$ $\dfrac{\text{Fixed costs}}{\text{Contribution per unit}}$

           $=$ $\dfrac{\$75000}{\$10}$

           $=$ 7500 units.

The break-even point is 7500, when sales income exactly balances the total cost of $112500 (labour and material 7500 x 5 = $37500 + fixed costs $75000). Output less than this amount would result in a loss, while greater output would make a profit. This profit or loss situation can be easily read off a graph, or calculated directly.

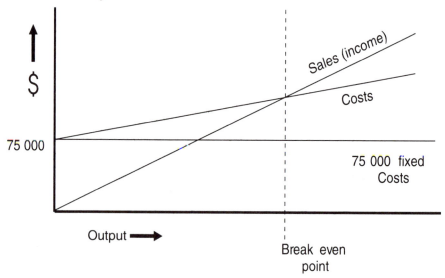

Figure: 4. Cost break-even analysis

This technique allows the project manager to see at a glance how profit varies with change in volume. It can also be used to show the affect on the cost structure by switching from say, manual to automatic machinery.

Break-even analysis can also be used to aid decision-making where two mutually exclusive projects present a different cost structure. Consider a project to install a heating system for an office block. Project A has a high installation cost but low maintenance, while project B has a low installation cost but high maintenance costs. Cost break-even analysis will indicate which system is the cheapest for a given period of time.

Exercise: Using the same technique as above find the following break-even points; (Solutions are at the end of the chapter.)

	Fixed costs	Selling price	Variable costs	Break-even point
a)	20 000	17	7	?
b)	60 000	20	5	?
c)	50 000	75	25	?

Cost-Benefit Analysis: The cost-benefit analysis evaluates a project by assigning a financial value to all the items under consideration. Although this topic is mentioned here as a project selection technique, it will be discussed in the project estimating chapter.

2.12 Sensitivity Analysis

Sensitivity analysis is part of the final stage in financial project appraisal. The techniques used are the same as those outlined in the project estimating chapter. In a situation where two mutually exclusive projects present similar returns on investment and there are only a few parameters exerting major influences over the results, then sensitivity analysis should be used. If, however, each parameter exerts only a limited change to the outcome then the additional effort of using sensitivity analysis may not be worthwhile.

If a company cannot objectively evaluate risk, personalities often dominate discussions on investment decisions. Where risk is recognised companies try to minimise their exposure by basing their selection purely on payback period. Such techniques miss one of the basic points about investments, which is that it is impossible to accurately evaluate potential return on investment without knowing the level of risk.

2.13 Summary

This chapter on project selection outlined how investment appraisal techniques are used to determine the financial feasibility of a project. It also quantified how mutually exclusive projects competing for limited resources can be ranked by profitability and suitability.

The project selection models were introduced as numeric and non-numeric types, where the numeric models were sub-divided into financial and scoring techniques. The non-numeric models used non-financial considerations, for example, production repair, maintenance, competitiveness, marketability and product expansion to aid selection.

The financial appraisal techniques developed were; payback period, return on investment, net present value and internal rate of return. The scoring technique used the factor model to broadened to scope of selection to include a wide range of factors which would not otherwise have been considered by the financial models.

The cost break-even analysis explained the relationship between fixed and variable costs to aid decision-making where two mutually exclusive projects present different cost structures.

Finally sensitivity analysis was discussed as the last resort to distinguish mutually exclusive projects with similar financial profiles. By simulating certain variables the exposure to risk and uncertainty can be determined.

Solutions: a)   2000   b)   4000   c)   1000

Chapter 3

Scope Management

This chapter on scope management will outline a framework for managing the entire scope of the project. The main subject headings will be developed around the Project Management Institute's Body of Knowledge.

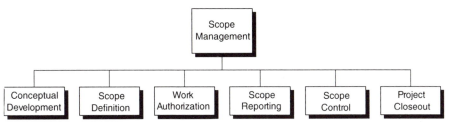

Figure: 1. PMI Body of Knowledge

The PMI define Scope Management as:

> "The scope of a project can be either the work content or component of a project. It can be fully described by naming all the activities performed, the end products which result and the resources consumed".

Effective scope management is one of the key factors determining project success. Failure to accurately interpret the clients needs or problems will produce a misleading definition of the scope of work. If this causes rework and additional effort, there may be project cost and time implications. Therefore project success will be self-limiting if the scope of work is inadequately defined.

Scope management will also outline how the project will be managed, progress monitored, reported and controlled. This need to plan ahead is fundamental to effective project management.

3.1 Conceptual Development

Conceptual development outlines a process for evaluating project selection within the company's requirements and market norms. The project should also meet the clients needs and / or provide a solution to a problem.

This section will set up a methodology for defining the client's needs, gathering information, identifying problem areas and constraints, listing and evaluating alternative courses of action before quantifying a set of project objectives which will satisfy the clients goals. At this stage the detail would be limited to summary level reporting.

Where appropriate the conceptual development will initiate a **needs analysis** to investigate the cause of the problem, recommend a solution and outline expected results. The financial implications can be quantified through a cost-benefit analysis, this will be discussed in the project estimating chapter.

Conceptual development will include the identification of problem areas and the different methods available to address them. It may also identify areas which require more research and information before an effective decision can be made.

The design philosophy should be documented to ensure that subsequent decisions made by the various groups are based upon a consistent rationale. The first step is to assess the clients needs and check the viability of the project.

To address conceptual development in a structured manner, a check-list should be developed to identify the specific requirements of the project and highlight problem areas based on past experience. The benefits of closeout documentation from previous projects can now be reaped (project closeout will be discussed later in this chapter).

3.1.1 Define the Client's Needs

The starting point for a project is usually to address a problem or a need, which may be internal or external to the company. The sponsor may start a project to implement a change, make a product or solve a problem. The following questions which are typical for product development will help to clarify and define the motivation for the project:

* The product must carry out a certain function at a predefined rate.

* The product must operate in a specific environment.

* The product must have a working life of x years.

* The project's budget must not exceed $ x.

* The project must meet certain specifications and standards.

* The product must meet achieve reliability requirements. These may be quantified as mean time between failures (MTBF).

* The product must be energy efficient. A car would quantify this requirement as miles / per gallon or kilometres / litre.

* The product must meet statuary health and safety regulations.

* The ergonomics must be consistent with the latest accepted practice.

* Ease of maintenance and repair must be incorporated into the design.

* A predetermined level of system redundancy and interchangeable parts must be achieved.

* The operational requirements must achieve predetermined manpower levels and automation.

* The product must be manufactured with a predefined value of local content.

* The product must provide opportunities for future expansion.

* The project must be operational by a predefined date.

* The product must be manufactured by approved and accredited suppliers, if necessary pre-qualified by an audit.

* All suppliers must have implemented an approved quality management system.

* All suppliers must have a good track record, supported by references.

* All suppliers must be flexible to accommodate any reasonable changes made by the sponsor during the manufacturing phase.

* All suppliers must be financially stable, supported by a bank reference.

* The end product must be marketable and profitable.

Although this list may seem lengthy it is by no means exhaustive, the intention here is to outline an approach, which should be intuitive for the experienced manager. The responsibility for developing such a list lies equally with both the client and the contractor.

Many of the above items may be mutually exclusive, which means there will have to be a trade-off. For example, it is generally not possible to achieve both minimum construction cost for a machine that also has minimum maintenance cost. These items of conflict need to be discussed and resolved during the early stages of the project, with all decisions recorded to form the basis of the design philosophy. This key document must be structured in such a way as to facilitate an audit trail of the decisions.

If the field of the project is specialized the client may employ consultants and specialists to assist defining the scope, on small projects this task may fall to the contractor's project manager himself.

3.1.2 Project Viability Check

The client may also need assistance checking the viability of the proposal. Will the product technically and commercially be fit for the purpose ? Has the client kept away from wish lists and pipe dreams ? These questions will form the basis of the clients feasibility study to which the contractor as a specialist in the field of the project, can have a valuable input.

* Consider the effect location has on the project. Can the logistic requirements during the project and subsequent operation be met through existing roads and ports ?

* Consider how the environment will affect the product, for example, a hotel in a hot country will require air-conditioning for a five star rating.

* Consider how the product will affect the environment, for example, CFC's will deplete the ozone layer.

* Calculate the optimum size of the end product. Economies of size are not always a straight line extrapolation, but pass through plateaus of optimum production.

* Are the aesthetics and style commensurate with modern day thinking?

* Define the target market. Who will buy the product? These questions can be quantified by market research.

* Assess the market supply and demand curve. What is the demand for the product now and forecast demand in the future?

* Assess the competition from other players in the market. How will an increase in your rate of production affect market share?

At the outset of the project it may not be possible to answer all of these questions. The questions will, however, indicate areas that need more information.

3.1.3 Information Gathering

Information is a pre-requisite for any decision-making function. This section will discuss the need for the timely supply of accurate and pertinent information. Information may be found in books, periodicals, technical reports, bureau specifications, sales and marketing brochures, estimating data base from empirical analysis of previous projects, product information and market trends.

A focused source of information would be the closeout reports from previous projects. It cannot be over stressed how important it is for a company to learn from previous experience, not only should the mistakes be noted, but also what went right, together with any recommendations for future projects.

The size of the company will influence how and where information should be kept. In a small company, information may be collected by individual managers, while the large company may have a corporate library. The responsibility for setting up a data base of information should lie with either the project department or the company's general manager.

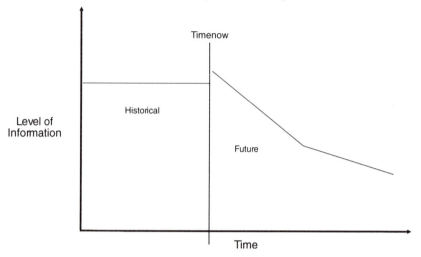

Figure: 2. Level of information against time

The figure shows how the level of accurate information varies with time. The highest level of information is required around Timenow, with this requirement moving forward like a wave as the project progresses.

3.1.4 Project Constraints

Project constraints can be considered as internal or external restrictions which may effect the achievable scope of the project. These anticipated limitations can be quantified under three sub-headings:

*   Internal project constraints.

*   Internal corporate objectives.

*   External constraints.

3.1.4.1 Internal project constraints: The internal project constraints relate directly to the scope of the project and ask basic questions about the product.

*   Can the product be made ? Consider Rolls Royce RB111 carbon fibre turbine blades which led to the company's liquidation.

*   Does the company have the technology ? If not, can the technology be acquired through a **technology transfer**, if so with whom ?

*   Should we start the project now with the present technology or wait until new and better technology is available ?

*   Is the new technology component greater than 10% ? Practitioners recommend the scope of innovation be kept below 10% so not to compound the risk and uncertainty.

*   At what point in the development should a design freeze be imposed ? From the figure, note the technology gap at the end of the project.

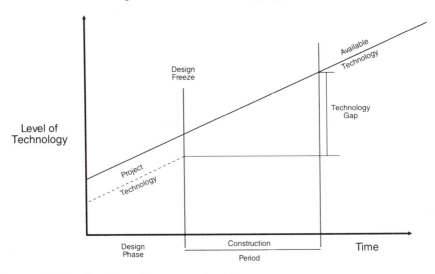

Figure: 3. Technology change against time

*   Can the resources be trained up to the required level of ability, or should outsiders be employed to meet the forecast skills requirement?

*   The multi-project resource analysis will consider the effect other projects will have on the supply of internal resources.

* Are there any special design requirements ?

* Are special machines and equipment required ? If yes, can these be sub-contracted out or procured ?

* Are there special transport requirements ? Can the product be transported to where it is required or does it need to be made piece small and assembled on Site ?

* Will any new management systems introduced be compatible with existing systems they interface with ?

* Can the project be completed within the budget ?

* What is the quality assurance requirement ? For example, is accreditation to ISO 9000 required ? Is the present quality system sufficient?

* Can the company meet the specifications ?

* Are there company and project procedures in place ? If not is there time to develop them ?

* Is the project office set up ? Has the project manager been appointed, the project team selected, the office space allocated and the equipment and information systems available ?

* Can the project meet the clients completion date and any intermediate key dates ?

* Can the company accept the time penalties ?

* Is the project risk and uncertainty acceptable ?

* Can the company accept the terms and conditions outlined in the contract document ?

All these questions relate directly to the project. The next section will show how the company can impose further constraints.

3.1.4.2 Internal corporate constraints: The company itself can impose further quasi constraints on the project. Corporate policy and strategy usually relates to long term issues which indirectly (and unintentionally) may impose limitations on the project.

Financial objectives: The project selection criteria may be based on a financial feasibility study quantified as, payback period, return on investment, net present value (NPV), internal rate of return (IRR) and a cost-benefit analysis. The acceptance criteria being set by company policy.

* The company may wish the project to maintain a positive cash flow.

* The progress of the project may be encouraged or delayed to meet company fiscal budgets.

* The share price may have an effect on the company's ability to borrow.

Marketing: The company may wish to diversify its products and enter new markets. This project will implement the technology transfer for the company to operate in this market.

* The current project is a loss leader to enter a new market. The project must accept sub-normal profits to get a ''foot in the door''

* Your project may be viewed by prospective clients as a true sample of the company's performance and ability. Word of mouth recommendation and return business are the most cost effective ways of marketing your products.

Estimating: Due to a down turn in the economy, the company's main priority may be to keep the workforce intact. The lower the bid the greater the probability of being awarded the next contract. The lowest a company can bid is to cover direct costs, with the overheads being written-off. If this is the case will the project's budget be based on the estimated cost or sales price ?

Partner: The company may wish to take on a partner who may have previous experience in the field of the project and also to spread the risk.

Industrial relations: Industrial unrest is often caused by conflict over pay and working conditions. The project manager may have little power to influence these conditions.

Customer service: The company culture may determine the level of customer service required, this may influence how frequently the client is entertained and the amount of scope flexibility.

Training: Your project may become the training ground for new recruits, in which case the learning curve will be an expense to the project.

* The project may be a pilot scheme to implement a new system.

* The project environment can provide an excellent management training ground, especially site work for the MBA graduate.

Exports: The company may influence the estimate in an effort to acquire exports to enter new markets or take advantage of export incentives. Where these company objectives are in conflict with project objectives the company objectives usually take preference. This often leads to increased project costs which must be included in the budget.

3.1.4.3 External Constraints: External constraints are imposed by parties outside the company's and project's sphere of influence. These constraints for the most part will not be negotiable.

* National and international laws and regulations.

* Material and component delivery lead times.

* Limited number of sub-contractors who can do the work.

* Logistic constraints, availability of transportation.

* Availability of foreign currency and currency fluctuations.

* Market forces, supply and demand curve.

* Environmental issues, Government legislation and pressure group activities, for example, Green Peace and CND. The nuclear, chemical and mining industries are particularly affected.

* Climatic conditions, rain, wind and heat.

* Political unrest.

These headings should not be seen as comprehensive, but as the forerunner of a company check list that ensures all the necessary questions are asked, which in turn should reduce the level of risk and uncertainty.

3.1.5 Alternative Analysis

The alternative analysis is the process of breaking down a complex product into its component parts before identifying different, and hopefully more effective methods of achieving the desired result.

The process should start with a check list to structure the thought process. This can be achieved through; the work breakdown structure (see WBS chapter), the project constraints or the project objectives.

The technical definition should aid the direct comparison between alternatives. With a machine for example the capital costs should be compared with the operating costs.

Although this process should be on-going during the project, the design freeze would usually signal the end of this phase. Once the manufacturing phase starts the emphasis would shift to considering manufacturing alternatives. The following check list outlines a number of the basic questions to be asked:

* Time: Can the project be completed quicker ?

* Cost: Can the budget be reduced ?

* Quality: Can the project be made to a lower level of quality which would be acceptable to the client but more cost effective and quicker to produce?

* Resources: Can the work be cost effectively automated to reduce the manpower requirement ?

* Technical: Can cheaper materials be used ?

* Is there a simpler design configuration ?

* Has the latest technology been considered ?

* Has the use of different equipment and machines been considered ?

* Is there a simpler build method ?

* Has the trade-off between cost, delivery schedule and technical performance been quantified ?

* Have alternative management systems been considered ?

When the client's needs have been structured and quantified using the above headings, the next step is to determine what the company and the project must achieve to meet these client requirements.

3.1.6 Define Project Objectives

The conceptual development phase should close with a document outlining the project objectives. These project objectives quantify what the project must achieve to meet the client's needs or provide a solution to the problem.

The level of detail will obviously depend on the level of effort and time spent preparing the report, at the conceptual development stage this may be limited to summary documentation. The project objectives can be structured by using the main headings from both the work breakdown structure (WBS) and the organisation breakdown structure (OBS), (see WBS chapter):

Viability: A statement confirming the viability of the project should be included.

Scope of Work: The scope of work outlines what the project will make or deliver. This may be quantified using the following headings:

* Drawing register.
* Parts lists.
* Specification register.
* WBS work packages.
* Method statement.

Time: The planning and scheduling using the CPM approach would generate the following documents:

* Network diagram.
* Scheduled barchart.
* Key date barchart.
* Procurement schedule.

Resources: The manpower resources would be linked to the schedule barchart:

* Manpower forecast.
* Resource availability.
* Resource smoothing.

Costs: The financial model would use:

* Activity budget.
* Cash flow statement.
* Profit and loss account.

Quality: The quality management approach would be quantified by:

* Project quality plan.
* Quality control plan.

Project Management: The project management objectives would outline how the project office would operate:

* Project team members.
* Project management systems.
* Document control.
* Configuration control.
* Information data base and filing system.
* Project procedures and work instructions.

Contract: The contract document is usually based on the company's standard terms and conditions of contract together with special contracts developed for the field of the project.

* Standard terms and conditions of contract.
* Tender document.

* General contract, usually prepared by an institute, for example, mechanical contract or electrical contract.

* Special conditions.

These basic objectives provide the foundation for the design and manufacture philosophy. It is advisable to request the client to approve the project objectives to ensure that the brief has been interpreted correctly.

The project objectives serve as a guideline for developing the scope definition and project initiation. This will be covered in the next section.

Self-test exercise:

1. Develop a viability check-list for a project you are familiar with.

2. Define project constraint.

3. Discuss how you would set-up your information gathering system.

4. At what point during the project would you implement a design freeze?

5. List five project objectives from a project you are familiar with.

3.2 Scope Definition

The scope definition outlines the content of the project, how the project will be approached and explains how it will solve the client's needs or problem.

Scope definition establishes a method to identify all the items of work that are required to be carried out to complete the project. The WBS can be used to provide a sub-division of the scope into manageable work packages to which responsibility can be assigned for accomplishment.

These work packages can be further sub-divided into a detailed activity list which forms a key input for Critical Path Method (CPM).

3.2.1 Scope Criteria / Constraints

The scope criteria outlines the parameters that need to be considered to define the project. The project objectives from the previous section, if acceptable, now form the scope constraints.

The constraints set the framework within which the project must operate to achieve not only the project's objectives, but also the client's needs.

3.2.2 The Management Plan

The purpose of the management plan is to document the overall guidelines explaining how the project will be organized, administered and managed to assure the project objectives are achieved.

3.2.2.1 The Organisation Structure: The project organization structure identifies the relationship between the project participants, together with defining their responsibility and authority.

Because of the dynamic nature of projects it is possible to have a number of organization structures running concurrently. These structures outline the relationship between the various participants and the lines of communication:

* Corporate hierarchy
* Project team
* Matrix overlay
* Responsibility / accountability matrix
* Project interfaces

Corporate Hierarchy: The corporate hierarchy simply outlines the relationship between the project manager and the senior corporate managers.

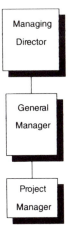

Figure: 4. Corporate hierarchy.

Project Team: The project team outlines the relationship between the project manager and the other team members. This structure may be dynamic, as seconded members move in and out of the project.

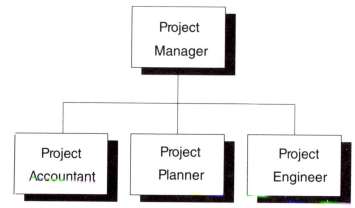

Figure: 5. Project team.

Matrix Overlay: The matrix overlay outlines the relationship between the project manager, other functional managers and their subordinates.

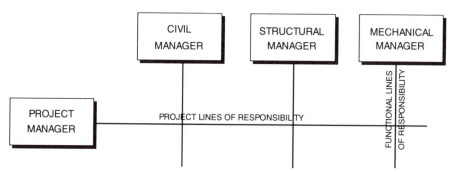

Figure: 6. Matrix overlay.

Accountability / Responsibility Matrix: Also called the **WBS / OBS** interface, links the scope of work with the responsible person. This matrix assures that the full scope of work is assigned to a designated person.

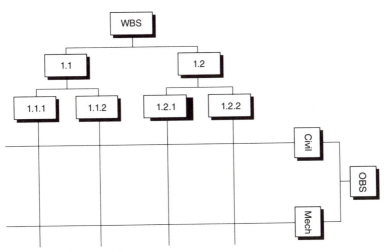

Figure: 7. WBS / OBS interface

Project Interfaces: The project interfaces outline the relationship between the project manager and the client together with all the outside companies used on the project.

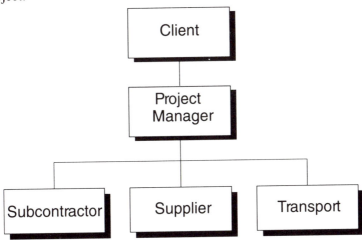

Figure: 8. Project interfaces

Although these structures outline the relationship between the various project participants they need to be supplemented with a job description or job evaluation to delineate responsibility and authority.

3.2.3 Job Descriptions

The job description develops the organization structure's positions into a further level of detail. The job description should contain the job title, the supervisor, a job summary, responsibilities and authority.

The framework of the job description can be supplemented with project procedures and work instructions, these will be discussed in the following section. A **framework** for a job description should include;

* Who the person reports to.
* Who reports to that person.
* What duties the person is responsible for.
* What authority the person has to issue instructions.

Using this basic framework consider an example of a project manager's job description:

Reporting to the general manager the project manager is delegated with responsibility and authority to:

* Achieve all the targets set out in the baseline plan.

* Select and manage the project team.

* Set up the project office and management system to manage and control the project.

* Represent the company at the client meetings.

* Process all project related correspondence.

* Authorise all reimbursable procurement and services required by the project.

* Negotiate and award all the sub-contracts.

* Process all non-conformance reports (NCR's).

* Issue the necessary project procedures.

*   Issue weekly / monthly progress reports and financial statements.

*   Approve all changes on behalf of the company.

*   During the development of the scope of work it is the project manager's responsibility to structure and co-ordinate the input and involve all interested parties (internal and external). This involvement is required to determine the technical and managerial requirements.

*   Some of the qualities the project manager requires include: an ability to communicate, negotiate, deduce, quantify dreams, quantify wish lists and interpret the client's needs correctly.

As the project manager is responsible for selecting the project team it can be assumed that he is also responsible for writing the job descriptions for the team members. These would normally include the following disciplines:

Project Accountant.
Project Planner.
Project Engineer.
Project QA.
Project Procurement.

The size of the project would determine the number of people in the team. On a small project one person may cover all these positions, while on a large project there may be a number of people per position.

The bottom line is that the project manager is the single point of responsibility and as such has a blanket responsibility for the project. The project manager's authority, however, may be limited. The key word here is to ensure that authority is **commensurate** with responsibility.

3.2.4 Project Procedures

Also called **work instructions**. Project procedures establish a guideline on how to manage certain aspects of the project. These can be tailored to the project's needs and generated by the project manager. A typical work instruction has three basic headings:

Purpose: The purpose will outline the scope of the work instruction.

Instructions: The instructions outline how to carry out a task, usually presented in a step by step format.

Reports: Sample reports are included to outline the required format of the document with explanations where appropriate.

Procedures should be developed when and where necessary, even for simple items like how to structure a letter and file it. Certainly the following procedure should be developed:

* Contract initiation
* Planning and progress reporting
* Engineering design and drafting
* Procurement and expediting
* Cost control and financial status
* Scope changes and configuration control
* Commissioning
* Invoices and payments

The main benefit these procedures offer is that they ensure all the team members are working to the same system, other benefits include:

* Mistakes can be prevented, or when they occur steps can be taken to ensure they do not happen again.

* Limits responsibility overlap and underlap, which could cause conflict.

* Encourages an expert system approach by capturing current experience.

3.2.5 Work Breakdown Structure (WBS)

The WBS is a hierarchical structure used to sub-divide the scope into manageable work packages. These work packages are then linked with the organisation breakdown structure (OBS) through the responsibility matrix. The work packages can be further sub-divided into activities for the network diagram and CPM calculations. This topic is developed in the Work Breakdown Structure chapter.

3.2.6 Scope Baseline

The scope baseline, also called **baseline plan,** is an aggregation of all the documents mentioned in the chapter so far. It essentially gives a summary description of the end product including basic activity budgets and scheduling. The baseline plan also provides a basis for making future scope decisions, verification measurements and evaluating changes.

The approval of the baseline plan is a key management function. This approval essentially commits company resources to the project. As with the project objectives the baseline plan should be submitted to the client for his approval.

The documentation and approval of the scope baseline is necessary before proceeding with the project, this should form part of a scope approval procedure.

Misinterpreting the scope of work: Misinterpreting the scope of work is a common cause of project failure (states *Kerzner* p.546), others include:

* Mixing and confusing; tasks, specifications, approvals, and special instructions.

* Using imprecise or vague language, for example, nearly, optimum, about or approximately can lead to confusion, ambiguity or misinterpretation.

* No pattern, structure, or chronological order. The WBS and CPM techniques have not been used.

* Wide variation in size of tasks and work packages, again caused by not using the WBS to sub-divide all the work packages to a common level of detail.

* Wide variation in how to describe work details.

* Failing to get third-party review or verification from the client, subcontractors and suppliers.

3.3 Work Authorization

Work authorization establishes a methodology to evaluate and confirm that the scope of work, planning documents and contractual requirements have been set up to accommodate the project and corporate objectives.

Work authorization establishes the WBS / OBS link where the lines of communication disseminate formal instructions and information to the responsible parties. The documentation should be controlled to provide an audit trail of instructions.

This process will entail examining the scope of work, planning schedules, budget, specification and contractual requirements to ensure they will meet the project objectives.

The formal authorization of commencement should be accomplished through instructions and directives and other documents as outlined at the handover meeting.

3.3.1 Handover Meeting

The purpose of the handover meeting is to formally commence the project or sub-contract. The attendance would normally include senior management, the project team members and other concerned parties. The purpose of the handover meeting is to set the scene for the project. The meeting would be chaired by the client. A typical agenda may include:

1. Outline what is being made or produced, scope of work, drawing register, parts list etc.

2. Outline the sub-contractors involvement.

3. Explain procedure for issuing instructions, format and who has authorization. Establish lines of communication between the companies and confirm the list of responsible persons.

4. Discuss how the project will be managed, reporting requirements; the content, format, frequency and circulation. Confirm the schedule of meetings, a typical agenda, attendance and venue.

5. Discuss how progress will be measured and reported, together with progress payments.

6. Contractual requirements, penalties, budgets, schedules and specifications.

7. List of client supplied items.

8. List of inclusions and exclusions.

9. Discuss configuration control; outline procedure for scope changes and identify the people with approved signing power.

10. Sign the minutes to confirm agreement.

Issuing of instructions: The issuing of instructions is the first step in the control cycle (see project control chapter). Work authorisation must ensure that the full scope of work is authorised to the responsible persons.

As the project is implemented there will be changes to the scope which need to be authorised. These would tend to be authorised by issuing a revised document, typical examples include:

*   Scope change, issue revised drawing.

*   Planning change, issue revised schedule.

*   Build method change, issue revised method statement.

*   Cost change, issue revised budget.

Transmittal of instructions: The procedure for issuing instructions discussed at the handover meeting will outline how the instructions are communicated. If controlled documentation is required then all instructions must be accompanied by a transmittal or delivery note. An audit trail of work authorisations should be maintained to provide traceability.

Self-test exercise:

1. Which organisation structure links the scope of work with the responsible people ?

2.   Develop a job description for your position for a project you are familiar with.

3.   Develop a project procedure to control the flow of correspondence.

4.   What is the difference between the WBS and the OBS.

5.   Why is the handover meeting important ?

3.4 Scope Reporting

Scope reporting establishes a project management information system to capture progress and status data, which is processed into information to quantify the project's productivity and performance.

Project data can be collected, processed and reported in many ways, this section will outline a few of the commonly used methods. The report formats, their frequency and circulation, need to be established during the start up phase of the project.

The reports should be designed to assist decision-making by the various levels of management so that they can ensure the project will meet its stated goals and objectives.

3.4.1 Status Reports

Status reports simply quantify the position of the project. This data capture function is the first link in the monitoring and reporting chain, all subsequent evaluations are based on this data.

Status reports may be specific and focus on the key areas of the project, like time, cost and quality, or they may be general and include a much wider scope.

Activity	Description	Status
010	Foundations	Material ordered work started on Monday -

STATUS REPORT at date:..............

Figure: 9. Status report

3.4.2 Earned Value

The earned value report integrates the variable parameter of cost with time, this technique can also be used to integrate manhours and time. The integration of data enables the planner to model the various parameters more realistically. For more information see the chapter on earned value.

3.4.3 Variance Reports

Variance reports quantify the difference between planned and actual. Their application is quite pervasive, being used basically for any parameter that can be quantified.

The first example shows a typical budget report where the original budget is compared with the revised budget. The variance is simply the difference between the two values.

Activity	Original Budget	Revised Budget	Variance
010	10 000	12 000	2 000
020	15 000	13 500	-1 500

Figure: 10. Budget variance report

The second example shows the schedule variance from an earned value report. This example addresses one of the problems of variance reporting by converting the variance value into a percentage.

When a variance is reported as the difference between two values, it does not take the size of the parameter into consideration. This problem can be addressed by converting the variance into a percentage of the planned value. Now the variance is expressed as a percentage of the original base.

Activity	Original Budget	Revised Budget	Schedule Variance	Schedule Variance %
010	1 000 000	1 010 000	10 000	1 %
020	400 000	420 000	20 000	5 %

Figure: 11. Schedule variance report

3.4.4 Trend Reports

Trend reports move away from the limited snap shot status reports to give a feel for the direction of the project. Trend reports extrapolate known data from timenow to the end of the project. The example shows the earned value graph where both BCWP and ACWP are extrapolated to show the current trend.

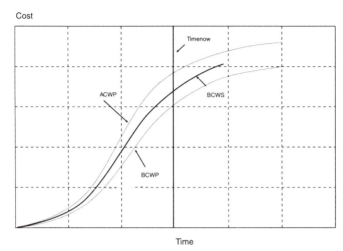

Figure: 12. Earned value trend report

3.4.5 Exception Reports

Exception reports are designed to flag an occurrence or event which is outside predetermined limits. This threshold can be set by the project manager as a guideline for the planner to follow. For example the planner may be requested to report:

*   All activities that have a float less than 5 days. This would highlight all the activities that could go critical in the next week.

*   Any item of material that has missed its planned delivery date. The project manager can now contact the supplier for a status report.

*   All non conformance reports (NCR) where the product has not attained the required condition as outlined by the specifications or contract.

3.4.6 Monthly Reports

On a long project, monthly reports give the project manager an excellent forum to quantify what is happening on the project and report it to senior management. The monthly report should roll up the weekly progress meetings and any other special meetings to give an overall picture of the project.

3.5 Control System

The Control System establishes a framework to monitor, evaluate and up-date the scope baseline to accommodate any scope changes. This will ensure that the baseline always reflects the current status of the project and that control is implemented to keep the project on track to meet its objectives. This section will focus on a control system to control scope changes.

3.5.1 Configuration Control

The configuration control system captures all the proposed scope changes from a variety of sources. Before the scope baseline is revised these changes must be quantified and approved by authorised personnel. Only then will the work be authorised for execution. Configuration control would incorporate the following phases:

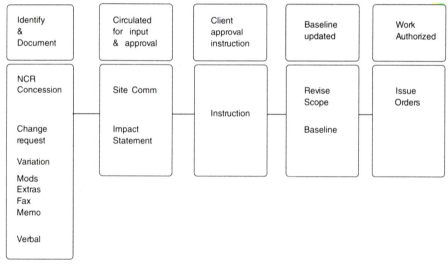

Figure: 13. Configuration control

It is important, particularly on large complex projects, that any scope changes are only approved by the nominated technical experts. This will not only prevent scope changes by unapproved personnel, but also ensure that all implications of the proposed change have been considered.

Scope changes: The system should allow for scope changes to be motivated by anyone working on the project. The following documents formalize the motivation:

* Non conformance report (NCR), usually motivated by quality control. This problem would either be corrected and fall away or motivate a concession.

* A concession, requests the client to accept an item which has been built out of specification. If approved this would not be shown as a scope change, but would be included on the as-built drawings.

* Change requests, modifications and variations are requesting the client to approve a change to the scope baseline.

* Written request would be by memo, letter, fax or minutes.

* As a matter of course all verbal instructions and agreements should be confirmed in writing. A simple fax will pay dividends later in the project if there is a dispute and also this letter can be referred to as the motivation for a scope change.

Change request: Using a numbered change request form is the preferred method of motivating a scope change. The form should describe the scope change, list affected drawings and documents, together with the reason for the change.

CHANGE REQUEST			
NUMBER		DATE RAISED	
INITIATED BY:			
CHANGE REQUESTED (Related Drawings)			
REASON FOR CHANGE			
APPROVAL			
NAME	POSITION	APPROVAL	DATE

Figure: 14. Change request

... I'LL BE ON SITE AS SOON AS THE PAPER-WORK'S DONE

Site communication: All the proposed changes are now captured by a site communication document which formally logs the proposed change and asks the client how the contractor should proceed.

SITE COMMUNICATION
NUMBER   DATE RAISED DESCRIPTION:
WE ACKNOWLEDGE YOUR ENQUIRY/INSTRUCTION VERBAL FROM: TO: WRITTEN FROM: TO: DATE:
PLEASE ADVISE HOW WE ARE TO PROCEED: 1.   START IMMEDIATELY AND QUOTE WITHIN 7 DAYS. 2.   START IMMEDIATELY ON RATES. 3.   DO NOT START, QUOTE WITHIN 7 DAYS. 4.   OTHER
REQUEST FROM: INSTRUCTION FROM: CONTRACTOR   CLIENT PROJECT MANAGER   PROJECT MANAGER

Figure: 15. Site communication

This essentially puts the ball in the client's court and forces him to give clear written instructions.

Impact statement: The impact statement quantifies the implication of making the proposed change. Formerly the impact statement follows the response from the site communication, but in reality it is usually issued at the same time.

An information pack is now compiled to collect input, information, comments and approval from the responsible parties.

IMPACT   STATEMENT

NUMBER   DATE RAISED

DESCRIPTION:

REFERENCE SITE COM:

IMPACT ON PROJECT: IF YES QUANTIFY:

SCHEDULE   YES / NO
COST: YES / NO
QUALITY: YES / NO

PLEASE ADVISE IF WE ARE TO PROCEED: YES / NO

REQUEST FROM: INSTRUCTION FROM:

CONTRACTOR   CLIENT
PROJECT MANAGER   PROJECT MANAGER

Figure: 16. Impact statement

All the above documents should be numbered, consecutively if possible and status reported on a summary sheet.

Flow sheet: To control the movement of the change requests and impact statements.

IMPACT STATEMENT FLOW SHEET			
IMPACT NO. SITE COM REFERENCE			
DESCRIPTION			
POSITION	DATE IN	DATE OUT	COMMENTS
PROJECT MANAGER			
DRAWING OFFICE			
ESTIMATING MANAGER			
QA MANAGER			
PROCUREMENT MANAGER			
PROJECT PLANNER			
PROJECT ACCOUNTANT			
PROJECT ENGINEER			

Figure: 17. Flow sheet

The flow sheet determines the sequence of circulation, it logs the document in and out of departments and collects comments, calculations, information, but most importantly it notes the acceptance or rejection of the change.

There are two possible methods of controlling the movement of the document:

    a)   Hub and spoke.

    b)   Consecutive.

Although the hub and spoke doubles the movement of the document, the project office knows where it is at any time. With the consecutive method the lines of communication may be shorter, but if the documents do not reappear timeously, it will require a time consuming witch hunt to find them.

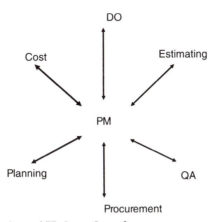

Figure: 18. Flow sheet / Hub and spoke

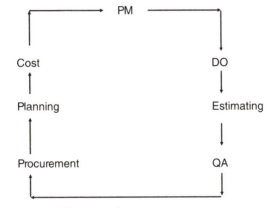

Figure: 19. Flow sheet / Consecutive

Scope change authorisation: The scope change authorisation formally authorises the contractor to carry out the work. It should be based on the impact statement findings which will have determined the feasibility of the change.

SCOPE CHANGE AUTHORISATION

```
NUMBER

DATE ISSUED:

REF IMPACT STATEMENT:

SCOPE                                                    AMOUNT




PLANNING


AUTHORISATION
```

Figure: 20. Scope change authorisation

With the implementation of the scope change into the production system, this completes the configuration control cycle.

3.5.2 Document Control

The purpose of document control is to ensure that the project is being made to the latest scope baseline. If the client authorises a change he expects to see the production department using documents which include that change.

The document control procedure for scope changes would first list all the documents to be controlled. On construction projects, for example, this would include the construction drawings, parts lists and specifications. Then against each document would be a circulation list. When the document is issued it is marked **controlled copy** and accompanied by a transmittal note which the receiver signs to confirm receipt.

Transmittal: A transmittal note or delivery note is sent with every controlled document. The addressee must sign the transmittal note and return a copy to the project office to confirm the document has been received.

```
┌─────────────────────────────────────────────────────────────┐
│                                                               │
│                    TRANSMITTAL NOTE                           │
│                                                               │
│                                                               │
│                                                               │
│  NUMBER                              DATE ISSUED:             │
├──────────────────────────────────┬──────────────────────────┤
│  FROM                             │ TO:                       │
│                                   │                           │
│                                   │ RECEIVED BY:              │
│                                   │                           │
│                                   │ DATE:                     │
├──────────────────────────────────┴──────────────────────────┤
│  CONTENT:                                                     │
│                                                               │
│                                                               │
│                                                               │
│                                                               │
└─────────────────────────────────────────────────────────────┘
```

Figure: 21. Transmittal note

It is the project office's responsibility to control the flow of these controlled documents. The project office must ensure that these controlled document reach their destination timeously. A control sheet is essential, each week the document controller should confirm receipt by telephone and ensure the signed transmittals are returned. A list of non-returned transmittals can be tabled at the progress meetings to encourage compliance.

DOCUMENT CONTROL					
TRANSMITTAL NO.	DATE ISSUED	DOCUMENT TYPE	DOCUMENT NO.	TO	DATE TRANSMITTAL RETURNED

Figure: 22. Document control sheet or Transmittal summary

Project Audit: A project audit is an official inspection of a declared system, in this case configuration control and document control. The contract would normally include a clause allowing the client to inspect the contractor's management system. The audit will determine how well the system is actually being carried out, report any deviations and make recommendations for corrective action.

Although the project audit is outside the framework of this chapter it is mentioned here because it provides the project manager with an excellent tool to ensure compliance.

3.6 Project Closeout

The project closeout can be sub-divided into three sections:

*   Compile historical data from previous projects to assist conceptual development.

*   Compile historical data from previous projects and the current project to predicting trends and problem areas on the current project.

*   Generate a closeout report which evaluates the performance of the current project against the project objectives and makes recommendations for future projects.

3.6.1 Historical Data

The search for historical data from previous projects will clearly show the benefit of effective closeout reports and filing, either through delight or frustration. Learning from previous experiences is the most basic form of development and what is more it is essentially free.

However, there are limitations with certain historical data becoming outdated and so misleading, together with the basic correlation between projects being tenuous. Consider the following:

*   The scope of work between projects is unlikely to be exactly the same.

*   The cost data will be influenced by inflation.

*   The manhours influenced by automation.

*   The build methods may be different.

*   The management systems may not have been computerised.

However, having made certain allowance for the limitations there may be a wealth of similarities. Look closely to see what went right and what went wrong together with any recommendations, because the same mistakes have an uncanny habit of happening again, particularly if the cause has not been addressed.

3.6.2 Project Closeout Report

A closeout report is generated during the final phase of the project before the project participants have dispersed. For best results a structured report format is recommended using the following steps:

Step 1.   Generate a comprehensive questionnaire and circulate to project participants.

Step 2.   Analyse responses and de-brief the key managers.

Step 3.   Compile draft closeout report for comments. This can also be used as an agenda for a formal closeout meeting.

Step 4.   Hold a formal closeout meeting attended by all participants.

Step 5.   Compile final closeout report, circulate and file.

Questionnaire: The main benefit of the questionnaire approach is to structure the responses. It must be made quite clear that this exercise is not a search for the guilty but an attempt to quantify what happened on the project. The net should be cast reasonably wide to include a broad range of opinions. The list of participants should certainly include the following:

*   The client.

*   The project team.

*   Corporate participants.

*   Suppliers and sub-contractors.

The questionnaire would typically be structured to include the following questions:

1. Identify your position in the project organisation structure and comment on the interfacing and co-operation with other disciplines.

2. Comment on the delegation of responsibility and authority.

3. Briefly outline your assigned scope of work.

4. Comment on planning schedules, budgets, quality and manpower performance. Where possible quantify performance with statistical data.

5. Give a candid assessment of your performance, analysing what went right and what went wrong. Comment on any NCR's with reasons for any deviations and the level of re-work. If audits were conducted comment on their findings.

6. Comment on the lines of communication, the issuing of instructions, the holding of meetings, the availability of information, procedures and reporting.

7. Evaluate design and technical changes, as-built drawings and operator manuals.

8. Comment on any scope changes and concessions. Evaluate how smoothly the configuration system worked, were the changes approved and implemented timeously.

9. Discuss the use of new technology, computerisation and automation.

10. Discuss any unexpected problems, how they affected the project and their solutions.

11. Comment on the performance of procurement suppliers and sub-contractors.

12. Comment on manpower performance, their training and any industrial relation problems.

13. Evaluate the accuracy of the estimate and list any recommended changes or amendments.

14. Evaluate the contract document.

15. General recommendation for future project.

This type of questionnaire provides the project manager with an excellent tool for accurate and meaningful feedback.

3.6.3 Recommendations for Future Projects

Learning by mistakes is one of the most important features of any project. These recommendations can provide an invaluable source of direction for future projects.

The closeout report should highlight any recommendation simply and clearly, because many years from now this may be the only section of any importance.

* Validating the project estimate is essential. Over estimating will generate good profits, but in a competitive market will reduce the chance of winning further tenders. While underpricing will simply reduce company profits. It is not sufficient to only look at the bottom line, validate at work package level to ensure competitive estimating on future projects.

* Wherever possible the analysis should indicate perceived trends, these may be in technology, build methods or management systems.

The final statement should comment on the overall success of the project and advise if the company is wise to tender on these types of projects again.

Storage: At the end of the project what happens to the files, are they moved to a storage area and dumped to be lost in the quagmire, or are they filed in such a manner to facilitate easy retrieval ?

Some companies file all their documents on micro fiche, although this process is expensive it does greatly reduce the storage area. A final word, beware **faxes fade**.

3.6.4 Project Handover

The project handover to the client indicates the end of the project. The key documents would include:

*   **Commissioning** report to demonstrate that the product has reached the required specification.

*   The handover of data books which document how the product was made together with operator instructions and user manuals.

*   The financial closeout would close the project account. No further payments will be accepted except for retention.

*   A letter of acceptance would confirm that all the contractual requirements have been fulfilled.

Self-test exercise:

1.   Develop a status report for a construction project.

2.   What is the difference between a variance report and management by exception ?

3.   Raise a document requesting permission to move the location of a door.

4.   Raise a document requesting the client to accept a design error.

5.   Develop a closeout report for a project you have worked on.

3.7 Summary

This chapter on scope management used the PMI's body of knowledge to structure the sub-headings. Each of these six sub-headings were developed separately.

Conceptual development: Outlined how a check list can be used to assess the client's needs or define the problem. It also outlined how to gather information, identify the constraints and consider alternative methods of achieving the project objectives.

Scope definition: Working within the constraining project objectives this section explained how to quantify the management plan. It also explained how the scope could be sub-divided into manageable work packages before being approved for execution.

Work authorisation: This section explained how the definition of project scope and associated planning documents are reviewed before being formally authorised. The work authorisation used the WBS / OBS link to establish the lines of communication and dissemination.

Scope reporting: This section outlined the different types of reporting formats generally used to quantify progress.

Scope control: This section developed the configuration control system as a viable control model to implement changes in a structured manner. It is important to keep the scope baseline up to-date.

Project closeout: Finally a structured closeout report was developed using a combination of questionnaires and meetings to determine if the project met its original objectives. Where necessary recommendations are made to benefit future projects.

There should be no doubt now, that effective scope management has to be a major concern for the project manager in his pursuit to achieve the project objectives.

Chapter 4

Work Breakdown Structure

The success of the whole planning and control function depends on the project planner being able to define the project's full Scope of Work quickly and accurately. The Work Breakdown Structure (WBS) provides a tool to address this need.

The WBS may be described as a hierarchical structure which is designed to logically sub-divide all the work-elements of the project into a graphical presentation, this is similar in structure to an organization chart, also called Organization Breakdown Structure (OBS). The full Scope of Work for the project is placed at the top of the diagram, then sub-divided uniformly into smaller elements of work at each lower level of the breakdown. At the lowest level of the WBS the element of work is called a **work package**.

The WBS is a prerequisite link between the Scope of Work and the Critical Path Method (CPM). The CPM requires a complete list of the project's activities which can be developed from the work packages.

Effective use of the WBS will graphically outline the scope of the project and the responsibility for each work package. Designing the WBS requires a delicate balance to address the different needs of the various disciplines and project locations. There is not necessarily a right or wrong structure because what may be an excellent fit for one discipline may be an awkward burden for another.

4.1   Components of the Work Breakdown Structure

The first step towards mastering the WBS technique is to fully understand the structured methodology for developing it. The main components of the WBS are:

* The structure.

* The description.

* The number or coding system.

* The number of WBS levels.

* The level of detail.

* The roll-up.

4.1.1 The Structure

Construction of the WBS is similar to that of an organization chart, where each successive level is drawn horizontally and represents a sub-division of the level above. Graphically the inter-connecting lines between the levels are drawn from the bottom of the higher element to the top of the lower element.

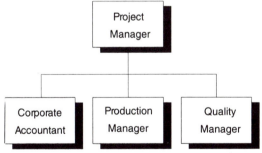

Figure: 1. Organization Structure

Each level is drawn horizontally except when space presents a problem (see figure 2). Here the lowest level work packages are drawn vertically. In this case, inter-connecting lines must join lower level elements from the side to indicate that they are on the same level.

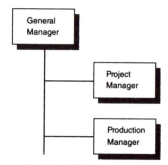

Figure: 2. Vertical Organization Structure

4.1.2 The Description

Each element in the WBS needs to be identified by a short description. Although the length of the description may be restricted the meaning should be clear.

When using project management software the length of the description allowed may vary from package to package. However, when using Lotus 123 as a graphics package the restriction would be the size of the paper and the printer.

At this point we need to visualize the WBS, consider figure 3 which shows a house construction project.

Level 1:   Represents the full scope of work for the house.

Level 2:   The project is sub-divided into its three main trades.

Level 3:   Each trade in turn is then further sub-divided at the third level to give the project's work packages.

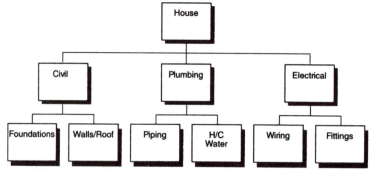

Figure: 3. WBS Structure and Description

NOTE: The work elements at the lowest level are called **work packages**.

4.1.3 The Numbering or Coding System

One of the main features of the WBS is its ability to uniquely code all the elements of work in a numerical and logical manner, which can later be used as an address (post box). The numbering system can be alphabetic, numeric, or alphanumeric (letters and numbers), in all the examples here the numbering systems will be numeric.

Level 1: The figure below outlines a coding system. The first number [1.0.0] represents the first work element on the first level. It is normal practice to have only one item at this level ie, the total project.

Level 2: At the second level the first work element will be numbered [1.1.0] and the second work element numbered [1.2.0]. Thus the other work elements will be numbered sequentially; [1.3.0], [1.4.0], [1.5.0] etc.

Level 3: These numbers are then further sub-divided at the third level from the element at the second level into [1.1.1], [1.1.2].

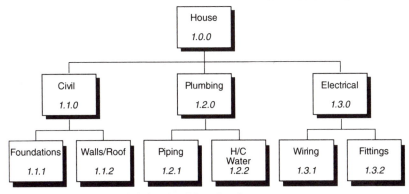

Figure: 4. WBS Sub-division by Numbering system

4.1.4 How Many WBS Levels

For practical purposes three or four levels seems to be the norm. However, there is no reason why the project cannot be sub-divided further (say 10 levels), but consider the large volume of data to be processed as the base of the **WBS** expands. Current PC software usually suggests four levels as the optimum.

If more than four levels are required this can be addressed by using sub-projects, where the highest level of one project constitutes the lowest level work-package of another. This situation is common on projects where a main contractor uses many sub-contractors. In this way, the **WBS** can effectively increase the number of breakdown levels, with each project manager focusing only on his area of responsibility.

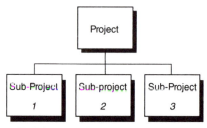

Figure: 5. WBS / Subdivision by Sub-projects

The figure below outlines another way of sub-dividing a house project, this time:

Level 1:   The first level is still the total project.

Level 2:   The second level is now sub-divided by location.

Level 3:   The third level sub-divided by Labour and Material.

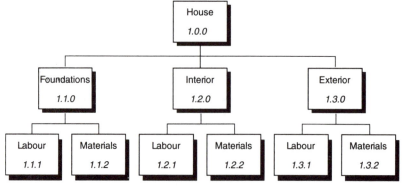

Figure: 6. WBS Sub-division by Location

Care should be taken when using a discipline / trade split at the lowest level, because it may not always lead to a tangible product whose completion can be assigned to a single manager.

The British Shipbuilding industry called this system ''demarcation'' which was a contributing factor to the industry's decline.

At the lowest level (work package) the preferred split would be by product or task under a single manager. This arrangement should encourage the various trades to work together to achieve a common goal.

4.1.5 Level of Detail

A guide to the appropriate level of detail would be to make each work package small enough to be considered as a separate work element for estimating purposes. Each work package can then be further sub-divided, if required, to form a complete list of work activities or tasks. These activities can then be logically related to form a Network Diagram. This will be developed further in the CPM chapter.

Time planning and control usually requires more detail than financial accounting. To accommodate this requirement the project may consist of a much larger number of work activities which roll-up to a single cost centre.

The work package's level of detail should be directly proportional to the level of control required and consistent with the other work packages at the same level. If the level of detail varies this will tend to produce a distorted plan.

The figure below outlines another way to sub-divide the project, this time using project phases or project life cycle.

Level 1:   The project.

Level 2:   The sub-division is now by project phase.

Level 3:   Work-package.

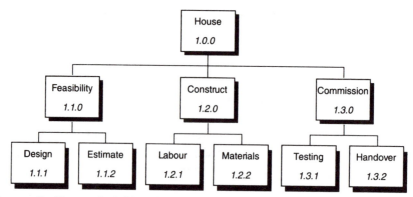

Figure: 7. Example 3 / WBS Sub-division by Project Phase

The figure below outlines other criteria for sub-division in this case by cost centre or accounting centre.

Level 1:   The Project.

Level 2:   Sub-division by cost centre.

Level 3:   Sub-division by account type / order number.

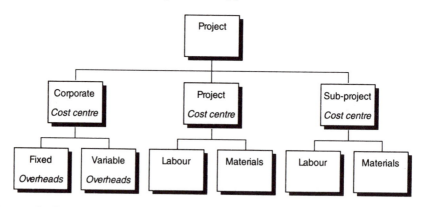

Figure: 8. WBS Sub-division by Cost Centre

Where possible the WBS numbering system should link the project accounting system with the corporate accounting system. (Where appropriate the client's cost accounting system as well). If this is achieved it will prevent unnecessary duplication of data capturing and processing.

As the single point of responsibility, it is important for the project manager to keep the project cost and resource control within his sphere of influence.

As these examples have shown there are many ways of sub-dividing a project, with some methods being more appropriate than others. The best results are generally gained by using an iterative and heuristic approach which considers a range of sub-divisions until an appropriate structure is derived.

Although location and discipline are popular criteria for sub-division, managers sometimes find difficulty thinking of ways to sub-divide their projects. In practice companies that use the WBS, set up a standard WBS proforma for their projects.

The figure below outlines a WBS where the second level is sub-divided by location, the third by discipline and the forth by expense. This format could be used as a standard WBS for the company. The only changes per project would be to the description rather than structure. Note: FOB = free on board.

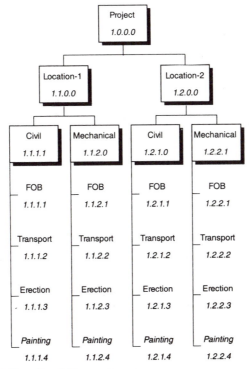

Figure: 9. WBS Standard Format

4.1.6 WBS Roll-up

Roll-up is the term used to describe the process where values (costs or manhours etc.) are entered at a low level (work activity or work package), then summated upwards and reported at a higher level.

Exercise 1: Try the following exercise where costs are entered at the third level. You are required to roll-up the costs and report them at the second and first levels.

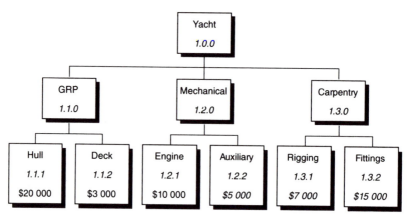

Figure: 10. Exercise 1 / Yacht project, roll-up the Costs

Solution to exercise 1.

Level 3:   The costs are entered at the work-package level, Hull $20000, Deck $3000 etc.

Level 2:   The costs are then **rolled-up** to the next level. The GRP costs are the addition of the Hull and Deck $20000 + $3000 = $23000.

Level 1: $60000 is the summation of level 2.

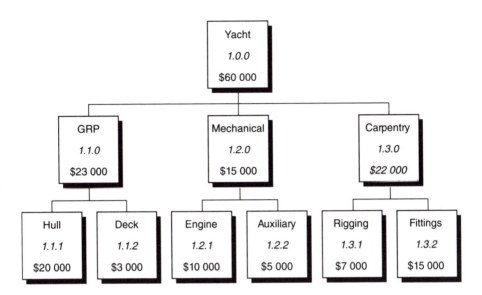

Figure: 11. Solution 1 / Yacht project

Exercise 2: Build a beach buggy. Roll-up the costs to find the total cost of the project.

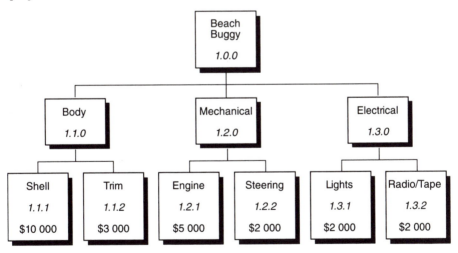

Figure: 12. Exercise 2 / Beach Buggy project

Solution to exercise 2.

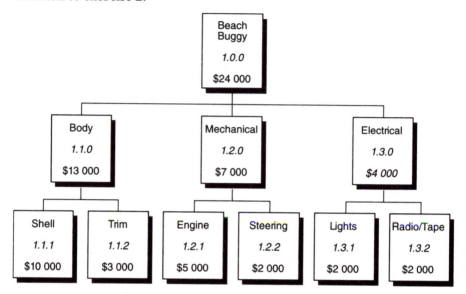

Figure: 13. Solution 2 / Beach Buggy project

The roll-up facility is normally used to roll-up project costs for budget planning and control purposes. By suitably structuring the WBS, budgets can be established per department, per location or per sub-contractor.

The WBS roll-up does lend itself to anything that flows in the project, ie. manhours, cubic meters of concrete thrown, tonnes of steel erected, bricks laid, drawings completed, square meters of paint etc. Any of these could be planned, tracked and controlled using the WBS.

Exercise 3: Consider a Drawing Office situation, where it would be more appropriate to plan and track your project with respect to manhours rather than costs. This is because the chief draughtsman can estimate time required to complete a drawing from experience, but may not have the data necessary to estimate the costs involved. Try rolling-up Exercise 3, where Mh represents manhours.

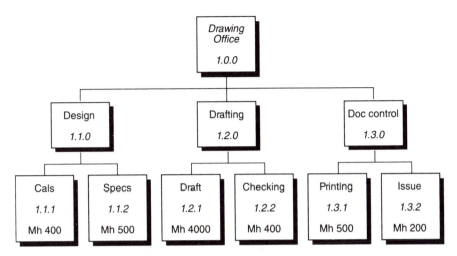

Figure: 14. Exercise 3 / Drawing office project

Solution to exercise 3.

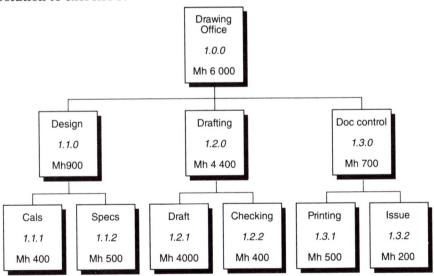

Figure: 15. Solution 3 / Drawing office project

In this exercise manhours are rolled up instead of costs. In industry and commerce manhours are often used to quantify the work content rather than costs.

4.2 Estimating

If your company wins contracts from competitive bidding it is important to have a system for generating accurate quotations quickly. The WBS can be used to sub-divide the project into work packages which can then be further sub-divided into work activities for estimating purposes. This will improve the estimating accuracy of each work package, as well as ensuring that all the costs have been included in the quotation.

The accuracy of estimates will increase in steps down the various WBS levels. As the work package's level of detail increases it should follow that the accuracy of the estimate will also increase. As a rough guide the level of accuracy should be at least the same as, or better than, the project's profit margin.

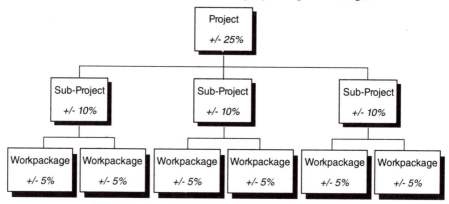

Figure: 16. WBS Level of accuracy

4.3 Responsibility

For a project team to operate effectively, all members must know what is expected from them and where they fit into the project. In your company each project may be significantly different in scope and have different team members, contractors and suppliers. The WBS can give a clear graphical breakdown of the project which makes it easier for those participating to understand the full scope of work and see where they fit into the project.

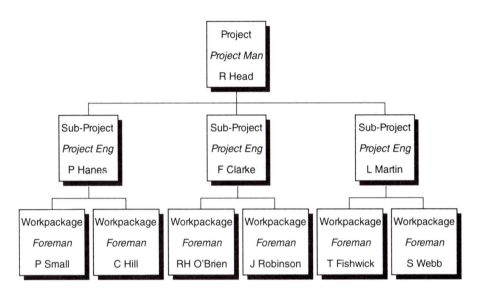

Figure: 17. WBS by Responsibility

The responsibility WBS, also called the Organization Breakdown structure (OBS), can be further developed by including the respective telephone numbers.

4.4 Foreign Currency

In some countries it is a legal requirement for certain industries to report **local content** by value. To comply with this, the WBS can be structured to report local and foreign currency separately.

When estimating projects which require imported components, the client may need to know his commitment for foreign currency so that he can make an application to the Reserve Bank to release these funds. If the WBS is appropriately structured to roll-up the different currencies it will save double processing of the data.

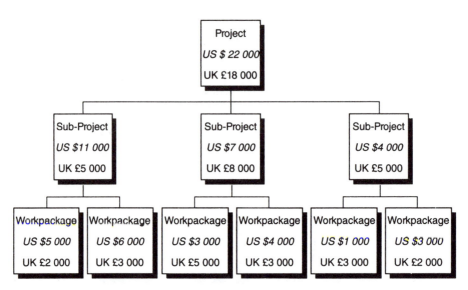

Figure: 18. WBS by Foreign currency

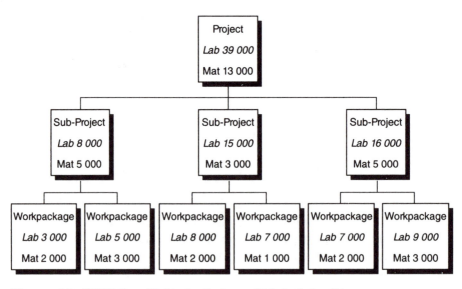

Figure: 19. WBS Sensitivity by Labour / Material split

4.5 Sensitivity Analysis

If the WBS is structured around the main cost types, then the roll-up will outline where the funds are being spent.

Example 4: A project comprising 90% labour costs and 10% material costs would be sensitive to pay increases. The project manager needs to identify the main cost parameters early on in the project.

Analysis would show that this project is more sensitive to increases in labour costs than material costs.

4.6 Summary

In this chapter we have explained how the WBS can be used to effectively outline the structure of the project. This summary will collate many of the advantages associated with using the WBS:

* Using either a top-down or bottom-up approach, the total project can be clearly described as a summation of sub-divided work elements.

* The project can be logically sub-divided using any of the following categories: project phase, location, disciplines (professional and trade), company departments, sub-contractors, technical, task etc.

* The WBS is the link between the scope of work and the CPM activity list. By generating a complete list of all activities this will help to ensure that the entire scope of work is included in the cost and time estimates.

* The WBS helps to develop a complete list of work activities at the same level of detail. This prevents a distorted view of the project.

* One or more work activities can be linked to a WBS work package, which allows activity costs to be grouped for financial, planning and control purposes.

* The values assigned to a work package can be anything that flows in the project: e.g. money, manhours, concrete, steel, drawings

etc. These values can be rolled up and reported at any level in the WBS.

* Costs and budgets can be quickly established for a quotation, the level of accuracy relating directly to the input level in the WBS.

* The WBS helps to set budgets for departments or cost centres which can be planned, tracked and controlled.

* Planning and control accuracy is directly related to the scope of the work package. This scope of work relates in turn to the number of WBS levels. It is therefore possible to achieve an optimum level of control by varying the scope of the work package.

* The number of levels can be increased to improve the estimating accuracy. There should be a direct relationship between the profit margin, the estimate and level of control.

* All work packages are uniquely identified by a numbering code which can link the project's accounts, the corporate accounts and the client's accounts.

* When the responsibility is assigned to a work package, this will link the WBS to the responsibility matrix or OBS. This link will also enable reports to be generated by responsibility or department.

* The WBS gives a graphical representation of the project which makes it easier for the project team to understand the project's scope of work and their responsibility. This in turn will help to gain their commitment and support.

* The WBS can be used to quantify the project's requirement for foreign currency.

* By suitable sub-division of the work, the sensitivity of the project can be established, e.g. labour, material or transport costs etc.

Effective use of the Work Breakdown Structure is axiomatic to project success. Once the scope of work has been sub-divided into work packages, the next step is to produce a complete list of activities to perform the Critical Path Method.

Chapter 5

Critical Path
Method

For the project manager to effectively plan and control a project, he needs to be able to process large amounts of data quickly and accurately to enable him to see order in a complex situation. Critical Path Method (CPM) is a structured approach to project planning which has been designed to meet this need.

This chapter will outline the techniques and practical applications of CPM, taking you step by step through the various planning stages from developing the logical network diagram through to establishing the critical path.

As the project planning software in the market uses **precedence network** in preference to **activity-on-arrow**, the precedence network technique will be developed. Although the diagram structure is different, the mathematical output from both methods is the same.

The network diagram and the activity scheduled barchart are two of the key planning documents which are axiomatic to successful time management planning, cost management planning and resource management planning. This chapter will introduce the time management planning function as a first step towards mastering the CPM technique. Cost management planning and resource management planning will be introduced in subsequent chapters.

CPM also provides the structure for **project control** and **earned value**, from tracking and monitoring project progress, to information processing and scope reporting. Project control and earned value will also be introduced in subsequent chapters.

CPM has become a generic term which can be used interchangeably to mean both time planning on its own, or to incorporate all the planning and control parameters of time, cost and resources.

5.1 Why Use Project Planning Techniques

It is useful at this point to establish a check list, outlining the purpose and benefits of project planning. It should always be remembered that project planning commits financial resources in terms of labour, equipment, materials and overheads, so it is not unreasonable for the project manager to be requested to justify the expenditure and substantiate the benefits of CPM. Here are some useful points to help structure your argument.

* CPM will identify the full scope of work, by developing the Work Breakdown Structure (WBS) to produce a complete list of project activities.

* Establish achievable objectives for the project, quantified in terms of activity time, cost and resources.

* Provide a scheduled barchart of activities to meet imposed deadlines using the available resources.

* Develop the project accounts, presented as a WBS cost roll-up, a cash flow statement, an expenditure curve, a cost "S" curve (BCWS) or an earned value table.

* Monitor and track the work done, evaluate progress by comparing planned with actual. Forecast progress trends and apply corrective action to keep the project on course.

* Identify areas of responsibility per WBS workpackage or activity.

* Provide a communication tool to disseminate scope information and issue instructions to the project participants.

* Reduce project risk and uncertainty, by identifying the critical activities.

*   Include time, cost and resource constraints in the contract document.

*   Provide the basis for a quantified cost-benefit analysis.

With the benefits of project planning fresh in our mind, let us now move on to the practical application of CPM by outlining the project planning steps.

5.2 Project Planning Steps

The CPM network diagram and scheduled barchart provide a highly structured and methodical approach to project planning. The following steps may be used as a guideline, or check list to develop the baseline plan. Within these steps are a number of iterative loops, which should be performed until an optimum solution is derived.

1.   Define the scope of work. Outline the method statement or build method, sequence of work and quality control plan.

2.   Define the project objectives with respect to time, cost and resources.

3.   Generate a responsibility matrix linked to the Work Breakdown Structure's (WBS) work package or activity. Develop the Organization Breakdown Structure (OBS) to identify the project's lines of communication through which instructions and information will flow.

4.   Develop the Work Breakdown Structure (WBS) to structure the scope of work and produce a complete list of activities.

5.   Estimate activity: time duration, cost expenditure, resource requirements and procurement lead times.

6.   Determine the relationships between activities and draw the network diagram.

7.   Develop the project calendar or workpattern.

8.   Perform the CPM time analysis (forward pass, backward pass) to establish an activity table consisting of Early Start, Early Finish, Late Start, Late Finish, Activity float and the Critical path.

9. Draw the scheduled barchart.

10. Analyze resources with respect to resource requirements, resource availability, resource loadings and resource smoothing. If necessary re-analyze project time to produce a resource levelled scheduled barchart. Integrate resources and time to produce a manpower histogram and ''S'' curve to plan and control productivity.

11. Generate project accounts and financial reports. Budgets per activity or WBS work package. Integrate cost and time to produce the cost ''S'' curve or BCWS.

All the above functions come together to form the project's **baseline plan** as show in the diagram below.

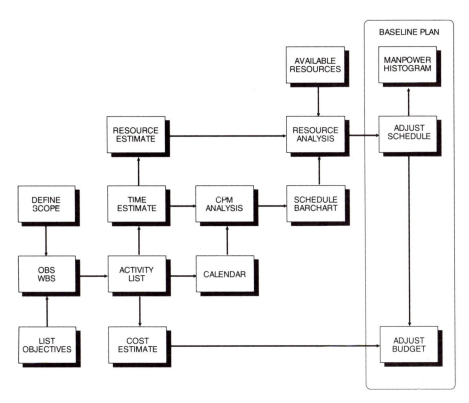

Figure: 1. Baseline plan

The level of detail will depend on the project phase:

Tender phase: During the tender phase these steps need to be performed quickly to produce a reasonably accurate outline of the project's requirements. The tender period which is usually imposed by the client may be considered as a small project in itself.

Execution phase: After the contract has been awarded, or authorized a detailed baseline plan should be developed. It is often a contractual requirement that the detailed planning be prepared for approval within 3 to 6 weeks after the contract has been awarded.

It is advisable to substantially complete the planning before the execution of the project. This will allow you the opportunity to plan and control the project before the project controls you. The execution phase will be controlled through the following steps:

12. Control the scope of work through the following documents:

Site communications

Impact statements

Non Conformance Reports (NCR)

Change requests and Concessions

Drawing revisions

Modifications and Variation Orders (VO)

Extras to contract

Specification and Configuration revisions.

13. Project expediting involves the follow up function to confirm that; orders have been received, materials have been procured, work has started and planned delivery dates will be achieved.

14. Project tracking and data capture, to quantify and measure project performance.

15. Analyze performance data to generate status reports and earned value analysis to clearly outline the project's actual progress against the baseline plan. Extrapolate forward to forecast and predict project trends.

16. Decide on corrective action where necessary to keep the project on track.

17. Issue instructions.

The control functions are shown diagrammatically below:

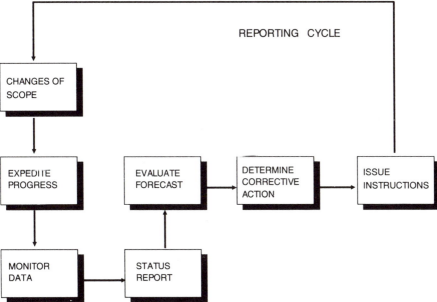

Figure: 2. Project control functions

These headings form the main structure for project planning and control. Mark this page for quick reference.

Self test:

1.   List at least five benefits of using Critical Path Method.

2.   What is the link between the WBS and the CPM ?

3.   What level of planning detail would be appropriate at the tender stage?

4.   What are the two must important CPM planning documents ?

5.   Prepare a 4 minute presentation explaining how your company develops a scheduled time plan for their projects.

Your planning flow chart should indicate:

1. How the data and information are captured.

2. How the activity list is developed.

3. How activity logic and time durations are estimated.

4. How the planning information is processed.

5. How the scheduled plan is presented.

6. If there are any iterative loops.

7. How responsibility is identified and communicated.

8. How risk and uncertainty are quantified and addressed.

Education objectives:

1. To assess if the student can provide a detailed description of a planning system.

2. To assess if the student can communicate and disseminate effectively how his company's planning system operates.

How did you do in the test ? Read through this part again if necessary, it is important for your comprehension and understanding to appreciate the sequence and relationships between the various planning steps.

5.3 Network Diagram (part 1)

The text is structured in a progressive manner where each section is only developed sufficiently to carry out a certain operation. This educational technique may be presented as a development spiral:

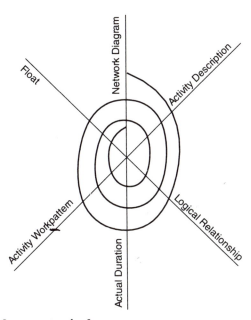

Figure: 3. Development spiral

The network diagram may be defined as a graphical presentation of the project's activities showing the sequence and relationship that the work must be performed in. In its simplest form only two items of information are required:

*   List of Activities.

*   Logic constraints, also called logical links, logical dependency or relationships between these activities.

The precedence network is a recent development of the ''activity- on-node'' concept where each activity is represented as a node or a box.

5.4 Definition of an Activity (part 1)

An activity may be defined as any task, job or operation which must be completed to finish the project. In the text the term activity and task will be used interchangeably. In the precedence diagram network an activity is always represented by a identity or number, which can be alpha or numeric and is presented in a box. Example activity 010 is to design a house.

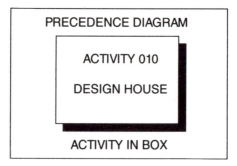

Figure: 4. Activity (Precedence Network)

5.5 Logical Relationships (part 1)

Before we can draw the network diagram we must define the logical relationships between all the activities. There are two basic relationships:

* Activities in series.

* Activities in parallel.

Activities in series: When the activities are in series they are carried out one after the other. When the network is first developed this would probably be the most common type of relationship used. An example of activities performed in series on a house project would be the foundation (activity A100), followed by the walls (A200), followed by the roof (A300).

Read the network diagram as you would a page of writing, the project starts on the left side and moves to the right and downwards.

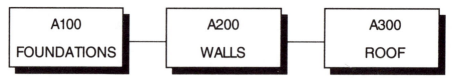

Figure: 5. Activities in Series

Think back to school, this presentation is similar to electrical resistors in series, while the next diagram is similar to resistors in parallel.

Activities in parallel: When activities are in parallel they may be carried out at the same time, hence this is a more efficient use of time. An example on a house project would be the installation of plumbing (activity B200) and electrical fittings (B300) simultaneously.

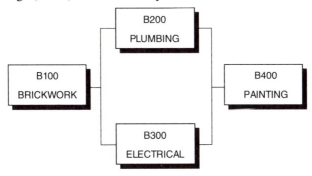

Figure: 6. Activities in Parallel

5.6 How to Draw the Logical Relationships

The terms logical relationship, constraint and link will be used interchangeably and are represented as lines between the activity boxes. The preferred presentation shows the constraint lines drawn from left to right, starting from the right side of one activity box into the left side of the following box. The normal practice is that the lines should only enter or leave from the sides of the box, not the top or bottom. Initially an arrow at the end of the constraint may help you to follow the direction of work flow.

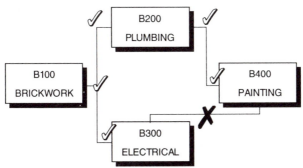

Figure: 7. How to draw activity constraints

The preferred and non-preferred methods of drawing the constraints are indicated on the diagram.

5.7 Activity Logic Table

For ease of reading, logic information is often compiled in a tabular format, with each record defining a relationship. Planning software usually term the before and after activities as preceding and succeeding activities as detailed below:

The table headings would be set up as follows:

BEFORE ACTIVITY	CONSTRAINT	AFTER ACTIVITY
----	----	----
----	----	----
----	----	----
----	----	----

or....

PRECEDING ACTIVITY	CONSTRAINT	SUCCEEDING ACTIVITY
----	----	----
----	----	----
----	----	----
----	----	----

Consider the following worked example where the activities and constraints are labelled.

Even if the logic table is not manually generated by the planner, the planning software will compile the logic data in this format. It is therefore useful for the planner to be familiar with this presentation to enable him to validate the network data.

We have just outlined how the planner can sketch out a rough draft of the network diagram using a pencil and plenty of rubber. The intention being to predict what will happen down-stream in the project. A common problem when developing the network diagram is to introduce activities on the basis of time rather than logic. At this point in the development of the network diagram think only of the sequence of the activities.

LOGIC TABLE

PRECEDING ACTIVITY	CONSTRAINT	SUCCEEDING ACTIVITY
START	C1	A100
A100	C2	A200
A100	C3	A300
A200	C4	A400
A300	C5	A500
A400	C6	A600
A500	C7	A600
A600	C8	FINISH

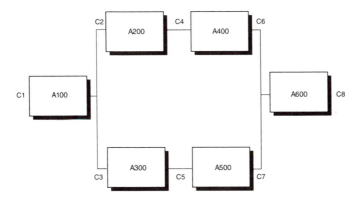

Figure: 8. Network Diagram

Self test:

1. What is an activity ?

2. What is a constraint ?

3. Draw activities in Series and Parallel.

4. What are the two basic requirements to be met before you can draw a network diagram ?

5. A number of logic diagram tests are set out in appendix 1.

5.8 Activity Durations (part 1)

We need two more items of information before we can proceed with the CPM time analysis:

* Activity durations.

* Activity calendar or workpattern.

Time units can be expressed as hours, days, shifts, weeks or months depending on the type of project. For simplicity the time units used in this book will be days unless otherwise stated. The time duration is the number of continuous working days from the start to the finish of the activity.

At this point we assume unlimited resources, the resource constraint will be introduced in the resource management chapter.

5.9 Calendar / Workpattern (part 1)

Calendar and **Workpattern** are common terms used in planning software to describe the activity's working profile, in other words on what days of the week the resources or activity will be working. As a first step we will assume the activity is working seven days a week, this is usually termed **continuous** working.

5.10 Critical Path Method Steps

We are now ready to perform the CPM time analysis to establish the start and finish dates for all the activities. Before we do, let us first recap on the CPM steps we have explained:

* Draw the logic network diagram.

* Assign durations to all the activities.

The information required as outlined above is usually compiled into two tables:

Logic Table

Preceding	Constraint	Succeeding

Activity Table

Activity Number	Description	Duration	Workpattern

In addition we need to set a start date.

Start date: We need to give the project a start date (this can always be changed later). The CPM analysis needs a start date to schedule the dates, if no date is given today's date will be used as a default option. By setting the start date the first iteration will give the planner a feel for the end date of the project using the given logic, activity durations and workpatterns. If a target completion date is given, the start can be adjusted accordingly.

CPM definitions: We need to understand the following terms before proceeding with the time analysis:

Early Start: The earliest date by which an activity can start.

Early Finish: The earliest date by which an activity can be completed.

Late Start: The latest date by which an activity needs to start before it will delay the project's completion date.

Late Finish: The latest date by which an activity needs to be completed so that it will not delay the project's completion date.

In addition to the calculated dates there may be a number of imposed dates, influenced by the delivery of materials, or access to sub-contractors.

Target Start: The date an activity is planned to start.
Target Finish: The date an activity is planned to finish.

The activity box: The key indicates where to position the values in the activity box.

EARLY START		EARLY FINISH
FLOAT	ACTIVITY NUMBER DESCRIPTION	DURATION
LATE START		LATE FINISH

Figure: 9. Activity box

5.11 Forward Pass

We use the term forward pass to define the process of calculating the Early Start date (ES) and Early Finish date (EF) for all the activities.

For convenience the Early Start date of the first activity in all the examples will be either day one or the first day of the month (i.e. 1st March).

Consider a simple project figure 10, with two activities A and B. The relationship between A and B is Finish-to-Start, this means activity A must be completed before B can start.

Activity	Duration
A	3 days
B	4 days

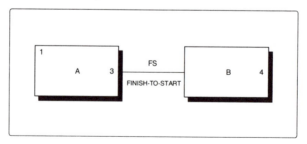

Figure: 10. Forward pass

The Early Finish date of an activity is calculated by adding the activity duration to the Early Start date, using the following formula.

EF   =   ES   +   Duration - 1

In the equation the minus one is required to keep the mathematics correct. Figure 11, will clarify this requirement. Shown as a barchart it can be clearly seen that a three day activity which starts on day 1 will finish on day 3.

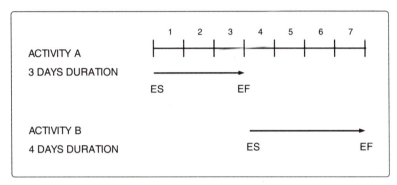

Figure: 11. Barchart

Using the above equation we can find the Early Finish date (EF) of activity A,

$$EF_A = ES_A + Duration_A - 1$$

$$= 1 + 3 - 1$$

$$= 3$$

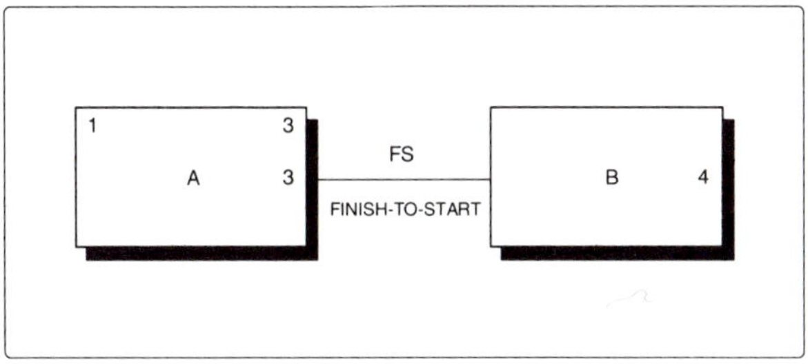

Figure: 12. Forward pass

To calculate the Early Start date (ES) of activity B use the following formula.

$$\text{ES}_B \quad = \quad \text{EF}_A \quad + \quad 1 \qquad \text{Activity (B) can only start the day after Activity (A) has finished}$$

$$= \quad 3 \quad + \quad 1$$

$$= \quad 4$$

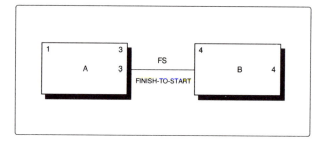

Figure: 13. Forward pass

To calculate the Early Finish date (EF) of B use the same formula as we used previously on activity A.

$$\text{EF}_B \quad = \quad \text{ES}_B \quad + \quad \text{Duration}_B \quad - \quad 1$$

$$= \quad 4 \quad + \quad 4 \quad - \quad 1$$

$$= \quad 7$$

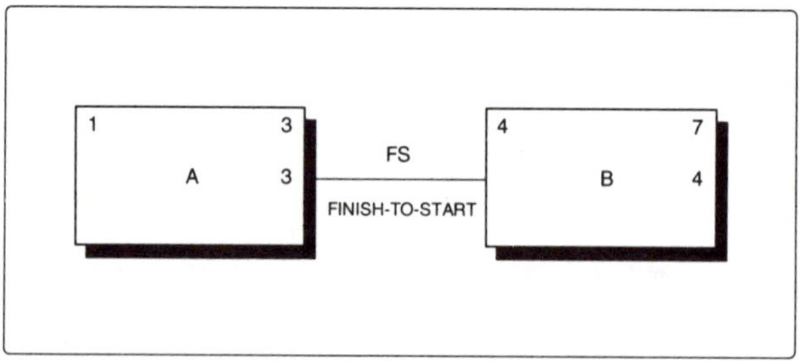

Figure: 14. Forward pass

To recap, the Early Start date of any activity is a measure of the time required to complete all preceding activities in the logical order outlined in the network diagram.

I have noticed while lecturing that managers like to work these numbers out on their fingers. I have therefore kept all the activity durations in the examples to less than ten days. Statistically most managers have 10 fingers. We now move on to the backward pass.

5.12 Backward Pass

Now that we have completed the forward pass the next step is to perform a backward pass to calculate the Late Start date (LS) and Late Finish date (LF). The Late Finish date for the last activity may be assigned, if not, use the Early Finish date as outlined in the following example.

$$LF_B = EF_B$$

$$= 7$$

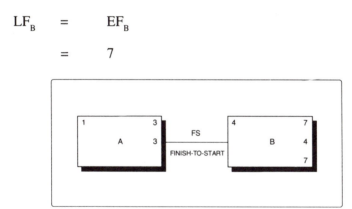

Figure: 15. Backward pass

To calculate the Late Start date (LS) of activity B use the following formula:

$$LS_B = LF_B - Duration_B + 1$$

$$= 7 - 4 + 1$$

$$= 4$$

Note the plus one in the formula to keep the mathematics correct.

$$LF_A = LS_B - 1$$
$$= 4 - 1$$
$$= 3$$

$$LS_A = LF_A - Duration_A + 1$$
$$= 3 - 3 + 1$$
$$= 1$$

To recap the Late Start date of any activity is a measure of the time required to complete all succeeding activities, in the logical order outlined in the network diagram.

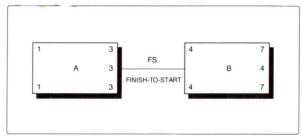

Figure: 16. Backward pass

Note: On large networks, when many activities lead into one activity on the forward pass, take the highest Early Finish value to calculate the Early Start date of the succeeding activity.

On the backward pass when many activities lead into one activity, take the lowest Late Start value to calculate the Late Finish of the preceding activity.

Take care, the intersection of activities is a common source of mathematical errors.

5.13 Activity Float (part 1)

Activity **float**, also called **slack**, is a measure of the flexibility of an activity, indicating how many working days the activity can be delayed or extended before it will effect the completion date of the project or any target finish dates.

Float is calculated by either of the two equations.

Float = Late Start - Early Start
Float = Late Finish - Early Finish

Mathematically they are both the same, therefore select the equation you are most comfortable with.

Using the previous example:

$$Float_A \quad = \quad LS_A \quad - \quad ES_A$$
$$= \quad 1 \quad - \quad 1$$
$$= \quad 0$$

The float for activity B is also 0. Where an activity has zero float this indicates it is on the **critical path**.

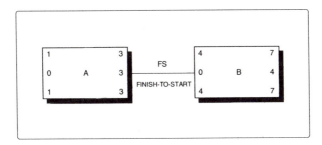

Figure: 17. Network Diagram

This now completes the forward and backward pass.

Worked example continued: We are now in a position to develop a complete CPM worked example. If we follow on from the first part of worked example we need the following activity information:

Activity Number	Duration	Workpattern
A100	2	Continuous
A200	2	Continuous
A300	1	Continuous
A400	4	Continuous
A500	2	Continuous
A600	2	Continuous

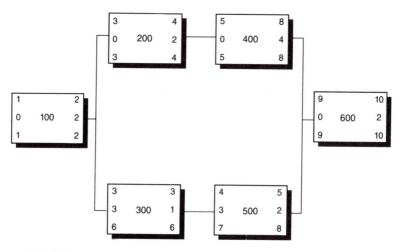

Figure: 18. Worked example

Work through this example before proceeding with the following exercises.

Self Test:

1.   What is a workpattern ?

2.   Why is a start date necessary ?

3.   What information does the forward pass give ?

4.   How is the activity float linked to the critical path ?

5.   At this point work through Appendix 4 up to the forward pass.

This completes the first cycle of the CPM development spiral. The second part will take the reader a step further, where the main headings from the previous sections will be developed in more detail.

5.14 Network Diagrams (part 2)

The network diagram also known as the Precedence Diagram Method (PDM) takes its name from the logical relationship between activities.

The precedence network has established itself, with the project planning software as the most popular form of network analysis and presentation. This has come about mainly because of the enhanced computer generated graphical presentation, the additional logical relationships and also the ease of including more activity information on the diagram.

Besides the basic finish-to-start there are four other types of constraints between activities. The abbreviation is shown in brackets:

* Finish-to-Start.   (FS)

* Start-to-Start.   (SS)

* Finish-to-Finish.   (FF)

* Start-to-Finish.   (SF)

* Hammocked activities.

Finish-to-Start (FS): The Finish-to-Start (FS) constraint is the most common type of relationship. In the example below activity 020 cannot start until activity 010 is finished, say activity 010 is completed on Monday then 020 can start on Tuesday.

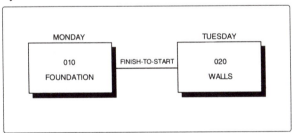

Figure: 19. Finish-to-Start

This relationship can be further developed by imposing a delay between the activities. Say activity 010 was laying a foundation and activity 020 was building the walls. If the concrete needs 2 days to cure and the foundation (010) is laid on Monday then the building of the walls (020) cannot start before Thursday. This relationship would be represented as follows.

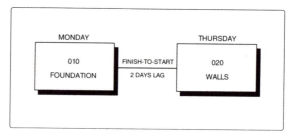

Figure: 20. Finish-to-Start with Lag

Or in barchart form:

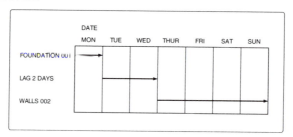

Figure: 21. Finish-to-Start barchart with lag

Start-to-Start (SS): The Start-to-Start (SS) constraint represents the relationship between the start dates of the two activities. Activity 060 can start 4 days after 050 has started. This could represent a fast tracking type of situation, where the project's duration is compressed by overlapping the activities.

An example of a SS constraint would be the laying of a pipe line. When the first km of the trench has been dug, the pipe laying can start. If the digging starts on a Monday and it takes 4 days to dig the first km, then the pipe laying can start on a Friday.

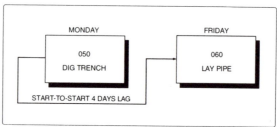

Figure: 22. Start-to-Start

Or in barchart form:

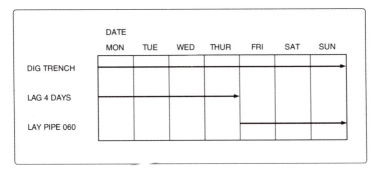

Figure: 23. Start-to-Start

Other SS relationships in this project would be the testing and back-fill of the pipe line. If the start of activity 050 is delayed, then activity 060 will also be delayed. The converse may also be true if resources are available.

Finish-to-Finish (FF): The Finish-to-Finish (FF) constraint represents the relationship between the finish of the two activities.

Activity 2000 can finish 3 days after activity 1000 is complete. An example here would be the fabrication and painting of a structure. Although there is no constraint concerning the start of the painting, the painters cannot start painting the last section until the fabrication is finished and then it will take 3 days to complete.

If the fabrication is completed on a Monday, then the painting can only be completed by Thursday at the earliest.

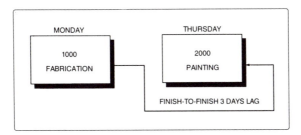

Figure: 24. Finish-to-Finish

Or in barchart form:

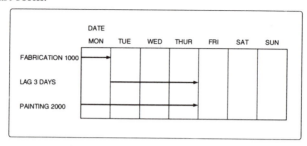

Figure: 25. Finish-to-Finish

Start-to-Finish (SF): The Start-to-Finish (SF) constraint links the start of the first activity with the finish of the following activity. This is a useful facility to assign an overall time duration to span two activities.

For example consider a crane hired for 6 days. The crane has two lifts which must be completed in 6 days. Therefore 6 days after Activity A100 starts A200 must finish.

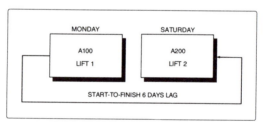

Figure: 26. Start-to-Finish

Or in barchart form:

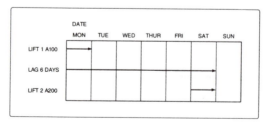

Figure: 27. Start-to-Finish

Feedback from industry suggests that this SF relationship is seldom used.

Hammock: A Hammock activity is used to summarize a number of activities into one activity. This is useful for keydate / milestone reporting to senior management, who only want to look at the important issues at a summary level.

In this example activity 1000 has the same Early Start date as activity 100 and the same Late Start date as activity 300.

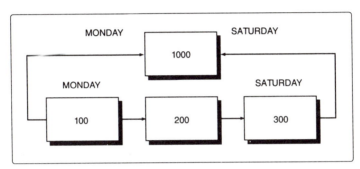

Figure: 28. Hammock

Or in barchart form:

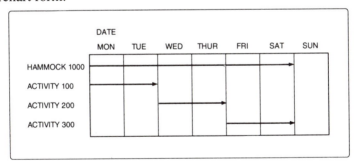

Figure: 29. Hammock

Note 1: A discontinuous option is available on some software packages where the activity is constrained both SS and FF. In this case the resource analysis will schedule the activities discontinuously to match the resources available.

Note 2: It may be the planners preference to impose a time base to the network diagram to enhance the presentation.

Leads and lags: A delay may be given to the start or finish of an activity. These delays are termed **lead time** before an activity and **lag time** after the activity. An example of each would be "waiting for plan approval" or "the curing time for concrete" respectively. The planner may want to keep these durations separate from the activity's duration, because if significant this would distort the cash flow statement and resource histogram.

5.15 Logical Errors

Before starting the time analysis it is important to validate the network's logic to ensure that there are no logical errors. Some packages perform a **topological sort** to compile the logic relationships into a suitable order, to ensure that no activity is processed before its logical predecessors.

There are a number of basic logic errors to be checked for in the network diagram. These are termed:

* Logical loop.

* Logical dangle.

* Redundant precedence relationship.

Logical loop: Consider the following logical loop which represents an impossible situation. Activity 020 follows 010, 030 follows 020, and 010 follows 030.

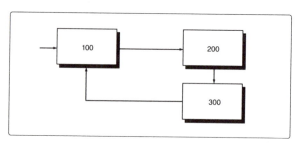

Figure: 30. Logical loop

The figure indicates that one or more relationships need to be re-assigned before processing.

Logical dangle: As the name suggests a logically dangling activity is where the activity either comes from nowhere or goes to nowhere. In this example activity 090 follows 050, but what follows 090 ?

Some software packages require the user to define the start and finish activity, as the start does not have a preceding activity and the finish does not have a succeeding activity.

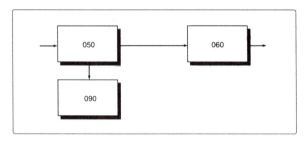

Figure: 31. Logical dangle

Redundant precedence relationship: When developing the network diagram it is only necessary to indicate an activity's immediate predecessors, for example, 200 is a predecessor of 300 and 100 is a predecessor of 200. Therefore implicitly 100 is a predecessor of 300. It is not necessary to explicitly specify this relationship, if you do this would be an example of a redundant precedence relationship.

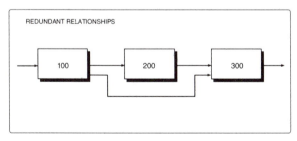

Figure: 32. Redundant precedence relationship

When using project planning software, the computer will perform the logical loop, logical dangle and redundant precedence relationship checks as part of the CPM validation. If errors are detected the time analyses (forward and backward pass) will not start and an error message will be sent to the screen. The error messages are usually structured to enable the planner to locate the error quickly.

This iterative process may need to be performed a few times before all the bugs are eliminated.

Self Test:

1. List the five types of constraints used in Precedence Network Diagrams.

2. What is the most common type of relationship ?

3. Which constraints would be associated with fast tracking ?

4. Why are Hammock activities useful ?

5. At what point in the CPM process should the logic be checked ?

5.16 Definition of an Activity (part 2)

With the introduction of project planning software, certain terms and norms have been established, it is the authors intention to use these terms wherever possible. The characteristics of an activity include the following:-

* An activity must have a unique activity code or number (A, 010, ABC100). The code may be alpha, numeric or alphanumeric. The numbers do not need to be in any sequence because the logical relationships will determine the position of the activity in the network diagram. If the numbers are in sequence, however, this may help readability.

* If multi-project resource scheduling is required the activity numbers from the various projects need to be different, otherwise some data will be overwritten. This can be achieved by either having a unique project code which forms part of the activity number, or assigning a control digit prior to processing.

* An activity must have a description. The description should be as informative and unambiguous as possible. Some computer packages

allow the user to define a short description and a long description to suit the report layouts. The description length is usually restricted to fit into the framework of a report. If longer words are used they may be truncated.

* There will be logical relationships between the activities.

* All activities will have a time duration for completing the task, even if it is zero.

* All activities will have a calendar / workpattern to indicate when the work can be scheduled. Even if it is seven days a week ie, continuous working.

* The activity can have target start and finish dates assigned. Certainly a starting date or finishing date for the project is required. Target dates would be influenced by delivery of bought-in items, availability of equipment or access to sub-contractors.

* An activity will use resources. When the resources are linked to an activity they can be scheduled to produce a resource histogram.

* As time and resources are linked to the activities they can be integrated to generate a manpower S curve against time for planning and control purposes.

* An activity will incur expenses. If these costs are linked to the activities the costs can be scheduled and rolled-up to produce a cash flow statement and planned expenditure curves (BCWS). See earned value chapter.

* If a Work Breakdown Structure (WBS) is used, the activities can be linked to the work packages. This will enable the costs to be entered at the activity level and rolled-up to be reported at a higher level.

* An activity may have material requirements. The ordering and delivery can be linked to the activity to give a material requirement planning (MRP) report and guidelines for expediting.

An example of an activity would be:

Identity   A100

Description   Dig the house foundations.

Workpattern   5 days per week / Monday to Friday

Duration   20 working days

Resources   5 men per day

Budget $ 20000

WBS   1.1.1

Logic   Relationship with other activities.

Target date   Assigned start or finish dates.

5.17 Calendar / Workpattern (part 2)

Up to now in the calculations we have assumed that the project is working seven days a week, this is usually not the case, so we use a calendar or workpattern to define when work will take place.

Before we can calculate an activity's start and finish date we need to know what days of the week the activity will be working. For example will the activity be working Monday to Friday, or Monday to Saturday or perhaps everyday of the week. We also need to know when the resources will take personal and company holidays together with public holidays.

The planning packages allow the user to define a number of workpatterns, which can be linked to either the activity or the resource.

It is preferable that, where possible, workpatterns are linked to activities, because in practice the same resource might work different hours on different activities. Listed below are the characteristics associated with a calendar / workpattern:

* The workpattern defines the days on which work can be scheduled. This takes into consideration access to the work place and availability of the resource.

* A number of workpatterns can be defined. They can be assigned to any of the trades or even one per manager if appropriate. Each workpattern being a unique combination of rest days and holidays.

* Rest days are the days of the week which are always taken off, ie. weekends, Saturday and Sunday. The computer software generally assume continuous working (default option is a seven day working week) except for the days the activity is not working (ie. the rest days and holidays).

* Holidays can be defined as public holidays, works holidays, or your own personal holidays. Essentially days on which the resource will not be available in addition to the rest days.

* Activities and resources can be linked to a workpattern number.

* If the activity does not have a workpattern, the planning software may flag an error or default to continuous working (seven days a week).

* The planning software sometimes limits the number of workpatterns one can create (about ten is typical), though two or three workpatterns are usually sufficient.

Example: The workpattern and start date can affect the duration of the activity, consider this example, if the workpattern is to work Monday to Friday, an eight working day activity could take either 10 or 12 calendar days depending on where the weekends fall.

					SAT	SUN						SAT	SUN	
	1	2	3	4	5	6	7	8	9	10	11	12	13	14	15
8 DAYS DURATION (TAKES 10 DAYS)															
8 DAYS DURATION (TAKES 12 DAYS)															

Figure: 33. Workpattern

Consider also activity 020 which has a Monday to Friday workpattern and is dependant on activity 010 which finishes on a Friday. Because of the workpattern activity 020 cannot start before Monday.

ACTIVITY	WORKPATTERN	FRI	SAT	SUN	MON
DATE		5	6	7	8
010	MON TO FRI				
020	MON TO FRI				

Figure: 34. Workpattern

5.18 Activity Float (part 2)

Float is a measure of the flexibility of an activity, indicating how many working days the activity can be delayed, before it will affect the completion date of the project, or any target finish date. Note: certain planning software packages relate the duration of the activity float to the workpattern.

The critical path is defined as the series of activities which have zero float. The critical path always runs through the project from the first activity, to the last activity. As a project approaches completion a number of network arms may become critical, giving more than one critical path.

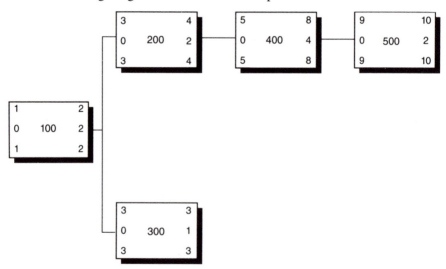

Figure: 35. Activity float

If a project has a number of finish activities on different arms of the network then each of these arms will become critical, if each activity takes its own Early Finish date as its Late Finish date. In the example, activity 300 although indicated as critical could finish up to 7 days later. To prevent all these from becoming critical either link them to the latest activity or assign a target finish date near the end of the project.

The presentation of the critical path is usually highlighted:

*   Heavy print.

*   Different type of line.

*   Red, if colour available (remember colours cannot be photocopied or faxed)

There are three main types of float in CPM and it is important to be able to distinguish between them to avoid confusion and errors.

Total float:	Here the float is shared with all the other activities in the arm. If the float is used by one activity, it will reduce the float available for the other activities on the arm. Care must be taken that one does not assume each activity has this amount of float to itself.
Free float:	This is a measure of the amount of float the activity can use up without affecting the Early Start of any other activity. This only happens when there is one activity in the network arm linked to a critical activity or milestone.
Negative float:	When calculations show that an activity must start before the preceding activities are finished, this is indicated as negative float. It is an unworkable situation which occurs when an activity falls behind planned progress. This value of the negative float indicates how much the activity's duration or logic must be shortened.

In precedence networks where there are both SS and FF relationships it is possible to have a start float and a finish float.

5.19 Summary

This chapter outlined CPM as a planning and control tool which would address the project manager's need to process large amounts of data quickly and effectively. A comprehensive list of benefits were presented to support the implementation of this technique.

The CPM technique was presented as a two cycle development spiral consisting of; the network diagram, activities, logical relationships and workpatterns.

The techniques and practical application of CPM were outlined by taking the manager step by step through the various stages; developing the network, checking for logical errors, forward pass, backward pass, calculating activity float to finally identifying the critical path.

This is an appropriate time to remind the reader that the purpose of this book is to manually perform the current techniques used by project management software. The long term goal should be for the reader to apply these techniques on the computer.

The next chapter will outline techniques to critically validate the information given by the CPM.

Chapter 6

Validation

Project validation is a method for critically examining and evaluating the quality of the information provided. The scope of validating extends to all the key areas of project management. This chapter will, however, use validation to scrutinise the planning and control function.

This chapter starts with a section outlining the basic validation questions before listing the benefits of acceleration and methods of acceleration. The time cost trade-off theory is then developed in detail before being explained through a worked example.

Critical Path Method (CPM) was originally set up as a validating technique to quantify the trade-off between project cost and project duration. CPM was able to quantify the difference in project cost associated with an extension or reduction in the project's overall duration.

On large scale complex projects it may be extremely difficult to examine all the activities in detail, it is therefore necessary to be able to set priorities to focus the project managers attention on the important issues.

To overcome this problem, CPM is used to identify the critical activities which determine the end date of the project together with other intermediate key dates. The planner can now focus his attention on those activities that will have the most significant impact on the project.

In theory it is easy to advise that the project's objectives should be clearly defined at the outset. In practice, however, there may not be sufficient information available. At the beginning of the project, the planner may not be able to appreciate how one objective may relate to another. It is not always possible, for example, to complete a project in the shortest time, at minimum cost and also achieve the highest quality.

6.1 Validation Questions

Validation is the process of asking pertinent questions which:

* Critically examine the quality of information.

* Determine if the project will meet its stated objectives.

* Analyse the time cost trade-off.

These questions can be structured around the main topic headings:

General: Is the information presented in an easy to assimilate and readable format ?

* Has the presentation been sorted and ordered in the most effective manner ?

* Is the project meeting the original goals and objectives ? If not, quantify the non-conforming parameter and the variance.

* Is the project control based on accurate feedback of project performance ?

* Are the meetings minuted ?

* Are the progress reports in sufficient detail to evaluate the project's performance ?

* Can an audit trail follow the main decisions ?

Scope: Does the scope of work outline the complete project and describe what is to be made ?

* Is the scope sub-divided into manageable WBS work packages ?

* Do the work packages define unique elements of work, a contractor, a department or location ?

Time: Does the planning information provide a network diagram and a scheduled barchart ?

* On the network diagram are all activities logically linked ?

* Has a structured walk through by the responsible parties been carried out ?

* Has the critical path been determined ?

* Does the scheduling information show if the project is meeting key dates ?

* Can the duration be reduced by either a logic change or crashing activities ? (Activity crashing or acceleration will be discussed later in the chapter.)

Costs: Has a budget per activity been allocated ?

* Does the financial information indicate if the project cash flow will be positive or negative ?

* Does the baseline plan integrate cost and time to give the budgeted cost for work scheduled curve (BCWS) or expenditure ''S'' curve ?

Resources: Has a manpower plan been produced ?

* Does the resource information indicate under and over resource utilization ?

* Is resource smoothing required ?

These are just a few of the questions one should be asking when validating the project's information.

Exercise: Develop a validating checklist for a typical project in your field of operation, based on your own experience.

6.2 Time Cost Trade-off

The main focus of the chapter is the validating of the CPM time cost trade-off. After completing the network diagram and the CPM calculations the next step is to critically examine and evaluate the quality of information being provided for the decision support function.

The purpose of time cost trade-off may be explained as developing the schedule that just balances the value of the time saved against the incremental cost of saving it. In simpler terms this means, when a power plant, for example, is taken out of the service its ''opportunity cost'' or lost income can be quantified per day. If an overhaul could be reduced by a few days, is the income from the time reduction greater than the cost of crashing the project ?

The need to reduce the duration of an activity may arise at any time during the project. The following list outlines some of the reasons and benefits associated with reducing activity and project duration:-

* The CPM calculations indicate activities with negative float. This problem will extend the end date of the project if not addressed.

* The company wishes to finish the present project quickly so that their resources can be used on another more profitable job.

* A bonus will be given for early project completion, road construction projects often offer this type of bonus.

* If the allocated budget is not spent within this tax or financial year, the excess funds will not be rolled forward to next year.

* If the project is running late, analyze the time cost trade-off between crashing the project or accepting the time penalties.

* Calculate the time cost trade-off associated with the opportunity costs while the component is out of action. This could apply to a power station, aeroplane or motor car. The opportunity cost is expressed as either the loss of income or the cost to hire a replacement.

If any of the above apply to your project, the next step is to look for ways of implementing a project acceleration.

Project Budget   vs   Project Schedule

6.3 Acceleration Methods

Project acceleration, also called **crashing,** is the process of reducing the duration of a project. Let us consider some methods of shortening an activity's duration.

* Once the critical path has been identified, resources can be transferred from non-critical activities to critical activities. This will shorten the duration of the critical activities, while extending the duration of the non-critical activities. Check that only the float is used up on the non-critical activities.

* Change the network logic along the critical path. Change activities which are in series to Start-to-Start (SS), Finish-to-Finish (FF) or parallel. This will shorten the overall duration of the project.

* Recalculate the estimate for activity durations along the critical path. With more information the contingency part of the estimate can be reduced which in turn, should reduce the duration of the activity.

* Change the calendar / workpattern to increase the working hours. For example work overtime, shifts or change from a 5 day week to 6 or 7 day week. Note: with the longer working hours expect a fall off in productivity and an increase in labour costs.

* When in-house resources are overloaded employ sub-contractors. However, first check that there is sufficient room in the work place for the additional workforce. Also consider the industrial relation impact, will the sub-contractors be accepted by the workforce ?

* If an activity's start is being delayed because of access, consider pre-outfit or modularization. In shipbuilding the accommodation is often pre-assembled in the workshops while the steelwork is being built on the slipway.

* If an activity is being delayed because of material delivery logistics, consider a quicker form of transport, for example, use air freight instead of sea freight or road transport.

* The use of incentive payments can speed up delivery of materials and other deliverables by ensuring a preferential service.

* Technical changes should be considered to make the work simpler and quicker. For example, using an alternative type of material, different method of assembly or erect components piece large.

* In the short-term productivity can be increased by offering various forms of incentive payments like a bonus, piece rate or job and knock. Job and knock means the workforce can leave when the job is finished, but they are paid for the whole shift.

* If the job involves a certain amount of repetition it is reasonable to assume there will be a learning curve, which will reduce the manhours per unit later in the project.

* Education and training of the workforce usually improves efficiency and effectiveness. The benefits unfortunately may only be reaped in the long term.

* Improving working conditions and focusing attention towards the workforce can increase production (Hawthorne experiment see **Handy** p162). Consider also the motivation theories expressed by Maslow, Herzberg and McGregor.

* If time and cost are the main objectives, consider reducing the project's scope of work.

* Project time could be reduced by further increasing the utilization of automation, machines and computers.

By skilfully using a number of these methods the project manager should be able to effectively shorten the length of the project.

6.4 Crashing Steps

This section will outline a sequence of steps required to crash an activity.

Step 1.   Identify the activities that need to be crashed (where an activity has negative float for instance). This can happen at any time from the initial project planning phase to project completion.

Step 2.   Identify the critical path. To crash non-critical activities is a waste of financial resources because it will simply increase the float on that activity without affecting the end date of the project. See figure 4.

Step 3.   Prioritise the activities to be crashed. When there are many activities which can be crashed which one will we crash first ?

a)   Select the activity with the least cost per day to crash.

b)   The easiest to crash.

c)   The activity which can be crashed soonest to bring the project back on course. As project manager you do not want to approach the end of the project with a number of activities running behind schedule and the prospects of further problems during commissioning.

Step 4.   Crash activities one day at a time, then re-analyze the network to see if any other activities have gone critical.

Continue this iterative process until there are no activities with negative float. These crashing steps may vary with the different types of projects. It should be evident that cost has been identified as a main consideration, the next section will show how to estimate the crashing expense.

6.5 Time Cost Trade-off Theory

This section will explain the theory behind the time cost trade-off concept. The first step is to define some terminology:

Normal Time: Normal office hours, 8 hours a day, 5 days a week.

Normal Cost: The cost of the activity working normal hours.

Direct Cost: Costs attributed directly to the project, labour and materials. These costs usually go up when the activity is crashed due to overtime, shift allowance etc.

Indirect Cost: Overhead costs which cannot be directly attributed to the project, for example, office rent and management salaries. These costs are usually linear with time, therefore, if the time reduces, the indirect costs also reduce.

Crash Time: The duration the activity can be reduced to, by crashing the activity.

Crash Cost: The new cost of the activity after crashing.

We will first discuss the way direct costs and indirect costs react when a critical activity is crashed.

Crashing (direct costs): The duration has been reduced but the costs have increased. These additional costs are caused by overtime, shift work and a reduction in productivity.

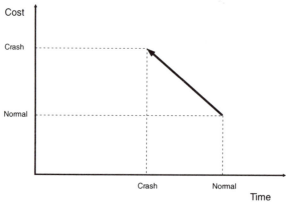

Figure: 1. Crashing direct costs

Crashing (indirect costs): The duration has been reduced but this time the costs have also reduced. The benefit has come from reduced office rental, equipment hire etc. Unfortunately project costs are usually split 80% direct, 20% indirect so the benefit of crashing indirect costs is usually overwhelmed by the far greater direct costs.

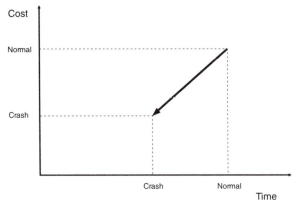

Figure: 2. Crashing indirect costs

When the direct costs and indirect costs are combined on the same graph an optimum position is derived.

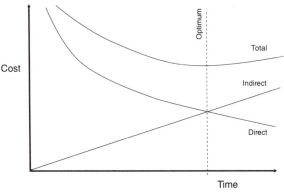

Figure: 3. Combined direct and indirect costs

Time cost trade-off: The time cost trade-off figure outlines graphically four different time costs positions. Starting at point A figure 4, this point represents normal time and normal cost. Consider first the effect of crashing all the non-critical activities, the project will move to point D. Notice there has been no shortening of the project's duration, but the costs have increased dramatically. This is not a recommended course of action as it only increases the float of non-critical activities.

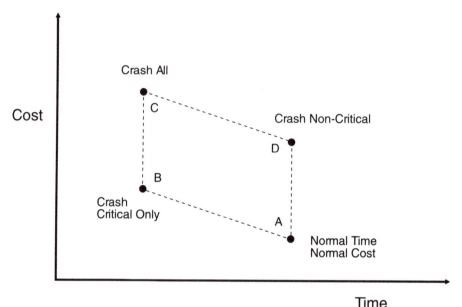

Figure: 4. The time cost trade-off.

The correct action would be to crash all the critical activities. The project moves to point B. Crashing the critical activities has reduced the duration of the project with a small increase in costs.

The fourth point on the graph, C, indicates the position when all the activities are crashed. Again this is not recommended because there has been no time improvement on point B, yet the costs have increased tremendously.

The moral of the story is **only crash critical activities**.

Worked example: The following calculations will show how direct costs increase with crashing, while indirect costs reduce. Consider the following activity to manufacture a garden shed.

When working normal time the activity will take;
5 men working 8 hours per day,
5 days per week for 5 weeks $\qquad$ = $\qquad$ 1000 man hrs.

The activity's normal costs will be:

Labour @ $20 per hour x 1000 man hours	=	$20000
Material	=	$ 5000
Preliminary and General @ $1000 per week		
$1000 x 5 weeks	=	$ 5000

Total	=	$30000

If the client now wants to manufacture the shed in less time, the crash cost can be quantified in steps of one day. To reduce the duration the men will have to work overtime, say 10 hours per day (2 hours overtime @ time and a half). Assume the additional hours do not effect the productivity.

The total manhours will still be the same at 1000 man hours / (5 men x 10 hours per day) = 20 days or 4 weeks. The extra hours worked per day will reduce the duration from 25 working days to 20 working days.

The crashing costs will be:

Labour: $20 x 20 days x 5 men x 8 hrs	=	$16000 (normal time)
$20 x 20 days x 5 men x 2 hrs		
x 1.5 (overtime)	=	$ 6000 (over time)
Material:	=	$ 5000 (no change)
P & G: $1000 x 4 weeks	=	$ 4000 (reduction)

Total	=	$31000

With this information calculate the additional cost to crash the activity by one day.

Additional crash cost $\qquad$ = $\qquad$ (Difference in cost)

per day $\qquad$ -----------------------

$\qquad$ (Difference in time)

$\qquad$ = $\qquad$ (31000 - 30000) / (25 - 20)

$\qquad$ = $\qquad$ $200 per day

This example clearly shows that to reduce the project by 1 week or 5 days the direct costs will increase while the indirect costs reduce. The overall effect is to increase the costs by $200 per day.

Crash cost priority table: Having decided to crash a project the next step is to set up a priority table to indicate the most cost effective order of crashing, i.e. crash the cheapest activity first.

A crash priority table is developed below, set-up columns A and B as normal time and normal cost, this information will be available from the original estimate. Assign the crash time and crash costs to columns C and D, this data will have to be calculated as outlined in the above example.

The additional cost to crash per day is calculated from columns A to D. If the table was set up on a spreadsheet this could be calculated automatically. Notice only activities on the critical path are considered and the priority of crashing is cheapest first.

Although crashing the cheapest first is recommended the timing of that activity should also be taken into count. If the project manager wants to crash the project **now** then obviously activities that do not start for a few weeks cannot be considered.

	A	B	C	D	(D-B)/(A-C)	
Activity Number	Normal Time	Normal Cost	Crash Time	Crash Cost	Additional cost to crash per day	Crashing Priority
010	25	30000	20	31000	200	2
020	10	5000	6	5400	100	1
030	12	9000	8	9200	50	Not Critical
040	15	21000	9	22500	250	3

Figure: 5. Crash cost estimating table

Self Test: Draw up an estimating table for the critical activities based on a project you have worked on.

6.6 Summary

In the discussion we have identified a need to critically examine and evaluate the quality of the information generated by the planning and control function.

The need to reduce the duration of an activity may arise at any time during the project. The text outlined a comprehensive list of ways to reduce an activity's duration, along with associated benefits to the project.

By skilfully using a number of these crashing methods the project manager should be able to effectively shorten the length of the project. The bottom line for most projects is cost, so it is important to appreciate the trade-off between cost and time.

Chapter 7

Scheduling

The scheduled barchart is a management tool used to graphically present planning information. This chapter will explain how to use the Gantt Chart and schedule barcharts as a planning and control facility. The text will show that they can either be used on their own or linked to the Critical Path Method (CPM).

The terms planning and scheduling are often used interchangeably. However, if a distinction is required, planning generally refers to the process of generating a time framework for the project which becomes a schedule when dates are assigned to the activities.

Barcharts are widely used on projects because they provide an effective presentation which is not only easy to understand and assimilate by a wide range of people, but also conveys the planning and scheduling information accurately and precisely.

7.1 How to draw a Barchart

The basic format of a barchart consists of a list of activities with start and finish dates imposed on a calendar pro forma. The normally accepted barchart format lists the scope of work on the left hand side, with a calendar scale along the top and sometimes the bottom of the page. The activities are listed down the left side, with a corresponding horizontal bar proportional in length to the duration of the activity indicating the activity's start and finish date. The calendar time scale is usually days or weeks.

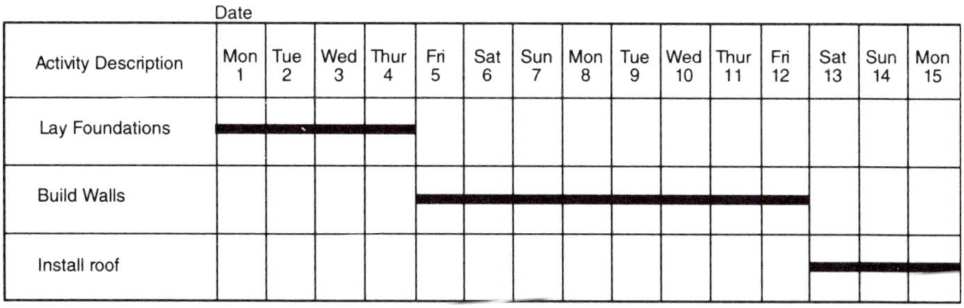

Activity Description	Mon 1	Tue 2	Wed 3	Thur 4	Fri 5	Sat 6	Sun 7	Mon 8	Tue 9	Wed 10	Thur 11	Fri 12	Sat 13	Sun 14	Mon 15
Lay Foundations	■	■	■	■											
Build Walls					■	■	■	■	■	■	■	■			
Install roof													■	■	■

Figure: 1. Simple barchart

7.2 The Gantt Chart

The history of project planning and scheduling can be dated back to the first World War when an American, Henry Gantt, designed the barchart as a visual aid for planning and controlling his projects. In recognition, planning barcharts often bear his name. In the text the terms Gantt chart and barchart will be used interchangeably.

The format of the Gantt chart is the same as a barchart, where the base is a calendar time-scale in days or weeks and the activities are listed on the left from top to bottom. Each activity is represented by a horizontal line (as a bar or characters), the length being proportional to the duration of the activity and the position indicating the scheduling of the activity.

The Gantt chart can be used for project planning and control as the following simple example will outline. The project is to decorate the front room of your house.

Activity Number	Description	Duration (days)
010	Buy materials	2
020	Paint ceilings	4
030	Paint walls	4
040	Paint woodwork	5

Date

Activity Description	Progress	Mon 1	Tue 2	Wed 3	Thur 4	Fri 5	Sat 6	Sun 7	Mon 8	Tue 9	Wed 10
010 Buy materials	planned actual	■■									
020 Paint ceilings	planned actual			■■■■■■■							
030 Paint walls	planned actual			■■■■							
040 Paint doors & windows	planned actual			■■■■■■■■■							

Figure: 2. The Gantt chart

7.2.1 Gantt Chart Symbols

Gantt used graphic symbols to add more information to the barchart without cluttering the presentation. The figure below shows a typical legend of symbols.

[	Scheduled Start
]	Scheduled Finish
—	Actual Progress
∧	Current Date
◊	Milestone Scheduled
◆	Milestone Achieved

Figure: 3. Gantt chart symbols

The type of symbol varies in practice to accommodate the available symbols on the planning software. A basic spreadsheet like Lotus 123 can be used to present a scheduled barchart as is the case with many of the barcharts in this book.

7.2.2 Gantt Chart Project Control

Besides planning and scheduling the project, the Gantt chart can also be used to track and monitor project progress.Once the project has started the next function is to show how the work is actually progressing. This is achieved by drawing a second line (bar or character) above, inside or underneath the original bar to compare planned with actual.

Progress information can be presented as either a percentage complete or remaining duration. For simplicity it is assumed here that there is a direct relationship between percentage complete and remaining duration, for example, when a 4 day activity is 50% complete, the remaining duration is 2 days.

Thus for the decorating project if the progress at timenow 4 was reported as follows:-

Activity Number	Percentage Complete	Remaining Duration
010	100 %	0
020	75 %	1
030	50 %	2
040	20 %	4

the Gantt chart would be drawn as below where activity 010 which is 100% complete, the actual progress bar is drawn the full length of the activity. For activity 020 which has a remaining duration of 1 day an actual progress bar is drawn up to day 5, thus indicating that this activity is 1 day ahead of the plan. Activity 030's progress is as planned, while activity 040 is 1 day behind planned progress.

Where barchart space is a premium the actual progress can be drawn inside the planned bar, thus removing a line. This type of presentation enables the project manager to see immediately the status of all the activities.

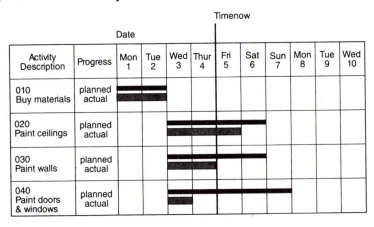

Figure: 4. Gantt chart showing progress

The next step is to analyse the Gantt chart at timenow 4:

* Activity 010 should have been completed and is finished.

* Activity 020 should have started and be 50% complete, but is actually 75% complete. This indicates the activity is 1 day ahead of planned progress.

* Activity 030 should have started and be 50% complete, and is actually 50% complete, indicating actual progress as planned.

* Activity 040 should have started and be 50% complete, but is actually only 20% complete. This indicates actual progress is behind planned progress by 1 day. This activity needs investigating to determine the problem, because without corrective action the end of the project will be extended.

Thus the Gantt chart shows that bars to the left of timenow are under performing, while those to the right of timenow are over performing. This type of progress reporting gives a very clear visual presentation which is easy to assimilate.

7.2.3 Gantt Chart List of Positive Features

The positive features of the Gantt chart may be summarized as follows:

* The barchart presentation is easy to assimilate and understand.

* The barchart displays activity progress very clearly and simply.

* Activity float is easier to comprehend when shown on a barchart.

* A scheduled barchart is a prerequisite for forecasting the resource requirement.

* A scheduled barchart is a prerequisite for predicting the project's cash flow.

* A barchart is an excellent management tool for planning and control.

* A barchart can be used to communicate and disseminate information.

*   A barchart is a key document for the management decision-making function.

We now move on to the Gantt chart's problems.

7.2.4 Gantt Chart Problems

The Gantt chart has two main limitations:

*   Interrelationships.

*   Multiple decision-making.

Inter-relationships: The Gantt chart does not explicitly indicate the sequencing and interrelationships between the activities. If an activity is accelerated or delayed it is not always possible on a complex project to see the affect this will have on the other activities.

Multiple decision-making: Before an activity can be placed on the Gantt chart three factors have to be considered and decided on simultaneously:

*   The logical sequence of the activities.

*   The activity's duration which depends on the resources used.

*   The resource allocation which depends on resources available.

An effective plan must address equally these three factors of logic, time, and resources. Unfortunately as projects became larger and more complex, the Gantt chart was found to be lacking as a planning and control tool if used on its own.

The Gantt chart's problem and shortcoming can, however, be overcome by using it in conjunction with network diagrams and CPM. The following section will outline how the tabular output from the CPM can be transposed into a Gantt chart.

7.3 Tabular Reports

Tabular reports as the name suggests contain information in rows and columns or (using computer terminology) records and fields. In the CPM chapter the output from worked example 2 (p.124) is now presented in a tabular format, before being transposed into a scheduled barchart.

Scope	Duration	Early Start	Early Finish	Late Start	Late Finish	Float
A100	2	1	2	1	2	0
A200	2	3	4	3	4	0
A300	1	3	3	6	6	3
A400	4	5	8	5	8	0
A500	2	4	5	7	8	3
A600	2	9	10	9	10	0

Figure: 5. Tabular format

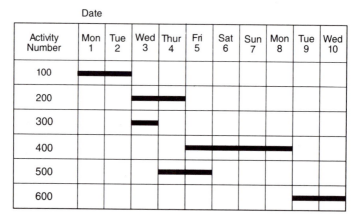

Figure: 6. Scheduled barchart

To transpose the data from the tabular activity table to the scheduled barchart requires the activities to be listed on the left side, with a bar drawn from activity's Early Start to Early Finish. Work through the example yourself until you feel comfortable with the technique.

Planning information is generally stored in a tabular format, certainly planning software data bases are structured this way. As seen above, the tabular report was a prerequisite for a scheduled barchart.

Planning information "packs" generally contain tabular reports, barcharts and other graphical presentations. Obviously the design of these reports should address the information need of the project.

7.4 Activity Float

The barchart presentation will now be further enhanced with the introduction of activity float. The accepted presentation is to show the float after the activity from Early Finish to Late Finish, and denote it as a dotted line with a symbol at the end, usually an up-turned triangle. The figure shows the float both before and after the activity bar.

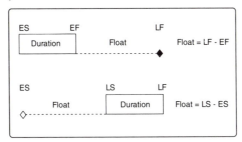

Figure: 7. Activity Float

It is generally assumed by implication that any activity without float is on the critical path, it is therefore important to show float to prevent this confusion. Using example 2, figure 5 again, add the float to the non-critical activities.

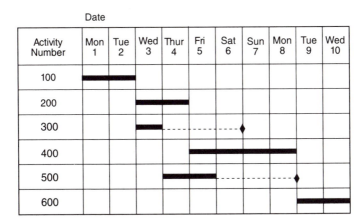

Figure: 8. Barchart showing Float

7.5 Select and Sort

Before developing the barchart further this is an appropriate point to introduce a few data handling techniques. These are generally termed by the planning software as; data ''Select'' or ''Filter'' and data ''Sort'' or ''Order''.

These processes are used to prepare the data for further calculations. It should be remembered that computers work in a highly structured and disciplined manner that requires the data to be in a particular format.

Although this chapter is looking at the manual methods of project planning it is the objective of the text to outline the current types of calculations used by the planning software.

Select: The first step is to indicate where in the data base the information can be found. To locate data the ''Select'' or ''Filter'' command is used:

*   ''Select'' where activity data is present, this may sound obvious, but remember planning software data bases can be extensive.

*   ''Select'' where float = 0   (This will select all the activities on the critical path).

*   ''Select'' where responsibility equals John, this will only select John's scope of work.

*   ''Select'' where Early Start > (greater than) 1 Jan and < (less than) 1 March. This will select the activities starting in January and February.

These are just a few examples of the select techniques available to extract information from a data base.

Sort: Once the data has been selected the next step is to arrange the data into a suitable order for processing, for example, the data can be presented:

* Numerical: Ascending or descending. This could be a WBS or activity number, activity duration or float. Also consider ordering by least cost for activity crashing purposes.

* Alphabetical: List names as in a telephone directory, or scope responsibility.

* Date order: Order the dates as in a calendar or activities by Early Start.

By skilfully using the above commands the data can be arranged in the format required for calculation or presentation. Sorting is an iterative process, with each sort the data becomes more structured. Using example 2, figure 5 again, select information where activity data is present and sort for Early Start.

Date

Activity Number	Mon 1	Tue 2	Wed 3	Thur 4	Fri 5	Sat 6	Sun 7	Mon 8	Tue 9	Wed 10
100	▬▬	▬								
300			▬	- - -	- - -	- - ◆				
200			▬	▬						
500				▬	▬	- - -	- - ◆			
400					▬	▬	▬			
600								▬	▬	

Figure: 9. Sort by Early Start

Note how the activities are now presented. The activities starting first are positioned top left.

7.6 Definition of an Event

The terms **activity** and **event** are often confused. In the CPM chapter we defined the term **activity**, here we will define the term **event** as it is a feature used in keydate scheduling.

An **event** may be defined as any point in time when something happens. This could be when the plans are approved, an order is placed, goods received or even the start and finish dates of an activity. An event is not concerned with the progress of the activity unless intermediate milestones are established. Although events are not used in CPM they can be linked to the start or finish of an activity as a keydate, which offers another facility for planning and control.

The characteristics of an event include the following :

*   An event has no duration, it is a point in time. For practical purposes it may be given a duration of 1 day.

*   An event may be the start or finish of an activity, WBS work package, project phase or the project itself.

*   An event is also called a keydate, milestone or a benchmark.

*   Data capture will be more accurate if the scope is sub-divided into milestones. This approach is developed in the project control chapter.

An example of an event would be the award of contract.

Identity   010

Description   Award of contract.

Budget   Nil

Duration   1 Day

Resources   Nil

Event planning and tracking lends itself to R&D type projects where it may not be possible to track and measure the progress of an activity in terms of percentage complete.

7.7 Keydate / Milestone Schedule

The keydate schedule offers another type of planning presentation, it can be used on its own or in conjunction with a scheduled barchart. If a project can be sub-divided into many activities with short durations, sufficient planning and control power can be achieved by simply tracking the start and finish of the activities. It would certainly remove any uncertainty introduced by monitoring percentage complete.

Using example 2, figure 5 again, identify the start and finish dates of each activity as milestones.

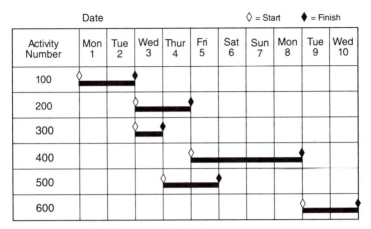

Figure: 10. Keydate / milestone schedule

Keydate schedules can be used for the following:

*   High level reporting.

*   Start and finish of project phases.

*   Access dates for sub-contractors.

*   PERT, events.

*   Start and finish of critical activities.

*   Start and finish of hammocked activities.

Key dates can thus be used on their own, or in conjunction with other formats. We now move on to the logic barchart.

7.8 Logic Barchart

The logic barchart shows the activity logical relationships explicitly on a barchart format. This technique is certainly appropriate for modest size projects, but on larger projects the sheer volume of activities may clutter the presentation.

The logical barchart addresses one of the main short comings of the Gantt chart, namely not showing logical relationship between the activities. Looking at example 2, figure 5 again, the relational links are shown.

Date

Activity Number	Mon 1	Tue 2	Wed 3	Thur 4	Fri 5	Sat 6	Sun 7	Mon 8	Tue 9	Wed 10
100	▬▬									
200			▬▬							
300			▬							
400					▬▬▬					
500				▬▬	- - - - - -					
600								▬▬▬		

Figure: 11. Logical barchart

7.9 Revised barchart

As a project progresses activities may not perform as planned (what an understatement !), they may under-perform or over-perform, either way the original plan will not reflect the current position and what work is required to complete the project. A revised barchart is therefore required to reflect the present status.

A revised barchart should be developed as frequently as the project demands. This will be influenced by a number of factors; delays, scope changes, speed of work and time to correct any problems. The reporting cycle would certainly be more frequent during the starting and finishing phases.

The revised barchart provides an important input to the decision-making and project control function. The drawing technique and the benefits of using a revised barchart will be developed in the project control chapter.

7.10 Rolling Horizon Barchart

On a large complex project it may not be convenient or practical to regularly update the whole project. In these situations the rolling horizon barchart is often used to outline the planning for a contractor or location for the next two or three weeks.

The rolling horizon barchart can be partly computerised by preparing a planning proforma, as shown below, which includes the scope of work, but no scheduling. The manager or foreman can then draw up the scheduling data by hand.

This type of barchart should be very accurate as it is based on the latest data and drawn up by someone working close to the action. It is quick to draw and only includes relevant information on the activities that are working.

Care should be taken, however, not to solely use the rolling horizon barchart on its own as planned activities which are not working may be conveniently forgotten.

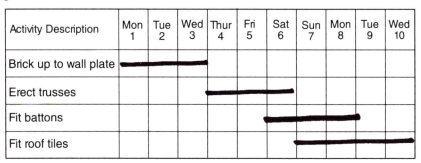

Activity Description	Mon 1	Tue 2	Wed 3	Thur 4	Fri 5	Sat 6	Sun 7	Mon 8	Tue 9	Wed 10
Brick up to wall plate	▬	▬	▬							
Erect trusses				▬	▬					
Fit battons						▬	▬	▬		
Fit roof tiles								▬	▬	▬

Figure: 12. Rolling horizon barchart

7.11 Line of Balance

The line of Balance is a production planning technique developed by E. Trimble (1968), while he was at the National Building Agency. The purpose of the technique is to calculate the required resources for each stage of production so that the following stages are not delayed and the target output is achieved.

Production systems are usually more efficient than project systems for a number of reasons:

* Economies of scale.
* Steeper learning curve.
* The tasks are performed repetitively.

It is therefore in the project's interests to identify areas of manufacture where production planning and control techniques can be applied.

To illustrate the line of balance technique a simple pipe laying project will be developed. The project has two operations per km: dig the trench and lay the pipe. This has to be repeated 7 times to complete the 7 km pipeline.

The network diagram of the project with durations and float is set out below, where 4 days are required to complete one cycle and the target completion of the whole project is 10 days.

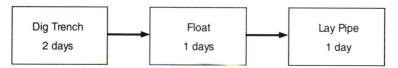

Figure: 13. Line of balance / Activity diagram

When this network diagram is incorporated with the production schedule the start and finish dates for each operation can be established, this is called the line of balance.

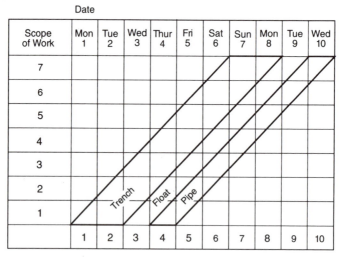

Figure: 14. Line of Balance / Production Schedule

The next step is to consider the resources required to meet this production schedule. Let us consider the trench diggers on their own and assume that there is only one gang. The figure shows their rate of production drawn on to the line of balance.

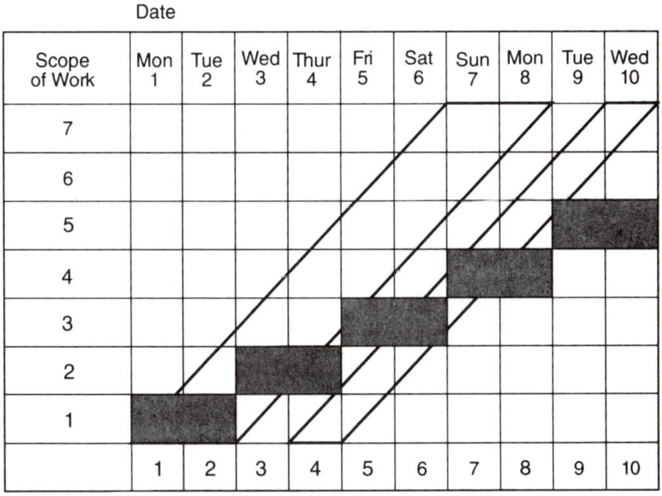

Figure: 15. Line of Balance / Rate of Production

The line of balance shows that after 10 days only 5 km of trenches have been dug, this will obviously delay the project. Consider now the progress when using two gangs.

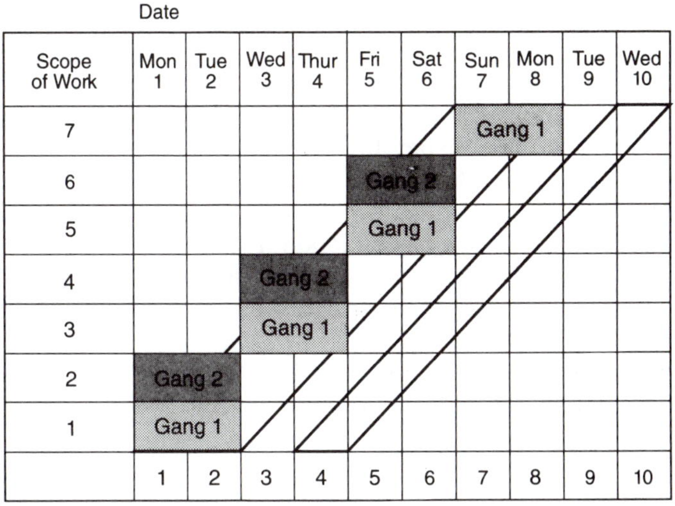

Figure: 16. Line of Balance

With two gangs the 7 km of trenches are dug in 8 days or 7 days if the two gangs can work together on the last section.

This is obviously a very simple application to illustrate the technique, if the reader requires more information try Lockyer, Production Management pp313-322.

The line of balance is particularly useful when the deliveries are not linear with time. To plan and control a single batch the following conditions must be satisfied:

*   There must be identifiable production stages.

*   Production times between stages must be known.

*   Delivery input dates must be known.

*   Resources can be varied as required to meet the production schedule.

In the project environment this production management technique can be very powerful.

7.12 Summary

This chapter on project scheduling focused on the schedule barchart as a key document to disseminate planning information. The development of the barchart can be attributed to Henry Gantt who used the barchart to plan and control his projects. The chapter first outlined how to draw a barchart before explaining how the Gantt chart can be used to plan and control a simple project.

The chapter also showed how tabular reports provide the link between the CPM analysis and the schedule barchart, together with the select and sort functions which were used to prepare planning data for further calculations.

The following types of barcharts were explained; the keydate / Milestone schedule, the Logic barchart, the Revised barchart and the Rolling Horizon barchart.

Finally the line of balance technique was developed as a useful planning tool within the project management sphere of operation.

Chapter 8

Resource Management

Project managers face a challenge with every project, trying to execute the tasks to meet the required quality standards, while expending minimum possible time, cost and resources. In the discussions so far, we have assumed an unlimited supply of resources, however, in reality this is obviously not the case, so here we will outline methods and techniques for integrating time planning with resource analysis.

A resource is usually understood to mean: manpower, machines, materials and financial funds. A resource is basically any commodity that is required to complete the task. In this chapter resource analysis will be directed towards considering the human requirements which play such a vital role in project management. The resource calculations will be used to:

*   Forecast and plan resource requirements.

*   Achieve full resource utilization.

The ideal situation is achieved when the resource requirement equals the resources available. Unfortunately, in project management this seldom happens, because it is not always possible to adjust supply with demand, so some form of compromise is essential.

When a resource is overloaded there are three basic solutions available to address the problem:-

*   Delay activities with float.

*   Resource-limited smoothing, where resources are assigned to a pre-determined limit and re-scheduled if necessary.

*   Time-limited resource smoothing, where the end date of the project is fixed and resources are increased to meet the revised manpower histogram.

Projects which are both resource-limited and time-limited, are unlikely to achieve their objectives without managerial input to redefine or release conflicting constraints. For simplicity in the text, unit time is assumed to be one day, but in practice it could equally be one hour, a week or a month.

8.1 Resource Estimating

The resource estimate is linked directly to the scope of work and Bill of materials (BOM). The scope of work may be expressed as so many tonnes of steel erected, or so many square meters of wall to be painted etc. From this description the estimator must convert the scope of work to manhours per unit "X".

The next step is to consider the direct trade-off between the resource requirement and the activity's duration. Consider **example 1**, if the work requirement is to erect 12 tonnes of steel and the estimator knows from past experience that the work can be done in 150 manhours per tonne and the men work 10 hours shifts, then the equation is:

$$\frac{(12 \text{ tonnes x } 150 \text{ man-hrs per tonne})}{10 \text{ hrs per day}} = 180 \text{ man days}$$

The resource / duration trade-off would then be as follows:-

Resource Men	Duration Days	Mandays
10	18	180
11	16.4	180
12	15	180
13	13.8	180
14	12.9	180

By varying the resource availability, the duration of the activity will change. As the time and cost parameters are the first to be planned, the scope for resource planning may have already been constrained. In this case the resource analysis function is to forecast the manpower resources required to meet the already agreed time and cost schedules. Factors which could affect the estimate:-

a)   A confined space will limit the number of people able to work there.

b)   Restricted access might affect the movement of materials and equipment, eg. building a house on a mountain slope.

c)   Limited number of computers and machines available.

d)   Safety requirements not permitting overhead working.

e)   Productivity is often directly related to effective supervision.

In the above example, the duration was expressed as a fraction of a day. In reality you may find that the smallest reasonable time unit is half a day or even a whole day, this will obviously depend on the scope of work and the flexibility of the workforce.

8.2 Resource Forecasting

The next step is to forecast the total resource requirement by discipline or interchangeable resource. This is done by compiling all the resource estimates and presenting them in a structured resource table. The following headings for the resource table are typical of those used by the project management software.

Activity Number	Resource Type	Quantity per day	Resource Duration	Lead Time
010	Welder	5	4 days	0

Activity number: The resource information is addressed through an activity number. Therefore the timing of the resource can be linked directly with the scheduling of that activity. It is therefore necessary to perform CPM analysis and activity scheduling before resource analysis.

Resource type: This field is used to distinguish the different types of resource. For example, it could be Mr Smith, an engineer or a welder.

Quantity / day: Use this field to enter the quantity of resource required per day.

Duration: Use this field to indicate how many days the resource will be working on that activity. This number can be less than the duration of the activity, but not more.

Lead time: The lead time is the difference in time between the activity's scheduled start and the resource's start, for example, if the painter is required for the last three days of a 10 day activity, the lead time would be 7 days.

If there is more than one resource working on an activity, use a separate line (record in computer language) for each resource. For example:

Activity Number	Resource Type	Quantity per day	Resource Duration	Lead Time
010	Engineer	3	6 days	0
010	Fitter	4	10 days	0

If the resource quantity per unit time varies, a number of entries are required to define the profile mathematically. The resource table can be developed by taking horizontal or vertical slices through the resource profile.

Consider **example 2**:

Item Number	Activity Number	Resource Type	Quantity per day	Resource Duration	Lead Time
A	030	Painter	2	2	0
B	030	Painter	4	4	2
C	030	Painter	3	2	6

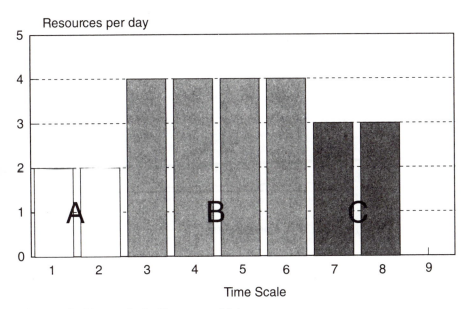

Figure: 1. Example 2. Resource histogram

Self Test: Express the above histogram as horizontal slices.

8.3 Resource Availability

At this point we know what resources are required to perform the work in the planned time. The next step is to see what resources are available in the company. The following points should be considered.

* The normal efficiency of the work force. An estimate made for a skilled workforce would be very different to that of an unskilled workforce.

* The existing commitments. If the company is involved in a number of projects which all draw from a common labour pool, the other projects' requirements must also be considered. This will be discussed further under the heading of multi-project resource scheduling.

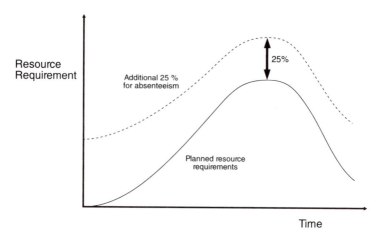

Figure: 2. Planning for 25% absenteeism

* The anticipated sickness and absenteeism rate. The author knows of a company that allowed 25% for absenteeism based on past experience.

* Resource availability can be increased by:-

a) Working overtime.

b) Using Sub-contractors.

c) Changing the workpattern. This will also change the resource - requirement profile.

Increasing resource availability in this manner usually carries additional costs which must be included in the cost estimate. Keeping the above points in mind, the resource availability table will be developed. Consider **example 3**:

Resource Type	Quantity per day	Available From	Available To
Engineer	3	1 Dec	13 Dec
Engineer	3	2 Jan	31 Jan

This profile would indicate the extent of the Christmas break when no Engineers are available.

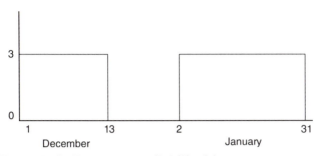

Figure: 3. Example 3. Resource availability histogram

The resource availability table is slightly different from the resource forecast table in that it is not linked to an activity. It simply identifies the resource and the quantity available between certain dates.

Company holidays, public holidays, religious holidays and any other shutdowns (for purposes such as maintenance) can be programmed in. This step ensures that no work is scheduled when the workforce is not available. A new line will be required in the resource table to define each non-working period, or where the number available changes.

8.4 Resource Histogram

The resource histogram is similar to a vertical barchart where the horizontal axis is a time base and the vertical axis is the resource requirement per day. The resource histogram is a popular planning tool because it gives a good visual presentation which is easy to assimilate and understand. The prerequisites for drawing the resource histogram are:

*   Early Start barchart, and
*   Resource forecast per activity.

By using the Early Start barchart it is assumed that the planner wishes to start all activities as soon as possible and maximise the activity float for flexibility. Once the resource requirements have been added to the Early Start barchart, the daily requirements are summed by moving forward through the barchart one day at a time to give the total resource required per day.

The total daily resource requirements are then plotted vertically to give the resource histogram. It is important to note that separate resource histograms are required for different trades that are not interchangeable. Consider **example 4**:

Task Number	Start Date	Finish Date	Resource per day
010	1	2	2
020	3	4	2
030	3	4	6
040	5	6	3
050	7	10	1
060	11	11	2

Step 1.   Draw the barchart.

Step 2.   Transfer the resource per day from the table above to the barchart.

Step 3.   Add the resource per day vertically to give a total daily requirement.

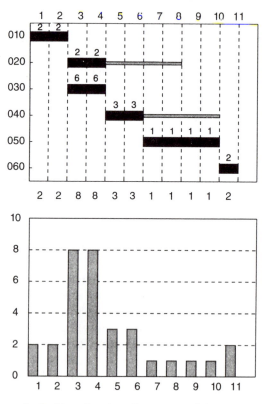

Figure: 4. Example 4. Barchart and resource histogram

Self Test: At this point draw the resource histogram in appendix 4.

8.5 Resource Loading

The resource forecast is now compared with the resources available and overloads and underloads reported. An overload is when the forecast exceeds the available resources, and an underload is when forecast is lower than the available resource.

A resource overload, where the requirement exceeds the resource availability, is obviously an unworkable situation. If this overload is not addressed it will cause the activity to take longer than estimated.

Consider **example 4** again and assume there are only 6 men available, the resource loading will be as below:

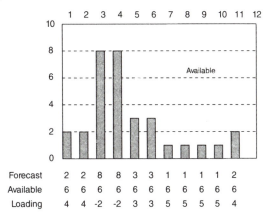

Figure: 5. Example 4. Resource loading

The resource histogram now shows the forecast and available manpower both as a histogram and numerically. The underloads and overloads can now be identified and addressed. Consider the following suggestions to address an overload:

Working overtime: This will increase the number of manhours available
                         without having to employ more staff, however over-
                         time may reduce productivity.

Working shifts:
This will increase the utilization of machines, equipment and also increase the number of manhours worked in confined spaces.

Increasing productivity:
Education and training should improve productivity in the long term, especially if it incorporates automation.

Job and knock:
When workers have finished a job, they can leave the factory, although they will be paid for the full day or shift. The benefit here is that the job is not stretched out.

Learning curve:
If the project involves a certain amount of repetitive work, the planner could expect to see the number of manhours reducing on subsequent units.

Consider **example 5**, the manhours to manufacture a series of similar yachts. This example shows a learning curve where the manhours per unit reduce exponentially until it reaches an optimum efficiency.

Scope	Manhours
Hull 1	15000
Hull 2	13000
Hull 3	10000
Hull 4	9000

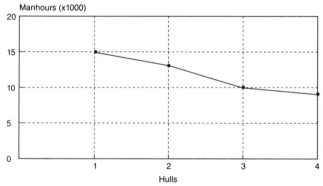

Figure: 6. Example 5. Learning curve

Sub-contractors: Using sub-contractors will increase the workforce in the short term, the benefit here is that there are no long term commitments, but the labour costs will be higher. Using sub-contractors can also be useful to check the performance of the in-house workforce. It is the author's experience that often company workers will increase their output in line with the sub-contractors. But keep a close watch on the work quality and team morale.

A **resource underload** can also be a problem, because these men will continue to be paid a salary and other benefits, even though they are not working. These incurred costs can be offset by:

* Moving unemployed resources to critical activities.

* Moving unemployed resources to fill-in jobs which either have a resale value or can be used by the company, eg. building a spec house.

* Hiring out resources internally or externally. The hire rate can be competitively reduced to at least cover their direct costs.

* Pre-manufacture to make components before they are needed. However, check the trade-off between resource utilization and the additional cost of the trial assembly, disassembly and handling.

* Maintenance of equipment during slack periods.

* Train your workforce to gain new skills which will make them more productive and flexible in the future.

* Send the under-utilized workforce on leave.

* Develop new systems to forecast resource utilization.

* Evaluate past projects to predict any resource utilization trends.

* Market the company's product to ensure resource utilization.

The profit of a company in the long term may well depend on the efficient utilization of its resources.

8.6 What-if Simulation

The "what-if" simulation has become a popular management technique, which enables the planner to vary certain parameters at will to determine the affect on the project. Remember when using project management software it is advisable to perform the "what-if" simulations on a backup copy of the project, in case you corrupt the data base or need to get back to your original starting point. "What-if" simulations can be applied to many applications, consider the following:-

*   Time-limited scheduling.

*   Resource-limited scheduling.

*   Workpattern changes. Increase the working week of certain resource types in steps of one day.

*   Increase the number of resources in controlled steps.

*   The time / cost trade-off of project time to resource cost. The ability to build a resource model and test the various parameters should be the ultimate goal for effective decision-making, planning and control.

*   Adjust activity durations to re-profile the resource requirement.

*   Split or sub-divide an activity into two or more parts.

*   Quantify the additional cost of using sub-contractors.

*   Adjust company holidays to coincide with forecast downturn in the work load.

The power to model and predict the future is the key to effective planning and control.

8.7 Resource Smoothing

Resource smoothing is the process of moving activities to improve the resource loading profile. The first step is to select the resource to be smoothed, because it is not possible to smooth for more than one resource at a time. To decide which resource to smooth consider:

* The resource that is most overloaded.

* The resource that is most used on the project.

* Least flexible resource. The resource that comes from overseas, is difficult to get hold of or is least available.

* Most expensive to hire.

After you have smoothed for the chosen resource, the other resources must follow the re-scheduled barchart. Unfortunately, you will have to accept this compromise with the other resources, because to smooth for another resource may put the first resource back into overload.

Resource smoothing involves the levelling of the resource overload to meet the resource available. The resource histogram can be levelled by moving activities away from the overloaded area by either:

* Changing the logic of the network.

* Moving non-critical activities within their float so that the end date of the project is not affected, while making sure the network logic is maintained.

* The author has found that managers often prefer to smooth manually, thus keeping control on the changes. This exercise is certainly made easier by the planning software where the barchart and resource histogram are shown on the same screen.

Continuing with **example 4,** the resource overload can be addressed by simply moving task 020 two days. However as the network diagram shows, task 020 has a finish-to-start relationship with task 040, therefore task 040 will also have to move forward by at least two days.

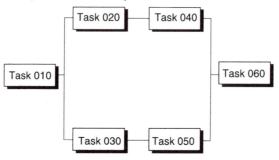

Figure: 7. Example 4. Network Diagram

The resulting barchart and smoothed resource histogram are shown below:

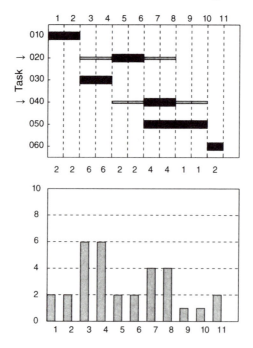

Figure: 8 Example 4. Barchart and smoothed histogram

Resource analysis requires a tremendous amount of mathematical calculation. It is therefore desirable to use computer software for this type of analysis. Planning software generally use the following steps :

*   Select where the data is to come from.

*   Order the data for the calculation.

*   Calculate the resource information using pre-defined algorithms.

Select: Selection of data is usually a simple matter of telling the computer where to look for information. Typically select where resource information is present.

Order: The ordering of the activities is the first step in building a priority list for the assigning of resources. Although there is no "right" or "optimum" priority list it is generally accepted that a set of decision rules will produce a better schedule than an "ad hoc" approach. On a large project it may not be physically possible to manually test all the resource conflicts so some routine must be set up. A typical priority order would be:

1st	priority	Early Start
2nd	priority	Total float
3rd	priority	Duration
4th	priority	Record number

In this example the priority would be established by first looking at the activity's Early Start. If more than one activity has the same Early Start, it then looks for the activity with the least float. If there is more than one activity with the same float, it then looks for the activity with the least duration and if that is not sufficient it then orders the activities by record number.

It is not always possible to justify your priority decision rules on logical grounds and the results cannot be assumed to be an optimum solution. The following points should, however, help to establish a framework for your priority.

*   On a long project it may not be realistic to schedule in any great detail many months from timenow, because as the project rolls forward the situation and trade-offs may well change. With this line of thinking, Early Start should have a high priority.

*   The size of the float is a measure of the amount of flexibility or movement an activity has. Resources should be assigned first to the activity with the least amount of flexibility, ie. critical or near critical activities.

*   The duration and cost would be a measure of the size of the activity, therefore, assign resources to the larger and more expensive activities first.

*   If no clear priority can be established using the above conditions, simply order by activity number or record number.

During the life of the project it is often found that the priority list might change to accommodate internal and external pressures. This can be easily incorporated during the regular progress revisions.

How to assign resources: There are two basic methods for the allocation of resources to constrained activities, namely serial and parallel. The serial method allocates resources (for the whole activity) by examining the activities in their established priority, one activity at a time.

The parallel method allocates resources (for only one day at a time) by examining resource availability on a daily basis regardless of activity duration. The scheduler does, however, have the option of specifying whether or not execution of the activity can be interrupted and split before completion.

The following is a brief explanation of the parallel method. If there are insufficient resources available to start the activity Early Start, sort the resources by means of the following steps:

Step 1:   Starting at the beginning of the project, compare the resource requirement with the resources available and attempt to schedule the activities by their Early Start.

Step 2:   If insufficient resources are available to begin the activity on its Early Start date, move the activity ahead by one calendar unit (day / week) assuming there is float, and again compare the resource requirements with availability. This process continues until:

    a) There are sufficient resources to begin the activity or.....
    b) The total float for the activity has been used up.

If the total float has been used up and the activity still does not have resources assigned, there are two courses of action to take:

a) Resource-limited scheduling.

b) Time-limited resource scheduling.

These resource smoothing techniques will now be explained.

8.8 Resource-Limited Scheduling

If there is a resource limit which cannot be exceeded, planned activities will have to be delayed until sufficient resources can be assigned. If this process delays a critical activity the end date of the project will be extended. This situation could occur in any of the following situations:

* Working in a confined space.

* Where there are limited facilities, for example the number of bunks available on an offshore platform.

* Information delays to contractors in the form of drawings and specifications.

* Limited amount of equipment, e.g. the number of computers, machines, drawing boards, lifts or scaffolding.

* Safety requirements may limit the number of workers in a certain area.

The extent of the restrictions imposed by resource-limited scheduling can be reduced by considering a number of the options outlined in the resource overload section.

8.9 Time-Limited Resource Scheduling

This type of resource smoothing is used when the end date of the project cannot be exceeded. In which case any resource overloads will have to be addressed by increasing the resources when they are required. This situation could occur when:

* The project has heavy time penalties.

* The project is part of another project with limited access dates, for example, an accommodation module for an offshore platform.

* Building a new hotel to meet the summer season.

* Opening toll roads to coincide with the heavy traffic during the summer holidays.

Once the end dates of project milestones have been contractually agreed, time-limited scheduling will become a powerful tool to assist the planner achieve these commitments.

8.10 Re-scheduling the Project

The initial CPM analysis was performed without considering the resource constraint. Now that the resource analysis is complete, certain activities may have been moved during the resource smoothing, in which case it will be necessary to re-schedule the baseline plan. Check all the related documents for changes, this will certainly include the following:

* The barchart schedule.

* The budget.

* The cash flow statement.

* The expenditure curves.

* The manpower plan.

* Procurement cycle.

If these reports are linked through an integrated system they will be up-dated automatically, otherwise a manual transfer of data will be necessary.

8.11 Project Tracking and Revision

After every reporting period the activity schedule may change, which in-turn means the manpower histogram will need to be recalculated and revised. The new schedule and manpower histogram will then form the plan for the next reporting period.

In practice the manpower availability does not usually fluctuate significantly on a daily basis, resources will, however, be increased if production schedules are not met.

8.12 Multi-Project Resource Scheduling

Up to now the manpower resources have only been considered for a single project. Here we will determine what happens when the company is running many projects at the same time, each calling on the same pool of resources.

Multi-project resource scheduling addresses this problem by joining all the projects together to form one large company project. This allows the total requirement of the projects to be compared with the total company pool of resources. Any smoothing will now consider all the projects at the same time.

In the CPM chapter it was recommended that all the activities, even of other projects, should have different numbers. The reason becomes evident when performing multi-project resource smoothing. If two activities have the same number the last activity entered will overwrite to the previous one, with disastrous results.

It is, however, a problem which can be simply addressed by assigning a prefix or suffix to the activity number. The latest software will handle this automatically.

Multi-project scheduling adds a further dimension to resource management enabling senior management to plan and control the overall manpower requirement. It further encourages the project manager to plan ahead and confirm the manpower he requires for the project.

8.13 Implementation

The resource calculations outlined above will indicate the optimum resource utilization to meet project objectives, but they do not address the human element. The project manager must bridge the gap, in terms of explanation and persuasion, between what should be done mathematically and what can be done practically.

It is generally accepted that a workforce will tend to be more adaptable and committed when given the opportunity to participate in the planning process.

8.14 Food for Thought

In compiling this chapter a few points came to mind which did not fit into any of the above sub-headings, they are presented here as an ad hoc collection:

* Certain industries work in multi-trade gangs, for example, bricklayer, plaster, electrician, carpenter and labourer will work together.

* When a project is running late bringing in more resources may well delay it even further.

* It may be possible to split activities which have float. In this situation workers would be moving between unfinished jobs. Concern here would be for the lost time of production while moving, setting up and reorganization. However, in reality this is quite common.

* Clients often require a manpower plan to check that the contractors have sufficient resources to meet project objectives.

* Offshore contracts often impose a penalty if the manpower usage exceeds +/- 5% of the agreed amount.

This concludes the chapter on Resource Management except for the summary.

8.15 Summary

This chapter developed the CPM analysis to include resource management. The term ''resource'' was explained, before going on to outline how to forecast resource requirements and draw the manpower histogram.

We then introduced the resource availability constraint which when compared with the forecast requirement, determined the overload / underload situation. A number of ''what-if'' techniques were outlined to model possible solutions to assist the decision-making function.

The resource smoothing methodology was then outlined under the headings of: smooth within float, resource-limited and time-limited smoothing. Finally we emphasized the importance of multi-project resource smoothing to integrate all the company's projects under one corporate project before assigning resources.

The following list is a summary of the resource analysis steps.

Step 1:   Estimate resource requirement.

Step 2:   Compile resource table. For each resource, assign the resource requirement per day to the Early Start barchart. Include lead and lag times as required.

Step 3:   Compile the resource availability table.

Step 4:   Draw the resource histogram.

Step 5:   Compare resource forecast with resource availability and report overloads and underloads.

Step 6:   Create new project for "what-if" simulation.

Step 7:   Smooth resources by moving activities within their float.

Step 8:   Perform resource-limited scheduling as required.

Step 9:   Perform time-limited scheduling as required.

Step 10:   Re-schedule the planning barchart.

Step 11:   Save the baseline plan for tracking and controlling of the project.

Step 12:   Track project to timenow and revise the resource histogram.

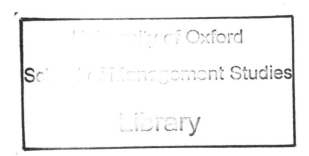

Chapter 9

Project Estimation

For the project manager to effectively plan and control a project, accurate estimating is essential. The estimator's task is to predict the projects' parameters by building a model of the project on paper.

The quality of the estimate should be seen as the best approximation based on:

* The time available.
* The information available.
* The techniques employed.
* The expertise and experience of the estimating personnel.

The accuracy of the estimate will depend on the level of detail it is based on, this information will come from:

* The scope of work.
* The contract.
* The specification.
* The extent of risk and uncertainty in the project.

The quality of the estimate can be improved as the project is executed when more detailed and accurate information becomes available.

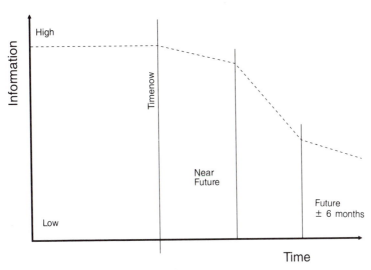

Figure: 1. Information rolling horizon

Unfortunately, the project manager usually has to commit his company finan-cially and contractually at the tender / quotation stage when the amount of data and information may be limited. For this reason alone it is important to be able to provide accurate estimates based on incomplete information at the tender stage.

Although estimating usually focuses on the financial aspects of the project, it is important to remember that the costs cannot be accurately established until the other factors of time, resources, materials and equipment have been quantified.

Estimating is an integral part of the project management and tendering process, which should be based on past experience together with market norms and standards. Although the estimate will have an input into all areas of the project here the investigation will be restricted to cost and time estimating.

9.1   Terminology

In commerce and industry it is common to label the estimate according to its level of detail and accuracy. This classification will depend on the quality of information available and the amount of effort put into compiling the estimate. The text will identify three types of estimate according to their purpose, scope of work detail and level of accuracy.

9.1.1 Conceptual Estimate

Also called; **Order of magnitude, Budget figure, Ball-park figure, Thumb suck** or **Plucked from the air (PFA).** The conceptual estimate addresses the needs of senior management who are presented with a number of possible future projects. They need an initial filter to select those projects which warrant further investigation. This would form part of the conceptual development phase outlined in the Scope Management chapter.

The conceptual estimate will be based on a limited scope of work using scale factors or capacity estimates to give a level of accuracy +/- 25%. A conceptual estimate should not be a legally binding document, however, professional competence could be questioned if the estimates were too far adrift. If the conceptual estimate looks promising, senior management will then allocate funds to finance a more detailed feasibility study.

9.1.2 Feasibility Study

Also called; **Preliminary estimate** or **Comparative estimate.** The feasibility study would also be made without detailed data, but when estimates are based on previous projects having a similar scope of work and capacity the accuracy can be improved to +/- 10%.

The feasibility study would use a number of other techniques to improve the quality of information available. These would include:

* Cost-benefit analysis
* Needs analysis

A cost-benefit analysis may be performed at this stage to establish the financial feasibility of the project. Cost-benefit analysis is generally based on the following principles:

* The Pareto improvement criterion.
* . The Hicks-Kaldor test.
* The willingness-to-pay test.

The basic concept is simply to express the costs and benefits in money terms. If the financial benefits exceed the costs, then the project passes the test.

The **Pareto** improvement criterion is expressed as where: ''The project should make some people better off without making anyone worse off.'' This situation may be difficult to achieve in reality.

The **Hicks-Kaldor** test seems more realistic. This states that: ''The aggregate gains should exceed aggregate losses.'' This framework will enable the people that gain to compensate the people that loose. For example, a dam project may have many benefits to the community, but might cause the silting up of the river. If the financial benefits of having a dam exceed the dredging costs of the river, this project will satisfy a Hicks-Kaldor test.

The **willingness-to-pay** test is simply to determine how much your clients will pay for your product. The economists model this test using the following techniques:

* The supply and demand curve. (Begg p.48)
* Monopolies and Oligopolies. (Begg p.212)
* Product elasticity. (Begg p.177)

These techniques will model the relationship between supply, demand and prices.

The **needs analysis** uses a structured questionnaire targeted on the project scope to quantify the status of:

a) The company's present position.
b) The company's planned target.
c) What the project must do to take the company from a) to b).

This focused audit if well prepared and executed, will provide a meaningful needs analysis report. This type of information should be seen as a prerequisite for project selection and scope of work development. The end product of the needs analysis should establish project objectives and critical success factors together with a recommended course of action.

9.1.3 Definitive Estimate

Also called; **Detailed estimate, Project control estimate, Quotation or Tender.** When the decision has been made to proceed with the project a high level of accuracy is required for the quotation.

The definitive estimate will be based on a considerable amount of data incorporating; a developed scope of work, detailed drawings, specifications, vendor quotes (which are now legally binding) and site surveys to give an improved accuracy of +/- 5%.

9.1.4 Costing

If an **estimate** is defined as a quick method for pricing a project based on incomplete data, then **costing** may be defined as a detailed price based on a complete parts list of materials.

Costing requires the following items to have been completed:

* The design.
* The scope of work.
* The parts list.
* The detailed planning.
* Firm prices from sub-contractors and suppliers.

In fact almost every aspect of the project must be quantified. With this high level of information and effort accurate quotations of +/- 1% can be achieved. There is, however, a time and cost penalty, as costing is expensive and time consuming to produce.

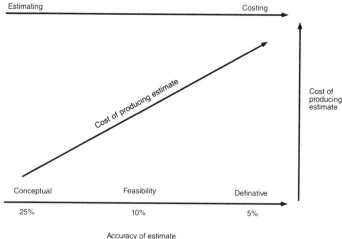

Figure: 2. Estimate accuracy

9.1.5 Accuracy of Estimate

The four categories of estimates may be described as milestones on a level of accuracy continuum, with the estimates accuracy varying from 1% to 25%.

The figure shows the relationship between a higher level of accuracy and the increasing cost of producing it. Although it is not the project manager's function to set the company's profit margin, he does need to know what the percentage profit is, as this will influence the accuracy of the estimate and subsequent data capture.

As a guide, the level of accuracy should be at least equal to, or greater than, the profit margin so that in the worst case scenario a cost over-run would be accommodated by the profit margin. Thus resulting in the project breaking-even rather than making a loss.

The accuracy of the estimate may be further constrained by the time available. When your boss says "I need it by nine o'clock tomorrow morning", you have my sympathy.

Self test:

1.   What is an estimate ?
2.   Why do we have estimates of different accuracies ?
3.   Why would you use the Hicks-Kaldor test in preference to Pareto's ?
4.   Develop a needs analysis for your current project.
5.   What is the trade-off between estimating and costing ?

9.2 Different Types of Costs

Since there are many different **costs** in project estimating the term **cost** should always be qualified, because it could be related to:

*   Direct costs.
*   Indirect costs.
*   Labour costs.
*   Material and Equipment costs.
*   Transport costs.
*   Preliminary and General (P&G) costs.

Listed below is a framework for sub-dividing the different cost types into their main parameters of management, labour, material, equipment and expenses.

9.2.1 Direct Costs

As the term implies, direct costs are those costs which can be specifically identified with the activity or project. The current trend is to assign as much as possible, if not all to direct costs, because direct costs can be budgeted, monitored and controlled far more effectively than indirect costs.

*   Direct management costs refer to the project office running costs. Salaries for the; project manager, project engineer, planner, accountant, secretary and QA.

*   Direct labour is the cost of wages attributed for the men working on an activity, e.g. boilermakers, welders or fitters.

*   Direct material costs are for the materials, consumable and components which are used for completing an activity. An allowance should be made for scrap and wastage.

*   Direct equipment costs refers to in-house charges for new machinery, plant, tools and buildings.

*   Direct expenses include bought-in services that are specific to the project, for example, plant hire, surveyor, designer and sub-contractor fees.

The distinctive nature of direct costs is that the total expense can be charged to the activity.

9.2.2 Indirect Costs: Fixed and Variable

Indirect costs, also called **overheads**, are those costs which cannot be directly booked to an activity or project, together with costs that may be incurred whether the project is executed or not.

*   Indirect management costs; senior managers, estimating department, sales and marketing, general office staff, secretarial, administration and the personnel department.

*   Indirect labour includes; reception, maintenance, security, cleaners. Basically it includes all the employees not working directly on the activity, but are required to keep the company functioning.

*   Indirect materials include; stationery, cleaning materials and maintenance parts.

*   Indirect equipment; Company computer, photocopier and fax.

*   Indirect expenses include; Training, insurance, depreciation, rent and rates.

Indirect costs are usually financed by an overhead recovery charge added to the earned manhour rate. Indirect overhead costs if not properly managed will eat away at the company profits. The acid test for the project vis-a-vis indirect costs and overheads, is to compare internal costs with the same services bought externally.

Another way of looking at the indirect costs is to sub-divide them into **fixed** and **variable** costs. **Fixed** costs are those incurred independent of the work load. For example, rent, rates and maintenance costs for the buildings, offices and equipment all of which do not fluctuate with the workload.

While indirect **variable** costs on the other hand fluctuate with the work load. For example, if a number of projects were running concurrently the telephone and secretarial costs would increase, along with heating and lighting etc, but because of their nature the costs could not easily be directly attributed to any one activity or project.

These fixed and variable costs are often centrally pooled with financial recovery apportioned as a percentage to the earned manhours.

Although companies tend to differ on how they distribute their costs, it is generally suggested that the leaning should be to apportion more to direct costs and less to indirect costs. The nature of direct costs allows them to be planned, tracked and controlled.

With high indirect costs the larger companies run the risk of them escalating under a cloud of uncertainty. In this situation the project manager must ensure that his project is not being lumbered with excessive overheads to finance an inefficient head office.

9.2.3 Labour Costs

The labour costs considered here are for the project workforce and thus a direct cost. Although the salaries of a workforce may be clearly identified there are also a number of other associated costs incurred which are necessary to keep the company ticking over. These costs need to be identified and quantified as they will form part of the labour rate.

The labour rate is calculated by aggregating the various costs and dividing by the number of manhours worked. This process is explained in the following worked example. Here the costs have been sub-divided into four main headings:

1.	Salary.	
2.	Associated labour costs.	
3.	Contribution to overheads.	
4.	Contribution to company profit.	

		Cost per month	Days lost per month
1.	Salary	$ 2000	

2.1	Medical insurances.	$ 50	
2.2	Sickness benefit.		1
2.3	Annual holidays.		1
2.4	Training courses.	$ 30	1
2.5	Protective clothes.	$ 20	
2.6	Car allowance.	$ 250	
2.7	Housing allowance.	$ 50	
2.8	Subsistence allowance.	$ 100	
2.9	Pension.	$ 100	
2.10	Tool allowance.	$ 20	
2.11	Private jobs.	$ 20	
2.12	Productivity bonus.	$ 100	
2.13	Standing time.		1
2.14	Inclement weather.		1
	TOTALS	$ 740	5

3.	Contribution to overheads. 30% of salary	$ 600	

4.   Company profit.
        25% of salary $ 500

Some of the above items may be difficult to quantify without recourse to statistical analysis, for example, days lost due to sickness and standing time. But they should be recognized as potential costs and a figure assigned if only as a contribution to an unknown amount. The end product of this analysis should be a labour rate per hour. The calculation is simply:

Labour rate   =   Total monthly costs

$$\overline{\qquad\qquad\qquad\qquad\qquad\qquad\qquad\qquad\qquad\qquad}$$

                Total no. of normal working hours per month

Where the average working month is 21 days and average days lost per month is 5 days.

Labour rate   =   2000 + 740 + 600 + 500

$$\overline{\qquad\qquad\qquad\qquad\qquad\qquad}$$

                (21 - 5) * 8

                = $ 30 / hr

As a rule of thumb the labour rate can be approximately established from the labour wages (which are known) by factoring the other expenses. Here the labour rate is split into thirds:

1/3   Labour wages.
1/3   All auxiliary costs listed above including contribution to overheads.
1/3   Company profit.

This bring us to an interesting question, based on the above how do we cost out overtime ? If all the auxiliary costs have been paid for by the contribution during working hours, one can assume they do not need to be paid for again. In which case costs need only be assigned to the following headings:

*   Labour wages.
*   Overtime rate (time and a half or double time).
*   Contribution to indirect variable costs.
*   Company profit.

In industry and commerce, however, the overtime rate to the client usually increases as a multiple of the employee overtime rate.

9.2.4 Material and Equipment Costs

Material costs relate to the materials used on the project. They can be identified as a direct cost from the parts list or bill of material (BOM). Material costs can be sub-divided into:

* Materials directly attributed to a job or project.

* Consumables which could be used on a number of activities (for example welding rods, paint etc).

* Handling of the material.

* Wastage and scrap.

It is normal practice to mark up the material costs by 10% to 20% to cover handling charges incurred whilst carrying out the following procurement functions:-

a) Purchasing: Procurement, vendor selection, adjudication of three quotes and place order.

b) Expediting: Checking-up on the order and follow through.

c) Warehouse transport.

d) Material handling: Off-loading and storage.

e) QA: Goods-inwards inspection and acceptance.

f) Warehousing: Storing, issuing, stock control and disposal.

Equipment costs generally relate to manual and automatic machinery items which are required to complete the activity. These may include:

* Office equipment: Computers, photocopier and fax.

* Site equipment: Cranes, plant, vehicles, generators, compressors, scaffold and hand tools etc.

* Shop equipment: Machines and special tools.

The equipment can be procured by either purchase, plant hire or lease. The choice will be influenced by your company's financial circumstances.

Equipment **purchases** may be new or second-hand, either way they usually attract capital investment tax allowances and depreciation allowances which will help to reduce costs. The insurance, maintenance and repair costs will need to be included in the budget. If in-house equipment is used this would be either charged to the project in the form of a labour rate or through the overhead recovery.

Plant hire although generally more expensive if hired per hour, this method however, will limit the equipment costs to the period of use. If plant is hired it is not the contractors responsibility to find work while it is standing idle. Insurance, maintenance and repairs need not be considered as they are covered in the hire rate. There will also be additional costs for transport to and from the plant hire depot together with erection and dismantling on site.

Leasing and hire purchase allow the contractor to obtain equipment now and pay for it later, usually in monthly instalments. Depending on legislation this form of procurement has certain tax benefits.

Independent of the method of procurement the running costs of equipment need to be included in the budget. This will include fuels, lubricants and in some cases a nominated operator.

Scaffolding, tarpaulins, power supply and temporary lights can be costed out either as a hire, erection and dismantle cost, or recovered through the unit rate of say brickwork at so much per square metre.

How does the estimator price material and equipment that has already been paid for on a previous project. What is the value of surplus material and equipment that has been written-off ? The estimator obviously has scope to price the old material and equipment from free issue to current market price. Company policy will determine stock rotation which could be a mixture of:

LIFO   Last in first out.
FIFO   First in first out.

The material and equipment estimate usually allows the procurement manager the scope to save 5% to 10% on material and equipment costs through negotiation with the suppliers. In a competitive market this saving would significantly enhance the project's profit.

9.2.5 Transport Costs

It is important to appreciate what additional costs may be incurred in delivering the goods from the suppliers factory to client's premises. There are a number of conventional terms used.

Ex-works: This is how much the product costs to manufacture the goods at the factory. It is the purchaser's responsibility to organize and pay for; delivery, loading, transport and insurance from the factory gate.

FOB: **Free on board**. The supplier will arrange for the goods to be loaded on board a ship, plane, train or truck at an agreed place. The supplier will pay for the port duties and export clearances, while the client is responsible for the transport, insurance and any import duties. It is important to clarify when the change of ownership and responsibility takes place. This is usually when the goods have been loaded.

CIF: **Cost, insurance and freight**. The supplier pays for the delivery of the goods to their final destination plus the insurance. The client pay for import duties.

DDP: **Delivered duty paid**. The goods will be delivered to the purchaser's front door. All the risks and costs relating to transport, insurance, duty etc, will be borne by the supplier.

To compete successfully on the world market and convert quotations into orders it may not be sufficient to simply quote ex-works; at a minimum the quote should be ''per container load.'' To quote in these terms will require the estimator to establish the weight and volume of the product needed to fill a container.

A more useful quote to the client would be FOB, for which it would be necessary to establish the cost of transport to the coast, but why not go further and quote CIF, or better still match other major international exporters and quote DDP delivery to the buyer's front door and in his own currency.

To offer these enhanced facilities will require the estimator to establish a data base of the ''total cost breakdown'', so that he can respond quickly and accurately to an inquiry. DDP will also have the added benefit to the exporting country of earning additional foreign currency from the insurance and freight-age.

9.2.6 Preliminary and General (P&G) Costs

The preliminary and general costs which are normally abbreviated to P&G's, are the costs which cannot easily be directly assigned to an activity or task. A typical construction project would use the following headings: (Note, many of these headings have been identified already under indirect costs)

1. Site supervision.
2. Insurances and performance bonds.
3. Plant-hire, equipment, cranage, tools, vehicles and generators.
4. Site establishment, huts, toilets and fencing.
5. Site security: Night watchman and guard dogs to protect the project from theft and vandalism.
6. Site services: Telephone, electricity and water.
7. Temporary access roads and sign posts.
8. Scaffolding and ladders.
9. Temporary lights and power supply.
10. Accommodation for the workforce.
11. Special travelling expenses to site.
12. Special training and testing of tradesmen.
13. Material handling: Receiving inspection, off-loading, storage and inventory control.
14. Removal of rubbish, waste and scrap.

The costs assigned to these headings should include the normal recovery percentage for overhead costs and profit. Check that these costs are not being recovered elsewhere in the estimate, for example, site services and security may be paid for by the client.

Self test:

1. What are direct costs ?
2. Calculate the labour cost for a company you are familiar with.
3. Calculate the overtime costs to the client based on employee rates of time and a half.

This concludes the section on terminology, we now move on to discuss estimating methodologies.

9.3 Estimating Methodology

We are now in a position to discuss some of the techniques the estimating and planning department can use to predict a project's parameters. The estimating techniques used by industry and commerce can vary tremendously from one company to another. It is therefore the author's intention to highlight a number of the basic techniques.

*   Operational estimating.
*   Factoring.
*   Time based indices.
*   Economies of scale.
*   Parameter costs.
*   Dayworks.
*   Nett and Gross Pricing.

9.3.1 Operational Estimating

Also termed **Jobbing** or **Job costing**. Operational estimating is the process of considering all the operations that go into executing the activity or task. These operations are then quantified in terms of labour, material, plant and equipment, transport and painting etc.

Activity	Description	Labour	Material	Plant & Equip	Transport	Painting	Total
100	Mark out	500	100				600
200	Dig Foundation	2000	100	600			2700
300	Lay Foundation	4000	15000	12000	3000		34000

Figure: 3. Operational estimating format

Projects tend to be activity driven, therefore for effective CPM planning and project control the estimates must be activity biased. The operational estimating steps are:

*   Establish the output of work per activity which is usually expressed in manhours.

*   Allocate resources to each activity.

*   The duration of the activity can be calculated from the equation:

Activity duration   =   Quantity of work

Output of resources.

Activity duration will be related to the resources used, for example, an activity to paint the wall of a house was estimated at 80 manhours, the duration of the activity is directly related to the number of painters assigned.

hr / day	men	duration (days)
8	1	10
8	2	5
8	3	3.3
8	4	2.5

In many industrial situations the workers tend to work in gangs, for example, in offshore fabrication a gang could consist of platers, welders, riggers and labourers all working together. Once the activity has started operational estimating enables the progress to be quantified because it provides:

*   A cost estimate for all the WBS work packages and activities.

*   After the activity has started the progress can be planned and tracked by determining a valuation for work in progress (percentage complete or remaining duration). This technique links in well with the data capture and project control.

*   When the activity is complete the profit or loss situation can be established. This data can also be used to ensure that the estimating data base is kept up to-date.

The operational estimating technique is a prerequisite for CPM planning and control. At the tender stage, however, there may not be sufficient time or need to produce an estimate with this level of detail. Certainly on award of contract operational estimating must be carried out as it is part of the CPM process. We therefore need to look at other estimating techniques that are quicker to produce, but still provide a reasonably accurate estimate.

9.3.2 Factoring

Also called **Component ratios.** Factoring is used when the work content is similar between projects such as the foundations of a house or the pipe work of a boiler. The estimated cost for the new project can then be expressed as a percentage of the previous project. Component ratios are derived from empirical analysis of previous projects, for example;

Management fee	5 % of contract price.
Quality assurance	1 % of contract price.
Foundations	2 % of machine price.
Pipework	20 % of generator price.
Profit	20 % of construction costs.

After execution it is the estimators responsibility to compare the planned and actual figures. The estimating data base should then be updated if the variances are significant.

9.3.3 Time Based Indices

Also called **inflation.** The project costs will change with time due to the non-reversible effect of inflation on the economy. If the current project is similar to a previous project completed a few years ago, the financial figures from the previous project can be used as the basis for the current estimate.

The upward effect of inflation can be established using a commercial available Cost Price Index (CPI) and inflation indices. One of the problems with this method is that commodities tend to escalate at different rates. This can, however, be addressed by sub-dividing the project into its component costs by CPI category, then applying an escalation factor to each separately.

	1990	1991		1992	
	Base	Inflation Rate	New Price	Inflation Rate	New Price
Labour	50000	10%	55000	8%	59400
Materials	40000	15%	46000	5%	48300
Totals	90000	12.2%	101000	6.6%	107700

Figure: 4. Inflation

Note: Inflation has a compound effect on the figures.

9.3.4 Economies of Scale

Also called **cost capacity factor**. The cost capacity factor relates mathematically similar jobs of different sizes. If a job is twice as big as the previous one will it cost twice as much? Usually not, for the following reasons:

Indivisibilities: In a production process there may be certain indivisibilities, or fixed costs which are required just to be in business, but not related to output. For example, a firm may require a manager, a telephone and a secretary. These costs are indivisible because you cannot have half a manager merely because you want to operate at a lower output.

Specialization: In a one man business all the project activities tend to be undertaken by that person. As the company grows, single repetitive tasks can be assigned to another worker, who will be able to handle them more efficiently - for example, TV production lines.

Technical: Large scale production is often able to take advantage of automated machinery. The high capital expenditure can be written off over large production runs. Thus reducing the unit cost, eg. car production lines.

Scaling: There is not always a linear relationship between dimensions and volumes, eg. on an oil tanker, the surface area increases at two-thirds the rate of the volume. Thus the tankers require proportionally less steel per cubic meter as they increase in volume.

These economies of scale effects have shown that as projects get larger their unit cost reduces and the production becomes more efficient, however, the opposite can also be true.

As the output increases there are some **diseconomies of scale** which are usually associated with the management function. When the organization structure becomes large and bureaucratic the co-ordination between the management levels and departments becomes increasingly more complex, costly and inefficient. Not only are the lines of communication longer, but enviably the number of unproductive meetings increases and internal memos proliferate.

These economy of scale which have a non-linear relationship can be quantified through a simple equation:

$$\$E = \$K \times (q1 / q2)^{\wedge}p$$

where $\$E$ is the estimated cost.
        $\$K$ is the known cost from a previous project.
        $q1$ is the size of the new project.
        $q2$ is the size of the old project.
        p is the cost capacity factor and ''$^{\wedge}$'' denotes raised to the power of p. The value of ''p'' is derived from empirical observations.

Consider a project to build a hotel with 1000 rooms. If a similarly constructed hotel of 500 rooms was built for $ 10000000 what is the estimate for this 1000 roomed hotel.

$$\$E = 10\,000\,000 \times (1000 / 500)^{\wedge}0.8$$

$$= 17\,411\,011$$

This indicates that although the number of rooms doubles the estimated cost only increases by 74%.

9.3.5 Parameter Costs

Also called **unit rates**. Although a project tends to be a unique undertaking, much of the work may be repetitive. Parameter costs are developed from unit rates for common items of work based on previous projects. This technique estimates a project's cost from an empirically developed book of unit rates. For example consider the following parameters:

Per linear metre: House piping and wiring.
                      Welding.

Per square metre: Decorating and painting.
                      Flooring.
                      House building.

Per cubic metre:	Concrete.
	Water supply.
Per page:	Reports and manuals.
	Photocopying.
	Printing a book.
Per tonne:	Ship building.
	Cargo freight.
Per HP or **KW**:	Engine and generator power.
	Electrical supply.
Per mile or **Km**:	Car hire.
	Transport and freight.
Per hour:	Labour.
	Machine time.

Parameter costs are used in conjunction with operational estimating to provide the activity or work package costs which can then be rolled up through the WBS.

Unit rates work well in a controlled work environment. Many projects by virtue of their location and scope of work may involve other considerations:

* Unit rate estimating is appropriate for a contractor with a record of small jobs within a limited geographical area.

* As the contracts increase in size so the data base samples will tend to decrease in number.

* Costs are influenced by remote locations, logistics, travelling distances and the conditions of the roads.

* Governmental laws and regulations.

* Environmental pressure groups.

* Weather conditions can be statistically predicted but what happens in practice may be very different.

*   Are there utilities available ? - Water supply, power supply, accommodation, public transport etc. Further considerations will be outlined in the estimating problem section later in this chapter.

Parameter costing is probably the most commonly used estimating technique and will form the basis of most estimates.

9.3.6 Daywork

Daywork is the term used to quantify the hourly or daily rate for labour, materials, plant and P&G's. The complete project could be financed on dayworks as a cost plus contract. This type of contract is quite common on military projects, but not on commercial projects where fixed prices are preferred.

On a fixed price project the client often requests daywork rates to be quoted at the tender stage to provide a framework for costing changes and additional work. The contractor's overheads and profit are included in the rate.

The contractor must ensure that the daywork sheets are signed by the client at the end of each shift. The client meanwhile needs to monitor performance to ensure good productivity.

9.3.7 Net and Gross Pricing

Net and gross pricing are terms for the different methods of building up the costs. The **net pricing** technique is built-up from:

Construction costs	$ .....
Overhead costs	$ .....
Profit	$ .....
Tender price	$ .....

The construction cost is an aggregation of the actual unit costs to make the product, while the overhead costs and profit are added on as a lump sum or a percentage of the construction cost. The tender price is then a summation of the construction costs, overhead costs and profit.

Meanwhile the **gross pricing** technique calculates the overhead costs and profit as a percentage of the unit cost. The aggregation of the unit costs will therefore give the tender price.

The estimator must decide which technique to use, both have their merits.

* The gross pricing will accommodate variations and changes simply by assigning the unit rates to the quantities, with the overhead costs and profit included.

* With gross pricing the percentage for overhead costs and profit will be rounded off, this could introduce a constant error.

* The net pricing simplifies the overhead costs and profit to two simple operations.

* Net pricing can use the gross pricing technique for variations to contract.

* Net pricing identifies the cost build-up, thus facilitating controlled negotiation.

Both net and gross pricing have their benefits, where possible a combination of the two methods may produce the best results.

9.3.8 Estimating Format

The final estimate will be a compilation of figures from different sources. Where this adds up to large amounts of data, some form of computerised system is required to produce a quick and accurate report.

It is essential to impose discipline and structure to the data capture to ensure that all parties are working to the same system, company policy and standard procedures. All of which will have been developed from the experience gained on previous projects.

The basic framework for structuring the estimate is to list the scope of work in the first column with a number and description. Then against each item assign the estimated costs. These costs are then totalled across and down.

Scope No.	Description	Costs			Total
		Labour	Material	Other	
1		10	20	30	60
2		10	15	20	45
3		10	25	15	50
4		20	15	10	45
Total		50	75	75	200

Figure: 5. Estimating format

The number system can use the WBS and CPM format to facilitate roll-up and integration with the planning and control setup. While the cost headings can use a combination of direct and indirect costs. Other advantages of a structured approach include:

* All working to the same data base of information.

* Clients prefer a consistent presentation format. This stops the ''back of the cigarette package estimating'', which at best is a thumb suck, but at worst is a gross under-estimation of the task.

* All the information on the computer can be backed up and saved, thus enabling quick disaster recovery of lost or corrupted information.

* If the estimate is structured activity bias and percentage complete, then this framework can be used to structure the data capture.

This approach should improve both the planning and progress reporting, making it more quantified and less subjective. From the different estimating techniques outlined, it is the estimator's responsibility to selection the most appropriate.

9.4   Cost, Price and Profit

The terms cost and price are often used interchangeably which can lead to confusion and ambiguity. The **cost** of a product is what you buy the goods for, whereas the **price** is what you sell goods for. Thus the price the seller asks for the goods is the cost of the goods to the buyer. Not wishing to confuse the manager these are normally expressed as the **selling price** and **buying cost**.

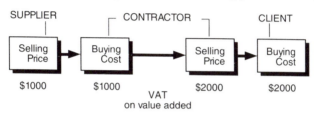

Figure: 6. Cost and Price

Note: VAT is paid on the difference or value added.

9.4.1 Pricing

There are a number of different pricing methods:

*   **Full-cost pricing**: Here all the costs are charged to the product. It is also called **absorption cost pricing** because the project absorbs all direct and indirect costs.

*   **Recovery rate pricing**: Here the overheads are linked to the product or labour price. A typical recovery rate would be expressed as a percentage of the manhour rate.

*   **Contribution pricing**: The contribution is to pay for fixed overheads and profit, expressed as:

	Contribution	=	Income - Variable costs
or:	Contribution	=	Income - Direct costs

* **Marginal cost pricing**: Here the costs are separated out into fixed and variable. With marginal costing the fixed costs are not apportioned to a project but left as a total sum for the corporate budget. This means that as long as the income covers the variable costs, the price can be reduced to attract additional business. For example, the railways often vary their prices with time of day for the same journey by righting off their fixed costs during peak periods.

9.4.2 Profit

The level of profit is usually determined by the state of the economy, market forces and the level of risk. Assessing these factors, however, is a senior management function. The project manager should concern himself with the project costs and ways of enhancing the profit (namely - complete the project for less than the estimated cost).

However, as the profit margin does have a direct bearing in the determination of the estimate's accuracy, the project manager needs to know what margin to work within. Neo-classical economics regard profit to be comprised of **normal profit, super-normal profit** and **sub-normal profit**.

Normal profit is the amount of surplus income less expenditure which the investor requires over a period of time to cover the minimum return of the investment. In the long term, normal profit may be considered as a quasi-cost, because if the company does not achieve at least normal profit it should cease trading and invest elsewhere. As a rule of thumb the normal profit should be greater than a low risk bank investment.

Super-normal profit is the profit earned in excess of the normal profit. This condition will depend on the state of the economy and competitiveness in the market.

Sub-normal profit, also called **buying work,** is when the profit margin is reduced below normal profit. There are a number of good reasons for this strange move:

* The company wishes to keep its workforce employed during a down turn in the economy.

* Accept a loss on the basic contract price, but expect to make good profits on the extras.

*   Enter a new field of business, use this project to gain experience and technology transfer.

*   Gain credibility with the client on a small project who has larger projects coming up in the future.

*   A prestige project may be seen as free marketing.

Buying work should remain a short term expedient, because this policy can quickly lead to serious financial problems. A firm losing money on one project may be tempted to finance it from a profitable project (rob Peter to pay Paul). A practice leading to further problems if this pricing policy is so manipulated over an extended period. Such a situation, if unchecked, can rapidly become a ''vicious circle'' and is a common cause of liquidation.

Profits can also be generated from a positive cash flow where a return on investment is made on the surplus funds. However, this may be difficult to identify if the project transactions pass through the corporate account.

Profit should be related to **risk and uncertainty**, the greater the risk the greater the profit. In practice this relationship may be difficult to quantify.

Every company in the long run must make normal profit, which as a guideline should be a few points above the local bank's interest rate. If this level of profit cannot be achieved then it would be financially prudent to accept the lower risk and move the investment to a bank.

9.4.3 The Pricing Dilemma

When tendering in a competitive market the contract price is one of the main factors considered during project adjudication. The pricing dilemma facing management is the trade-off between reducing their profit and improving their chance of winning the contract. The considerations here are:-

Reducing the profit margin will improve the chances of your quote being selected, but if the quote is significantly lower than your competitors this will unnecessarily erode your profits. Therefore before quoting a low price, first assess the market competition, the clients budget and the state of the economy.

On the other hand if the estimate is too high and the contract is awarded to your company, this will increase profits in the short term, but reduce the chances of further work if the same estimating data base is used on subsequent tendering.

It is refreshing to note that despite the competition in the market the lowest bidder is not always the automatic choice. Other factors are being considered as part of the adjudication process, for example, the ability of the management team, information systems, quality assurance programme and past performance.

9.5   Contingencies

So far the estimating has assumed that normal working conditions and practices will prevail. Unfortunately the real world does not work that way and allowances should be made for the risks and uncertainties. These allowances tend to get lumped together under the contingency heading which includes cover for the following non-recoverable items:

* Under estimate work content due to lack of scope definition.

* Additional work caused by design errors.

* Rework caused by production mistakes.

* Rework and replacement caused by material or component failure.

* Labour and equipment standing idle caused by import delays and inclement weather.

* Lost production caused by industrial action; strikes, work to rule, go slow or variable labour output.

* Limited supply of skilled labour locally.

The contingency allowance is usually added as a percentage to the estimated cost of the project. The size of the contingency will depend on many factors;

* Type of project.

* General efficiency and competence of the company.

* Degree of risk and uncertainty.

These headings are difficult to accurately quantify, performance on previous projects is probably the only reliable pointer.

9.6   Escalation

The term escalation in commerce and industry has come to mean the increase of the contract price due to inflation. The main elements causing inflation are; salaries, materials, transport, services and foreign currency fluctuations. Where there are fluctuations in the costs the contractor can sub-divide these into recoverable and non-recoverable, in whole or in part.

It is obvious, therefore, that quotations should include adequate cover for non-recoverable fluctuations. Several methods are available to predict the future position, a popular method is to establish the trend to-date and extrapolate. The affect of inflation may be identified as a risk in the project, the question is "who is going to accept that risk ?". The contractor accepts the risk in a fixed price tender, whereas the client accepts the risk if the project is escalated. The mechanics of an escalation clause are:

* The client and contractor agree on which escalation index to use.

* The contractor gives a quote based on "today's prices" with no contingency for inflation.

* Progress claims are escalated using published indices.

If the contractor fails to make adequate allowance for non-recoverable fluctuations this will lead to a reduced profit margin. Should the allowance be excessive the project will probably be awarded to a competitor.

9.7   Foreign Currency

The rate of exchange between your currency and your trading partners can change significantly during the course of the project. To assess the affect currency fluctuations will have on your project:

* Quantify the requirement for foreign currency.

* Quantify your currency's recent performance and extrapolate.

Although you may be a passive user of the exchange markets there are a number of steps to reduce your exposure to risk:

* **If your currency is appreciating**: Delay paying for imports as long as possible, any appreciation in your currency will effectively reduce the purchase costs.

* **If your currency is depreciating**:

   a) Buy forward cover. If you need $1m in six months time you can enter an agreement with the bank to sell you the required amount at a defined rate. Although you may have paid a premium, the bank now accepts the currency fluctuation risk.

   b) Buy the foreign currency as soon as possible before the exchange rate depreciates further. Invest short term in the other currency until required, check the differential interest rates between currencies.

   c) Let the client pay for all imported goods, this passes the risk to the client, but it might also mean you lose the opportunity to mark up the imported goods.

   d) Buy components from your home market if available at competitive prices.

It is often a tendering requirement to outline the need for foreign currency. If the WBS is suitably structured the foreign currency requirement can be easily estimated. This allows the client to assess the need for foreign currency which may have to be approved by the reserve bank.

9.8   Sensitivity Analysis

Sensitivity analysis is one of the final estimating undertakings. It investigates the effect cost changes have on the other cost parameters. It should be clear at this stage which parameters are exerting the greatest influence on the estimate and only these important parameters need be considered.

The mechanics of sensitivity analysis are to vary the estimate of each item in turn by a given percentage, say 10% and determine what the effect this variation has on the final result. If the effect is large, the project may be said to be sensitive to that item. For example, consider labour and material costs when they are divided as follows;

Cost Centre	Cost	Change	New Cost	Percentage Rise in Total Cost	
Labour	$80	10% Increase	$88		Labour
Materials	$20	nil	$20		Simulated
Total	$100		$108	8%	
Labour	$80	nil	$80		Material
Materials	$20	10% Increase	$22		Simulated
Total	$100		$102	2%	

Figure: 7. Sensitivity analysis

This indicates that for every 10% rise in costs the labour component costs will increase by 8% and materials 2%. Therefore this activity is more sensitive to labour than material costs. Should the trade unions demand a 10% rise total cost will go up 8%, but if the material supplier puts his costs up 10% the total will only rise by 2%.

It is good practice to isolate the key parameters the project is sensitive too. The estimator can now focus on these key items and hopefully improve the level of accuracy of the quotation.

9.9 Estimating Time

There are many approaches and techniques to estimating an activity's duration, planners usually develop these through experience. The problem occurs, when you don't have the experience or a comprehensive data base of historical information. In situations like these the following points may assist. Where possible seek advice and information from the people who will perform the work and co-ordinate their input.

* Establish the purpose of each activity in as much detail as possible, documenting all discussions.

* Establish any fixed dates, target start date, target finish date or other milestones. These may be internally or externally imposed.

* Assign durations where possible, state level of accuracy as a measure of your confidence. This may be stated simply as high or low. The accuracy field can be used later when the critical activities have been identified and you want to reduce the level of risk and uncertainty by improving the estimate on the critical activities.

* Sub-divide uncertain activities, estimating duration where you can.

* Make a stab at the uncertain activities and process the network. If the activities are not critical ensure there is sufficient float to cover the uncertainty.

* Now that the critical activities are known, you can spend more time gathering information to improve the quality of the estimate.

* At all times be realistic and assume normal working conditions.

* At the initial stages of CPM development we assume unlimited resources. Resources are brought in as a further constraint after the network has been validated.

The estimating function should first quantify the work input for each activity in terms of manhours. The duration can then be calculated by dividing the manhours by the number of men assigned to the activity. This process is repeated with each CPM iteration.

9.10 Types of Contract

Contracts are usually classified by referring to the method of payment, so far the estimating techniques outlined have all been concerned with providing a fixed price for the contract. There are, however, a number of other contracts where a fixed price is not always required. This section will outline five different types of contract.

9.10.1 Reimbursable, Plus-Fee Contract

Also called a **cost plus contract**. The reimbursable, plus fee is considered to be the most flexible type of contract, where all the direct costs are paid by the client plus an agreed fee or percentage profit to the contractor.

This type of contract is often used at the beginning of a project when there may be many design changes, requiring close client / contractor liaison, thereby allowing work to proceed while the details are still being discussed. Once the scope of work is finalized the type of contract may change, for example, the channel tunnel contract changed from cost-plus to a fixed price.

Cost-plus contracts are usually criticized on the grounds that the contractor has little incentive to control costs and increase productivity, since his fee is proportional to the total cost of the project. It is therefore up to the client to closely monitor the contractors performance.

9.10.2 Fixed Price Contract

Also called **lump sum**. The contractor gives the client a fixed price for completing the project. This contract will include all the costs associated with labour, material, plant, inflation and risk. A detailed scope of work is required from the client before the contractor can tender, this effectively prevents "fast tracking" between design and construction. Once the project has started any changes in the scope of work will have to be negotiated.

The preparation of a fixed price quote may cost the contractor 1 to 3% of the contract price. It is therefore, in the client's long term interest to limit the number of contractors tendering as the cost of tendering will ultimately be passed onto the client. This type of contract is becoming more popular with clients because it passes much of the project risk onto the contractor. The inflation risk, however, is often accepted by the client in the form of an escalation clause.

9.10.3 Unit Rates

Also called; **billed rates, parameter costs** or **schedule of rates**. This type of contract works on the basis of negotiated rates for specific work. All payments will be based on measurement of the work completed using the unit rates. At the tender stage the quote will be based on a **bill of material** (BOM).

This type of contract is suitable for the project where the client cannot supply sufficient data for the contractor to give a lump sum quote. Thus the client can start his project sooner than if he had to wait for a lump sum price. Even on a fixed price contract, unit rates can be agreed at the outset as a framework for costing additional work.

Unit rates do offer the contractor an incentive to maximize his profits through efficiency. The client will be responsible for the measurement of the work done, which can be integrated with the planning and control function.

9.10.4 Turnkey Contract

Also known as the **design and construct contract**. Here the contractor is responsible for the whole project, from the design phase right through to the commissioning phase. This reduces the client's input to a minimum while contractually ensuring that the contractor is responsible for making the project work.

9.10.5 Professional Project Management Contract

A firm of project managers are hired by the client to plan, monitor and control the project. The project managers will be responsible for the day to day running of the project. The advantage of using professional project managers is that they are experts in this field of management. They act as an extension of the client's management team who may lack project management expertise.

The project managers will have a wealth of project related experience to fall back on, along with integrated systems developed from previous projects. Better managed projects usually benefit all parties.

The different types of contract offer a continuum of employer's risk against flexibility. This is outlined in figure below. (Thompson p43).

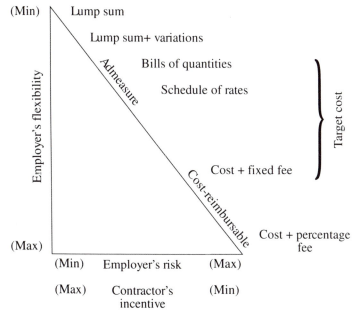

Figure: 8. Types of construction contracts

9.11 Estimating Problems

The following list is a collection of points to be considered when estimating. Some of the common pitfalls to be aware of include:

*   Misinterpreting the scope of work and omissions.

*   Poorly defined or overly optimistic schedule.

*   An unskilled workforce can give a variable output.

*   Risk and uncertainty not considered.

*   Escalation not considered.

*   If work is priced out at the department average, regardless of who is doing the work, this simplifies the estimating but the client may not be happy paying engineers' rates for tradesmen.

* The performance of individuals within a trade can vary considerably depending on ability and commitment.

* Lack of historical data, especially if this is a new type of project for the company.

* When negotiating the contract, mention a high figure to the client, and reduce it until you receive a favourable response, but what will be the profit ?

* When estimating symmetrical projects like a ship, it is normal to cost half the ship. Do not forget to multiply the figures by two.

* Keep new technology to a minimum, between 5% to 10% is recommended. Use the Japanese slice by slice approach. For example, Japanese cars tend to incorporate modifications on a frequent regular basis, every six months or so, while the British tend to make mega jumps every ten years (Concorde). By reducing the level of new technology, this will help to keep the amount of teething problems to a minimum.

* The main contractor will be at risk if he has to give a fixed price quotation to his client based on budget estimates from his sub-contractors. The sub-contractors prefer to give fixed quotations when the detailed drawings are finished and these are often only ready just-in-time for construction.

* Some managers prefer not to document their problem: "If my project fails the last thing I want around is hard data to nail me."

* Make sure that costs are debited to the appropriate activity and not off-loaded to the activity with the fattest budget.

* Consider your response to this reaction when requesting information, "My people have no time to collect data, they are too busy doing the work."

* If your project involves a certain amount of repetitive work it is not unreasonable to assume a "learning curve", which will tend to increase productivity by reducing manhours per unit.

* Make sure objectives do not become a wish list. All objectives should be attainable.

* A NASA astronaut was asked what concerned him most about the flight ? He replied, "It's not sitting on a potential fuel bomb that concerns me most, but the 10 000 components which were made by the lowest bidder. Also see the film "Capricorn 1".

* Expenses often forgotten when estimating include:-

a) Commissioning and customer acceptance.

b) Training of the client's technicians to use the installed equipment.

c) Protective painting.

d) User manuals.

* Terms and conditions of contract not quantified.

* Validity of quotations, which is usually 30 days, is not stated.

9.12 Summary

This chapter outlined how the success of a project can be directly related to effective and accurate estimating. The main estimating terminology and techniques were explained to provide a sound basis for project estimating.

It was shown that the estimate should provide the prerequisite information at an acceptable level of accuracy, at a reasonable cost to enable the project manager to make budget decisions.

The different types of costs and estimating methodologies were explained in detail to give the estimator the management tools necessary to compile a comprehensive quotation.

The pricing dilemma facing management was outlined, this being the trade-off between trying for higher profit on the one hand and reducing profit to improve their chance of winning the contract on the other. Risk analysis was addressed through the techniques of contingencies allowance, escalation and sensitivity analysis.

The different types of contract commonly used in project management were outlined. It was explained how the estimating function can vary with the type of contract.

The role of the senior managers and the project manager was outlined with respect to setting the profit margin and the estimate's level of accuracy. It was shown that the estimate's level of accuracy should relate directly to the profit margin.

As a final word on estimating, your current project can provide valuable estimating information for your future projects, therefore, you must document what is happening. Because managers who do not study the history of their previous projects are condemned to repeat their history of poor estimates and cost overruns.

Chapter 10

Cost Management

This chapter on Cost Management will outline the scope of responsibility for the project accountant, who is sometimes also called the cost engineer. On small projects of course all the accounting tasks may well land on the project managers desk. The cash flow statement will be developed, which is one of the most powerful tools available for cost management. If effectively used the cash flow statement has all the advantages of an explicitly designed financial planning and control system.

Statistics clearly indicate that more companies go into liquidation because of cash-flow problems than for any other reason. Managers must therefore keep a close watch on the project cash flow status. This chapter will also discuss expenditure curves, retention and escalation.

Project accounting should not be confused with financial accounting and management accounting which are used within the corporate environment. From the definitions, however, you will see there is common ground.

Financial accounting keeps a record of all the financial transactions, payments in and out, together with amounts owed and owing. This information gives the financial status of a company using the generally accepted accounting principles. The three main reports are; the balance sheet, the income statement and the cash flow statement.

While **management accounting,** also called **cost accounting**, uses the above financial information particularly from the profit and loss account to analysis company performance. This analysis will assist management in decision-making with respect to estimating, planning, budgeting, implementation and control.

10.1 Cash Flow Statement

The cash flow statement is a document which models the flow of money in the project. The time frame is usually monthly so as to coincide with the normal business accounting cycle.

The cash flow statement is based on the same information used in a typical bank statement, except that here the incomes (cash in-flows) and expenditures (cash out-flows) are grouped together and totalled. In a project the contractors income would come from the monthly progress payments, while the expenses would be wages, materials, overheads, interest and bought-in services.

The cash flow statement uses a structured format as shown below:-

Cash Flow Items	Month A	Month B	Month C
Opening balance Income			
Total available			
Expenses			
Total expenses			
Closing amount			

Figure: 1. The cash flow statement format

Consider example no. 1 where:

*   The brought forward amount for January is $5000.

*   The incomes: January $10000
                                     February $15000
                                     March $20000

*   The expenses: January $8000
                                     February $12000
                                     March $16000

Use the following steps as a guideline to solve the exercise.

Step 1:   Set up the cash flow statement headings. Use monthly headings (fields / columns) to cover the duration of the project.

Step 2:   The brought forward (B / F) for January is given ($5000).

Step 3:   List the in-flow of cash items from the income statement for January, February and March, $10000, $15000, $20000 respectively.

Step 4:   Calculate the total funds available for January by adding the total income to the brought forward.

Step 5:   List the out-flow of cash items from the expense statement for January, February and March, $8000, $12000, $16000 respectively.

Step 6:   Calculate the total out-flow of funds for January.

Step 7:   Calculate the closing statement for January, funds available minus expenditure.

Step 8:   The closing statement for January now becomes the B/F for the next month February.

Repeat this procedure every month for the rest of the project.

Solution: Cash flow example no. 1:

Cash Flow Items	Jan	Feb	Mar
Opening balance	5000	7000	10000
Income	10000	15000	20000
Total available	15000	22000	30000
Expenses	8000	12000	16000
Total expenses	8000	12000	16000
Closing amount	7000	10000	14000

Figure: 2. Worked example no. 1

Follow the calculations through the worked example to ensure understanding before moving on to the next development.

10.2 Cash Flow Timing

There is a catch unfortunately. The cash flow statement as the name suggests is a measure of the cash in and out of the projects' account. The catch is that this may not be the same as the sales figures or expenses for the month, because of the timing of the payments. Listed below are typical examples of cash flow timings:

* Part payment with placement of order, this is often used to cover the manufacture's cost of materials and ensure purchasers commitment.

* Stage payments; often required by companies building a component which will take months to complete. The payments are to cover the manufacture's costs.

* Payment on purchase; this is normal practice with retailers.

* Monthly payments; labour, rent, telephone and other office expenses.

* 30 or 60 days credit; normal terms for bought-in items.

* 90 days credit; large hypermarkets will pay their suppliers 90 days after delivery, even though they may sell the products in the first month. This means that even if they sell at cost they can still make a profit on the return from the positive cash flow.

It may help the learning process to look at the data presented the other way round.

* Labour costs are usually paid in the month they are used.

* Material costs can vary from an up-front payment, cash on delivery (COD), to 1 to 3 months credit.

* Bought-in services and plant hire costs can be paid within 1 to 3 months after delivery.

* Income from client; up-front payment, stage payments or progress payment one month after invoice.

These figures are usually compiled monthly on a creditors and debtors schedule. It is the project accountants responsibility to chase up late payments.

Non cash flow items: Company assets should not appear on a cash flow statement as they do not represent a movement of cash. Although appreciation and depreciation may present a flow of value, it does not present an inflow or outflow of money physically. This also applies to the revaluation of property and the value of the company's shares.

10.3 CPM Cost Model

When using Critical Path Method (CPM) for project planning, the accounts are generally assigned to activities and not to suppliers or departments. For ease of calculation the activity's cost is usually assumed to be linear over the duration of the activity. How accurate is this assumption ?

Labour costs are generally uniform over the duration of the activity. Whereas the cost of materials and other bought-in items may need to be qualified, as they can vary from up-front payments to 1, 2 or 3 months later depending on the supplier.

When considering the project as a whole, if there are more than a hundred activities any distortions caused by non-linear cash flow would tend to be smoothed out. However, if there are activities with disproportionate material or equipment payments, these can be separated out to form new activities with appropriate durations to match the expense profile.

Exercise: Cash flow no.2

Before going any further let us consolidate the above information by trying another exercise. Using the following information produce a cash flow statement for the months January to June.

* Brought forward for January is $5000.

* Sales forecast @ $10 each unit. The Clients take two months to pay a/c.

Nov	Dec	Jan	Feb	Mar	Apr	May	Jun
1000	1500	1600	900	500	1200	1300	1400 (units)

Cost of sales: [1]   Overheads are $300 per month.
                [2]   Material $2 each. Supplier gives one month credit.
                [3]   Labour $1 each unit. Paid in month used.
                [4]   Loan repayment: Feb $14000 May $15000
                                         Apr $22000 Jun $2000

Cash Flow Items	Jan	Feb	Mar	Apr	May	Jun
Opening balance Income						
Total available [A]						
Cost of Sales Overheads [1] Materials [2] Labour [3] Loan [4]						
Total expenses [B]						
Closing amount [A-B]						

Figure: 3. Cash flow statement proforma

Before looking at the solution, try the exercise yourself. Build up the cash flow statement one step at a time.

Step 1:   Using the cash flow statement proforma provided check all column and row headings.

Step 2:   The brought forward figure for January is given, insert this into the opening balance cell.

Step 3:   The income in January will come from sales in November because the client takes 2 months to pay a/c. The sales for November, being 1000 units @ $10 each, gives $10000. Enter this figure in the income cell. The sales figures for the remaining months will have the same stagger.

Step 4:   The overhead costs are $300 per month running throughout the project. Enter this in the overhead expense row.

Step 5:   The material expense for January will come from the purchases made in December since the supplier gives 1 month credit. 1500 units @ $2 each is $3000. Place $3000 in the material expense row for January. The other months will once more follow the same stagger.

Step 6: The labour expense occurs in the month of use, so for January 1600 units @ $1 each gives $1600. Enter $1600 in the labour expense row for January and so on for the other months.

Step 7: The loan repayments in this example have been preset by the bank, enter $14000 in the loan expense row for February and so on for the other repayments.

Step 8: All the data should now be positioned in the cash flow statement. The next step is to run the calculation through the months from January to June. The total funds available for January are the brought forward $5000 plus the income $10000 giving $15000.

Step 9: The total expenses for January are overheads $300, materials $3000, labour $1600 and zero for loan payment, giving $4900.

Step 10: Subtract the total expenses ($4900) from the total funds available ($15000) [(8) - (9)], giving $10100. This is the closing amount for January.

Step 11: The opening amount for February is the same as the closing amount for January, $10100.

Cash Flow Items	Jan	Feb	Mar	Apr	May	Jun
Opening balance	5000	10100	6700	20100	10600	-3400
Income	10000	15000	16000	9000	5000	12000
Total available [A]	15000	25100	22700	29100	15600	8600
Cost of Sales						
Overheads [1]	300	300	300	300	300	300
Materials [2]	3000	3200	1800	1000	2400	2600
Labour [3]	1600	900	500	1200	1300	1400
Loan [4]	0	14000	0	16000	15000	2000
Total expenses [B]	4900	18400	2600	18500	19000	6300
Closing amount [A-B]	10100	6700	20100	10600	-3400	2300

Figure: 4. Worked example no.2

These calculations are repeated for every month of the project. A negative amount can be printed as -10 or (10). Accountants like to use brackets like this (100) to indicate negative cash flow. Any negative cash flow will either need to be avoided or financed by an overdraft. Unless up-front payments have been organised, the initial stages of a project usually experience negative cash flow due to all the setting up costs and material procurement.

10.4 Stocking and Destocking

The cash flow statement will also show the differential cash flow effects caused by stocking and destocking. Stocking refers to increasing sales while destocking refers to decreasing sales.

Exercise: Cash flow no.3. Consider the following situation where a company has a steady sales turnover of machines each month.

* Sales: 6 machines per month @ $10000 each.
* Overheads: $4000 per month.
* Raw material: $5000 per machine.
* Labour: $1000 per machine.

Cash Flow Items	Jan	Feb	Mar	Apr	May	Jun
Opening balance	0	20000	40000	60000	80000	100000
Income	60000	60000	60000	60000	60000	60000
Total available [A]	60000	80000	100000	120000	140000	160000
Cost of Sales						
Overheads [1]	4000	4000	4000	4000	4000	4000
Materials [2]	30000	30000	30000	30000	30000	30000
Labour [3]	6000	6000	6000	6000	6000	6000
Total expenses [B]	40000	40000	40000	40000	40000	40000
Closing amount [A-B]	20000	40000	60000	80000	100000	120000

Figure: 5. Worked example no.3

The cash flow statement shows that the company is making $20000 per month profit which is being carried forward each month. Now let us make the situation a little more complicated. The company has in stock all the manufactured machines it needs for the following month's sales plus the raw material for the machines it is going to make in the following month. So it has a machine stock and a raw material stock.

Now consider what effect the cash flow timing will have on the cash flow statement:

* Sales: 6 machines per month @ $10000 each. 3 months credit.

* Overheads: $4000 per month. Paid in the month of use.

* Raw material: $5000 per machine. 2 months credit.

* Labour: $1000 per machine. Paid in the month of work.

In the steady state the cash flow statement will look the same as the previous example. But what happens when the sales decrease from 6 to 4 machines per month.

Exercise: no.4

* Sales reduce in January to 4 machines, but the income is not reduced till April because of the 3 months credit.

* The overheads remain the same.

* The finished machine stock after sales is 2 machines. This is because only 4 of the 6 machines were sold. Therefore in January only 2 machines need to be manufactured to bring the finished machine stock up to 4 machines. From February, 4 machines will be made per month.

* As only 2 sets of the raw material stock were used in January, 4 of the 6 remain. Therefore in January no more raw materials are required. From February order 4 sets of raw material per month. The supplier gives 2 months credit, so the expense will not change until March when it will be nil, from then on the costs will be for 4 sets of raw material per month.

Surprise! The monthly profit for the first three months actually increases, before finding the steady state of $12000 per month. This cash windfall phenomenon is known as **destocking** when the immediate effect of a drop in sales is to make the company temporarily flush with cash.

Cash Flow Items	Jan	Feb	Mar	Apr	May	Jun
Opening balance	0	24000	46000	98000	110000	122000
Income	60000	60000	60000	40000	40000	40000
Total available [A]	60000	84000	106000	138000	150000	162000
Cost of Sales						
Overheads [1]	4000	4000	4000	4000	4000	4000
Raw Materials [2]	30000	30000	0	20000	20000	20000
Labour [3]	2000	4000	4000	4000	4000	4000
Total expenses [B]	36000	38000	8000	28000	28000	28000
Closing amount [A-B]	24000	46000	98000	110000	122000	134000

Figure: 6. Worked example no.4

Exercise: no.5   Now consider the cash flow situation when the sales increase from a steady state of 4 machines to 6 machines per month.

* The sales increased to 6 machines in January but as the client has 3 months credit the change in cash flow income occurs in April. (Sales $60000).

* The overheads remain the same at $4000 per month.

* The finished goods stock for January is 4, but need 6, therefore make 2 more machines quickly. The total for January is then to make a total of 8 machines (Labour $8000). For the following months make 6 machines (Labour $6000).

* Raw material stock in January is 4 units, but need to make 8 machines, therefore need 4 more units, plus 6 units for next months raw goods stock. In January order 10 units (Material $50000 paid in March). For the following months order 6 units (Material $30000 from Apr).

We now have the destocking situation in reverse. In the first month we must restock the finished machine stock and the raw material stock. This will effect results by reducing the monthly profit for the first three months, before reaching its steady state of $20000 per month. In this example the cash flow actually went negative in April which would have required external financing. This exercise clearly shows the difference between profit and cash flow, and how a business

Cash Flow Items	Jan	Feb	Mar	Apr	May	Jun
Opening balance	0	8000	18000	-2000	18000	38000
Income	40000	40000	40000	60000	60000	60000
Total available [A]	40000	48000	58000	58000	78000	98000
Cost of Sales						
Overheads [1]	4000	4000	4000	4000	4000	4000
Raw Materials [2]	20000	20000	50000	30000	30000	30000
Labour [3]	8000	6000	6000	6000	6000	6000
Total expenses [B]	32000	30000	60000	40000	40000	40000
Profit per month	8000	10000	-20000	20000	20000	20000
Closing amount [A-B]	8000	18000	-2000	18000	38000	58000

Figure: 7. Worked example no 5.

can run into cash flow problems as any increase in sales will require more working capital to fund the expansion. This condition is called **over-trading**. Once the transition period is over the company will reach a higher level of profit, the problem is getting there.

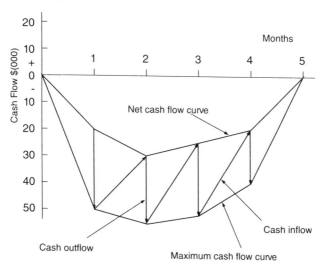

Figure: 8. Cash flow envelope

10.5 Cash Flow Envelope

In the text so far we have not considered the timing of the cash flow within the monthly time frame itself. The worst condition would be for the accounts department to be paying all the expenses to your creditors at the beginning of the month, whilst the income arrives at the end of the month. Although the balance at the end of the month may be positive, during the month the account would have been overdrawn. To represent this situation graphically see figure 8 (Fellows p195). From the graph the following points can be deduced:

* The area between the net cash flow curve and the x - axis shows the long term finance requirement.

* The area between the maximum cash flow curve when negative and the lower of either the x - axis or the net cash flow curve, will show the short term finance requirement.

* The project is completely self financing when both the net and maximum cash flow curves are above the x-axis

10.6 How to Draw an S Curve

Another method for modelling the cash flow is to use **S curve** analysis, which provides the link between the CPM and the budget. Experience has shown that a project's accumulated costs tend to follow the **S curve** shape. To draw the **S curve** use the following procedure on the worked example Appendix 4, p. 363.

Step 1:   Draw an Early Start barchart for the project.

Step 2:   Assign values linearly per day. Activity 010, for example, is $100 over two days, giving $50 per day.

Step 3:   Add the cost values vertically to get daily totals. For the 3rd March add the daily amount for activities 020, 030 and 040 which are $50, $10 and $50 respectively, giving a daily total of $110.

Step 4:   Plot the daily total costs on a graph of costs against time to obtain the daily rate of expenditure curve.

Step 5: Accumulate the daily values from left to right. To give the total to timenow. Thus the accumulated total for the 3rd March is the sum of the daily totals; $50, $50 and $110, giving $210.

Step 6: Plot accumulated figures on a graph of cost against time. This will produce the distinctive **S curve**.

	DAYS															
Activity list	1	2	3	4	5	6	7	8	9	10	11	12	13	14	15	16
010	50	50														
020			50	50	50	^	^	^	^	^						
030			10	10	10	10	10	I0								
040			50	50	^	^	^	^	^	^	^	^				
050							10	10	10	10	10	^	^	^	^	^
060									30	30	30	30	30	30	30	
070					30	30	30	^	^	^	^	^	^	^	^	
080																50
Expenses per day	50	50	110	110	90	50	50	20	40	40	30	30	30	30	30	50
Accumulated expenses	50	100	210	320	410	460	510	530	570	610	640	670	700	730	760	810

Figure: 9. Barchart

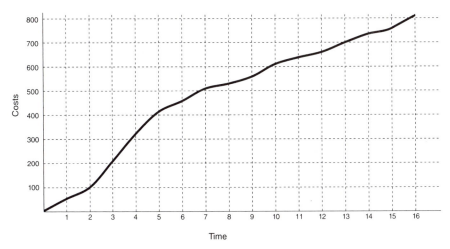

Figure: 10. S curve

Banana Curve: If the **S curve** for the Early Start and Late Start (p. 364) are drawn on the same graph they produce a distinctive banana type curve.

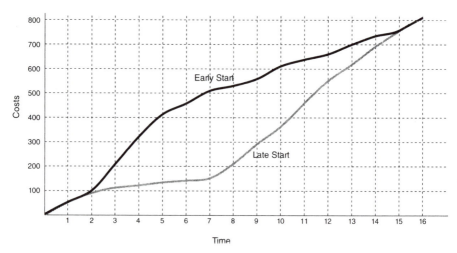

Figure: 11. Banana curve

The banana curve indicates the different timing of the cash flows of activities starting Early Start as opposed to activities starting Late Start. Project planners normally schedule activities Early Start to ensure all the float time is available.

However, the accountant may see things differently and feel that activities should begin Late Start. The advantage with activities starting Late Start is that the payments will be delayed and finance charges reduced.

This approach, however, could backfire on the accountant in the later stages of the project if there are delays, because now there is no float available to accommodate these delays, so the activities must be crashed if the project is to finish on time. This means the float that was freely given away in the early stages of the project may now be expensive to buy back.

10.7 Analysis of the Cash Flow Statement and S Curve

When the project manager is presented with a cost model of the project, he needs guidelines to direct his response.

If the closing amount is **negative**, try:

a)   Delaying expenditure payment or arrange longer credit periods.

b)   Bring forward the income payments. If your project is financed by stage payments, make sure these are completed as soon as possible.

c)   If the negative cash flow is being caused by the purchase of materials, ask the client to pay the suppliers directly. (Note: You may loose your mark up and discount).

d)   Arrange finance well in advance. Bank managers do not like to receive calls late Friday evening to arrange finance for your company salaries. The bank managers also have to plan their cash flow.

e)   Delay working on activities with float.

If the closing amount is **positive**, try:

a)   Looking into ways of investing the money at the best rate of return.

b)   Start activities earlier than planned, thereby finishing the project sooner.

All these possibilities are best tested through a **what-if** type simulation. The what-if simulation simply changes the values in the cost model to see what effect this will have down stream in the project.

Having worked through a few examples, you should now appreciate that when there are changes to the income or expenses, all the following values will change. If calculated by hand, this process would be extremely time consuming, fortunately computer spreadsheets have come to our rescue.

10.8 Retention

Retention may be defined as holding back payment of a certain amount of a contractor's income for a period of time to ensure good workmanship. The normal practice is to withhold 10% per month until 5% of the contract value is reached. This sum will then be held by the client against agreed defects for a period of up to one year after commissioning.

For retention to work effectively, checks must be made to ensure that the contractor is not over claiming.

Why use retention ?

*   To ensure that the contractor will finish the project within the agreed conditions.

*   To have something tangible to hold against the contractor in the event of substandard work or default.

*   Provide funds if another contractor is required to complete the activity.

*   "Money speaks louder than words".

Performance bonds can be used instead of retention. Here a legal document is drawn up by a bank guaranteeing the client the same conditions as a retention.

10.9 Benefits of Using a Cash Flow Statement

Although statistics clearly indicate that more companies go into liquidation because of cash flow problems than for any other reason, the full benefits of cash flow management are not always appreciated. Listed below are some of the many benefits associated with using cash flow modelling techniques.

*   The manager can plan ahead by knowing what funds are required, when they are required and how much is required.

*   It gives timely warning of negative cash flows which need to be financed and positive cash flow which should be invested.

*   It gives a forecast rate of invoicing (FRI) to your client so that they can produce their cash flow statement. This is often a contractual requirement with some of the larger corporations.

*   The cash flow statement is the main item of a business plan, as it will show the bank manager or lender how much you need, when you need it and most importantly when you will pay it back. It will also show that you have done your homework.

*   A cash flow loan reduces the amount of paperwork when compared with secured lending.

*   Cash flow will set the lending and repayment dates which usually makes the loan cheaper than an overdraft. With an overdraft the bank has no idea when the company is going to borrow or payback, so the bank builds up an extra margin to cover its own funding costs.

*   ''Secured'' lending, even if it is based on the borrower's assets, still depends on the borrower's cash flow to pay for the loan. For assets are only worth as much as an outsider is prepared to pay for them and that valuation is likely to be based on the asset's ability to produce cash.

*   The cash flow statement can be developed into expenditure curves, rates of expenditure and accumulated expenditure, all of which are required for earned value project control.

*   The cash flow statement can be used to perform **what-if** simulation which will indicate where the project's sensitivity lies. This forms the basis of the sensitivity analysis.

*   It can be used as a data source to calculate an investments payback period.

*   The cash flow can be discounted (DCF) which introduces a time value to the money.

*   It can be the data source for the company's asset register, asset depreciation and company taxes.

These benefits clearly indicate how the cash flow statement can be axiomatic to effective project cost planning and control.

10.10 Summary

In this module we have discussed how cost management can be effectively planned, tracked and controlled through the cash flow statement and expenditure curves. The importance of cash flow management is borne out by statistical evidence which indicates that more companies go into liquidation because of cash-flow problems than for any other reason.

The banks have also learnt through bitter experience the value of the cash flow statement to assess not the assets of their borrowers but whether they can pay back the loan from their cash flow.

Examples of how differential creditors and debtors affects the cash flow situation were developed, together with a stocking and destocking exercise which clearly showed the difference between profit and cash flow and how a business can run into cash flow problems due to an increase in sales which required more working capital to fund the expansion.

The cash flow envelope was used to indicate how the timing of the cash flow within the month can effect the finance requirements. Another method for modelling the cash flow, the **S curve** analysis, was shown to provide the link between the CPM and the budget. The full importance of this technique will be borne out later when it will be used in the earned value chapter to outline an integrated cost / time curve plan for the project.

Finally retention was shown to be an effective tool to ensure compliance from sub-contractors.

Chapter 11

Project Control

The development of a project plan completes the first phase of the planning cycle. The text now moves on to project control using the **baseline plan** as an outline of the required condition. This chapter will develop the project control cycle with respect to progress and time, while the next chapter will focus on the **earned value** technique.

Needless to say planning is a pointless exercise unless the execution of the plans are tracked and controlled by obtaining accurate feedback on performance. Project control is expensive and to warrant this expenditure the benefits of project control will be discussed and quantified.

A structured approach to planning and control is recommended by experienced practitioners, because through this disciplined system all parties will know; what is expected of them, their required performance and the reports they must generate. It also addresses the famous management quote "**Please no surprises!**".

The baseline plan may be seen as a number of documents which indicate the path the project should follow. Consider the comparison with the course a ship sails, by taking bearings, the captain can plot the ship's position. If the yacht has gone off course the captain will apply steering control to bring the ship back on course.

Similarly the project's baseline plan is the course to steer, with the tracking and monitoring functions ascertaining the project's position with respect to time,

---

cost and resources. If the project is off course, control in the form of corrective action must be applied.

It is essential for effective project control that performance is measured while there is still time to take corrective action. This chapter will show that not only is it cheaper to take effective action early on in the project, but as the project approaches the final phases, the project manager may in fact be powerless to take any corrective action at all.

11.1 Benefits of Project Control

Effective project control is expensive. To warrant this expenditure the benefits of project control must be substantiated. This section will show that the timely identification of a deviation, followed by prompt corrective action will result in a cost effective project control function. The influence cost curve figure below indicates two important features:

a) The project manager's changing level of influence over the project.

b) The changing cost of scope changes.

These two parameters are both plotted against time.

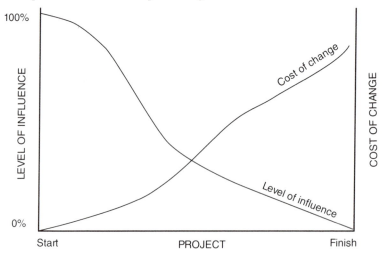

Figure: 1. Influence / Cost curve

From the figure it can be seen that initially the project manager will have a high level of influence on the project's direction and the cost of any scope changes would be small, expressed in terms of manhours spent redesigning the product. For instance the powering of a ship could change from gas turbine to diesel by simply changing the design.

As the project progresses the design will converge on an optimum scope of work. The level of influence the project manager now has over the direction of the project will be reducing all the time, while the cost of any scope changes will be rapidly increasing.

Consider the ship project again, if the client requests to change the main engine after the construction of the hull the cost could be substantial, especially if the engine beds, control system, electrics and piping are already fitted and have to be changed.

This model not only shows that changes at the beginning of a project are easier and cheaper, but also implies that the feedback on the project's status must be timely and accurate.

The effect of over optimistic reporting: As projects get larger and more complex the progress reporting needs to move from a subjective assessment to a more structured approach. The unsuspecting project manager should beware of the over reporting trap.

If the progress is over reported and not corrected in the early stages of the project the problem will rear its ugly head in the final stages of the project when the over reporting catches up with itself.

This phenomenon is shown in the over optimistic reporting diagram, where the three lines represent planned progress, reported progress and actual progress. In this case the progress was over reported throughout the project until, at about 90% complete it becomes obvious that there was something wrong and for the next few weeks the reported progress remained static.

If the actual progress had been reported accurately, the under performance trend would have prompted corrective action. But now at 90% complete the project manager may be powerless to bring the project in on time and any changes he could implement would probably be expensive.

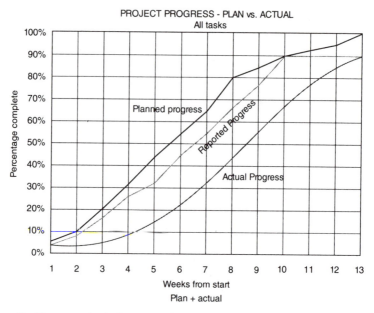

PROJECT PROGRESS - PLAN vs. ACTUAL
All tasks

Figure: 2. Over optimistic reporting

11.2 Scope of Control

It may be argued that as the project manager is the single point of responsibility, he is then responsible for everything that happens on the project. To structure this section the main project management headings will be outlined. Against each heading its purpose will be explained together with a list of typical planning and control documents.

Scope Management: The scope of work defines what the project is making or the end product. The control of the scope of work is also called **configuration control** and was developed in the scope management chapter.

Planning documents: Work Breakdown Structure
                                              Activity list
                                              Drawing register
                                              Specification register
                                              Parts list
                                              Contract

Control documents:	Site communications
	Impact statements
	Variations and Modifications
	Change requests
	Concessions

Estimating: The estimating function includes all the main parameters to predict what will happen during the project.

Planning documents:	Project selection model
	The quotation and tender
Control documents:	Closeout report on performance
	Revised estimating data base

Time Management: Outlines how the scope of work will be carried out. CPM will define the sequence of events together with activity start and finish dates.

Planning documents:	Method statement
	Activity list
	Network diagram
	Scheduled barchart
	Keydate schedule
	Rolling horizon
Control documents:	Progress report (planned vs actual)
	Gantt chart
	Revised barchart
	Earned value
	Trend documents

Cost Management: Cost management allocates department or activity budgets based on the estimate.

Planning documents:	Activity budgets
	Department budgets
	Cash flow statements
Control documents:	Expenditure reports (planned vs actual)
	Revised budgets
	Earned value

Resource Management: Resource management integrates with time management to forecast what is required to make the project happen. This is usually related to manpower requirements.

Planning documents:	Resource forecast
	Resource availability
	Resource levelled manpower histogram
Control documents:	Time sheets
	Revised manpower histogram

Procurement Management: The procurement function identifies all bought-in items. These must be procured to the time schedule and within budget.

Planning documents:	Parts list
	Procurement schedule
	Material requirement planning (MRP)
	Procurement budget
Control documents:	Expediting status report
	Revised procurement schedule and budget

Communication Management: The communication function is to disseminate information and instructions to the responsible parties, also called **document control**.

Planning documents:	Lines of communication
	List of controlled documents
	Schedule of meetings and agendas
Control documents:	Transmittals
	Minutes of meetings

Quality Management: Outlines how the company will assure the product will achieve the required condition.

Planning documents:	Project quality plan (ISO 9000)
	Quality control plan
	Parts lists and specifications
Control documents:	Inspection reports
	Non conformance reports (NCR's)
	Concessions
	Change requests
	As-built drawings
	Data books and operation manuals
	Commissioning

Technical Support: Technical support from the design office and drawing office extends from interpreting the client's brief to addressing day to day problems within statuary regulations and good building practice.

Planning documents:	Client's brief
	Statuary regulations
	Specifications
	Design calculations
Control documents:	Configuration control
	Commissioning
	As-built drawings

Human Resource Management: This function sets the framework for the human factors.

Planning documents:	Project organisation structure
	Responsibility matrix
	Job descriptions
	Work procedures
Control documents:	Team building reports
	Performance evaluations

Environmental Management: This function considers all the external issues that may effect the project.

Planning documents:	Laws and regulations
	Environmental issues
Control documents:	Environmental report

Although this list is rather extensive, the intention here was to show the reader that the range of items to be controlled relates to all aspects of the project.

11.3 Control Cycle

Project control can be effectively achieved through a control cycle. The control cycle outlines a series of steps from issuing instructions, tracking progress through to applying control on deviations. The control cycle forms a closed-loop flow of information as outlined in the figure below.

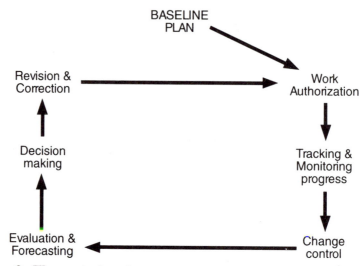

Figure: 3. The control cycle

The frequency of the reporting cycle should reflect the needs of the project. Short reporting periods, when there is a high level of change and uncertainty in the project, long periods when there is little change. For example, during project start up and commissioning the reporting cycle may be reduced to daily or even hourly. Under normal conditions the reporting cycle is usually weekly or monthly.

As a rule of thumb the reporting cycle should leave sufficient time to implement corrective action to bring any project deviation back on course. If the reporting is reasonably accurate the worst that can happen in a week, is you loose a week, unless of-course something is broken or damaged.

This section will focus on the control of progress and time, the control of scope and costs have already been covered in their respective chapters. The main items of a control loop will be briefly introduced before being developed individually.

The Baseline Plan: The baseline plan may be considered as a portfolio of documents which indicate how the project's objectives will be achieved. These documents should be produced before the execution phase of the project starts.

Work authorisation: This function communicates and disseminates information and instructions to the responsible parties.

Tracking and Monitoring Progress: This data capture function records the current status of the project.

Change Control: The change control function ensures that all changes to the scope of work are approved by the designated people before being incorporated in the baseline plan.

Evaluation and Forecasting: The evaluation and forecasting function is to quantify the project's present position within the CPM model and extrapolate current trends. It may also develop **what-if analysis** to simulate areas of uncertainty.

Decision-Making: The decision-making function collates all the information and decides on an appropriate course of action.

Revision and Correction: Based on the project manager's decision the baseline plan is revised and corrective action outlined.

Applying Control: This function will implement the revisions and corrections.

The planning and control cycle is now complete and the loop is closed. The next iteration is conducted to coincide with the reporting frequency. The above headings will now be developed individually.

11.4 Baseline Plan

The Baseline Plan may be considered as a portfolio of documents which indicate how the project's progress and schedule objectives will be achieved. These documents should be produced during the planning phase. The baseline plan is the starting point for project control. It quantifies what has to be executed, how the work is to be carried out, what standards to achieve and who will be responsible for the work.

11.5 Work Authorisation

The issuing of instructions to the appointed contractors and other responsible parties signals the start of the execution phase of the project. The WBS / OBS link determines what work will be done by whom, while the CPM determines the budgets, scheduling and manpower resources.

The method for authorising work will follow the lines developed in the scope management chapter, where the instruction formats are to be agreed. The schedule barchart usually is accepted as the key document which may be supplemented with exception reports to highlight areas of concern. This section will also develop a method for controlling the many verbal and informal instructions issued to the project participants.

It is advisable to keep lines of communication as short as possible, because long lines of communication will not only slow down the dissemination time, but may also lead to data corruption and distortion.

11.6 Tracking and Monitoring Progress

If one considers the project to be like a ball, once it starts rolling it must be tracked and controlled to keep it on course. The tracking and monitoring function establishes the project's current position with respect to progress and schedule. This section, which forms the largest part of this chapter, will develop data capture and progress reporting techniques under the following sub-headings:

* Data capture.
* Revised barchart.
* Data capture barchart.
* Rolling horizon barchart.
* Progress trend barchart.
* Quality control plan.

Data capture: Accurate Data capture is an essential element for successful project control. Data capture quantifies the current status or position of the project.

Data capture is part of the progress tracking and monitoring function where information is regularly reported back to the project manager on the project's progress and status. The figure outlines a very simple model showing where the data capture function is positioned with respect to the rest of the information system.

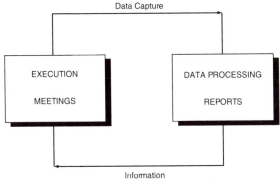

Figure: 4. The information and control system

The data capture function may be assumed to be at the start of the information cycle, therefore the accuracy of the subsequent calculations are based directly on the accuracy of the data capture. It is therefore extremely important for the data capture to be at an appropriate level of accuracy.

The appropriate level of accuracy will depend on a number of factors:

* The cost of gathering the data.
* The quality of the information.
* The quantity of the information.

It is up to the project manager to find the optimum level of project control. The accuracy of the data capture may be influenced by any the following:

* The data capture feedback proforma should be structured in line with the original estimate. This will help to make the data capture less subjective.

*   The accuracy of data capture can be improved by reporting percentage complete against a complete list of activities. This technique will be explained in the drawing office worked **example (1)** developed later in this chapter.

*   The person responsible for the quality of the data capture needs to be clearly identified by the project manager. One method of improving data capture, is to make the department that uses the information responsible for updating it. This should encourage the users to ensure that the data input is accurate.

*   A common integration problem with data capture and the subsequent analysis, occurs when the tracking categories are set up within one structure, while data is collected through another structure. An example would be the planning department having information activity biased, while procurement has its information supplier biased. In this case the baseline plan is no longer suitable for tracking the project's progress because there is no basis for comparison.

*   What data capture accuracy is required ? The accuracy of the data capture will directly affect the accuracy of any reports generated. Data capture with an accuracy of +/- 20% will give reports an accuracy of +/- 20%, or greater if the errors are compounded in the processing. As a guide the accuracy of the report should be the same or better than the profit margin of the project.

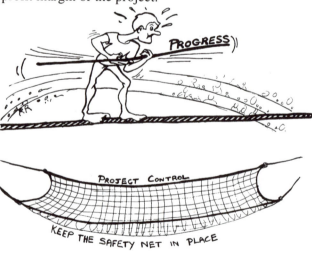

*   A higher level of accuracy is required on critical activities, because any delays on these activities will extend the project's duration.

*   Negotiate the design of your reports with the people who will use them. Try to make the reports simple and easy to use, this will help to ensure accuracy and commitment.

*   The use of written communication should be encouraged because it addresses the human failing of misinterpretation and forgetfulness.

*   Managers should have a propensity for one page reporting, giving quality not quantity. People are more likely to read a one page document than a 50 page report.

*   The data capture should be pertinent, relevant and to the point. Ask the question, "Will the information be used ?," if not, is it worth communicating ?

*   Progress can be recorded through other departments, for example monitoring quality inspection hold points. This would certainly give good feedback on key dates, but not progress between the milestones.

*   If information is received after the decision has been made, the value of the information is reduced to being historical.

If these points are used as a guideline for data capture the quality and accuracy of the information should improve.

What data can be captured ? Project progress and scheduling can be quantified with feedback from the following parameters:

*   Actual start.
*   Actual finish.
*   Remaining duration.
*   Percentage complete.
*   Bought-in delivery status.
*   Materials consumed and bought-in services.
*   Manhours liquidated.

The following example will show how to use a number of these key parameters.

Example (1): This data capture example from the drawing office illustrates how a simple matrix can be set up to capture and process data to give an overall percentage complete. This method should help to make the reporting more quantified and less subjective. In the drawing office the data capture could use the following format.

	Weighting	Accumulate % complete
1. Design	25%	25%
2. Drawing	50%	75%
3. Checking	10%	85%
4. Redrawing	10%	95%
5. Final check	5%	100%

The first column lists the five operations per drawing. The weighting column indicates as a percentage of the total the weighting of each operation. For example, in the past if the design operation has taken about a quarter of the effort, then it will be assigned a weighting of 25%. Obviously the total weighting must add up to one or 100%. These weightings should be based on experience and adjusted accordingly.

This structure is transposed on to an activity bias format with the five operations as column headings. In this case the activities are identified as drawing numbers. The calculation row is shown for the readers benefit. In practice this format would be set-up on a spreadsheet, the operator would simply enter the percentage complete for each item and the computer would calculate total PC for each drawing together with the total PC for the drawing office or project.

Drawing Number	Design 25%	Drawing 50%	Checking 10%	Corrections 10%	Final Check 5%	Total 100%	
	100	50	0	0	0		Reported Progress
	0.25x100%	0.5x50%	0x10%	0×10%	0×5%		Calculation
	25	25	0	0	0	50	Total % complete

Figure: 5. Data capture format

The data capture quantifies the percentage complete of each section from 0 to 100%. Consider the worked example. Here the reported progress is 100%, 50% with the rest zero. The design is 100% complete for 25% of the work, therefore the total is 1 x 25 = 25%. This calculation is repeated for the other items and totalled. This is obviously a very laborious exercise which lends itself to a computerized spreadsheet. The format for a number of other work situations are included for the readers benefit.

Drawing Number	Slinging	Fit and Tack	Welding	Test	Butt list and fix	Hand-over	Accumulative Percentage Complete
Planned%	20%	20%	35%	15%	5%	5%	

Figure: 6. Data capture proforma for pipe erection

Drawing Number	Columns	Beams	Gratings Handrails Ladders	Final Alignment	Punch list and fix	Hand-over	Accumulative Percentage Complete
Planned%	20%	20%	40%	5%	10%	5%	

Figure: 7. Data capture proforma for steel structures

With all the managers using the same system the accuracy and consistence of the data capture should improve.

Revised Barchart: The original scheduled barchart essentially outlines the timing of the activities, while the revised barchart reflects the current status of each activity. The Gantt chart was the first revised barchart to present on the same page both the original plan and the revised plan.

As a project progresses activities may not perform as planned. They may under-perform or over-perform, either way the original plan will not reflect the timing of the activities required to complete the project as planned. The revised barchart is therefore required to reflect the present position and highlight where control needs to be applied. The revised barchart has a number of possible formats, the main ones are:

1. Original bar with revised bar underneath.
2. Original open bar with progress measured along the same axis.
3. Progress is measured up to timenow and extrapolated.
4. Progress is measured as a percentage of the original duration.

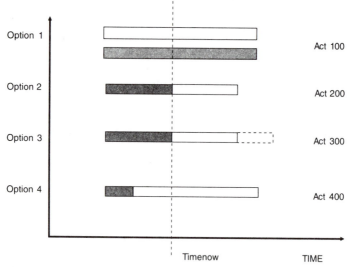

Figure: 8. Revised barchart format options

The worked example will use options 1 and 3, showing the original open bar with the revised bar underneath together with progress drawn up to timenow and extrapolated by the remaining duration. This process requires three documents:

* The network diagram showing the logic between activities.
* The data capture to timenow 4.
* The revised barchart.

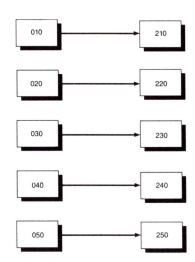

Figure: 9. Network diagram

The data capture quantifies the projects progress, these figures have been chosen to simulate a wide range of the possible events. Progress is quantified by determining remaining duration or percentage complete. Ideally remaining duration and percentage complete are directly related, where conflict exists the remaining duration takes priority.

Act No.	Act Dur	Actual Start	Actual Finish	Remaining Duration	Percentage Complete
010	2	1	2	0	100
210	4	3	-	2	-
020	4	1	4	0	100
220	2	-	-	-	-
030	6	1	-	2	-
230	3	-	-	-	-
040	6	2	-	3	-
240	2	-	-	-	-
050	6	1	-	1	-
250	2	-	-	-	-

Figure: 10. Data capture at Timenow 4

Using the progress measured to Timenow 4 the revised barchart is drawn.

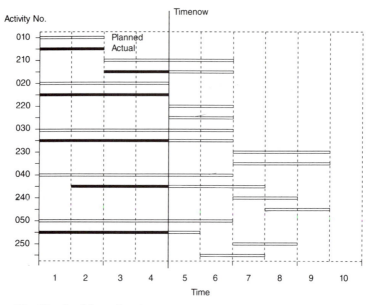

Figure: 11. Revised barchart

Each activity will be explained in the sequence presented.

Activity 010 and 020 have started and finished as planned. Activity 210 follows 010 to Timenow with remaining duration 2 days.

Activity 220 logically follows 020, therefore, it is assumed to start on day 5.

Activity 030 has a remaining duration of 2 days as planned, therefore, assume 230 will start and finish as planned.

Activity 040 started 1 day late, the remaining duration is 3 days, therefore, assume 240 will start and finish 1 day late.

Activity 050 started on time and has progressed better than planned needing only 1 day to complete. Assume 050 will start and finish 1 day early.

Analysis of this revised barchart would indicate that control may need to be applied to activity 040, especially if it is on the critical path.

Barchart data capture: The schedule barchart itself can be a useful format for data capture. Ask the foreman to mark on the last issued barchart what has been completed to Timenow and what work he intends to do in the next period. This information should be accurate because the foreman is at the operational end of the project. The report is also quick and easy for him to complete in a format he is familiar with.

The rolling horizon barchart: The rolling horizon barchart offers another use for the barchart, where the focus is on the plan for the next two or three weeks.

This type of barchart lends itself to a manual presentation as the scope of work is limited to just the activities that are working.

If a computerised presentation is preferred a simple pro-forma can be set up on a spreadsheet, with the bars drawn by the computer or by hand.

Progress trend barchart: The progress trend barchart enables the project manager to judge the direction and trend of the project at a glance. This is achieved by marking on the original barchart the successive weekly progresses. The points of interest are:

* Activities which are behind schedule. Are they catching up?

* Activities which are ahead. Are they maintaining their position ?

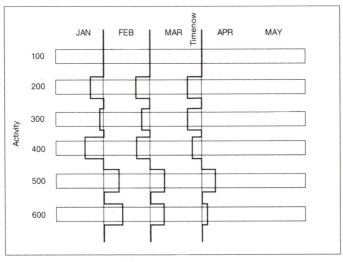

Figure: 12. Progress trend barchart

The progress trend barchart shows a number of possible situations:

Activity 100 progress as planned.

Activity 200 progress behind and steady.

Activity 300 progress behind and getting worse. This would be an area of concern.

Activity 400 progress behind but catching up.

Activity 500 progress ahead and steady.

Activity 600 ahead but loosing ground, keep an eye on this one.

This simple but effective presentation is drawn by hand on the original barchart and photocopied for circulation. To quantify the overall performance use this progress trend barchart in conjunction with the earned value presentation.

Quality control plan (QCP): The quality control plan integrates the quality requirements with the sequencing of the work. Although the planning schedule in conjunction with the network diagram and the method statement outlines the build method, the production department usually perform the work on a day-to-day basis to suit their resource availability.

The quality control plan offers the facility to impose a pre-determined work sequence. Consider the following example which highlights the need for this type document.

There are four key activities to build a warehouse;

1.   Erect steel columns.
2.   Install roof trusses.
3.   Brickwork between columns to roof height.
4.   Fit roof sheets.

The plan calls for these activities to be carried out in series, but the site foreman decides it is more efficient to start the brickwork before the roof trusses are installed because the scaffolding is in position. The brickwork starts, but the engineer stops this activity when he visited the site. The engineer explains to the foreman that the swaying of the unsupported columns will crack the mortar.

When the roof trusses are installed the foreman decides to fit the roof tiles at the same time because all the men are up on the roof. Remember the brickwork has not been completed. With the next strong wind the majority of the tiling is ripped off and besides the cost of damage to property there was a serious risk to life with these giant frisbees flying around.

The quality control plan comes to the rescue to enforce compliance. This is achieved by introducing an inspection hold point after each of these key activities. This means no work can commence on a subsequent activity until the previous one has been inspected and approved by the nominated person. A typical QCP is shown below:

Scope	Requirement	Inspection	Signature
Foundations	Spec 100	Surveillance	
Brickwork	Spec BS ???	Inspection	
Roof	Spec DIN ???	Witness	
Road	Spec ABS ???	Hold	

The scope of work heading outlines the operations, tasks or activities to be completed. The requirement or acceptance criteria outlines the standard or specification to be achieved. The inspection outlines who is to inspect; client, contractor or third party and the type of inspection; hold point, witness or surveillance. The signature is to confirm compliance.

11.7 Change Control

The change control function, also called **configuration control**, considers the impact any changes will have on the project schedule. When the impact statement is circulated it will request the planner to quantify the time and resource requirements to accommodate these scope changes and report if the original scheduling objectives are still attainable.

11.8 Evaluation and Forecasting

The evaluation and forecasting function is to consider how the progress status reports, together with any scope changes will affect the project and give prior warning of any impending problems. Using the CPM model the effect these items have on the schedule can be investigated. A what-if approach can be used to derive an optimum solution by varying key parameters. The decision-making function relies almost entirely on accurate reporting from this section.

11.9 Decision-Making

One of the main management functions is to make decisions. In-fact it may be argued that the sole purpose of generating information is to make decisions. The following steps outline a typical decision-making process:

* Define project objectives.
* Define the problem.
* Collect information.
* Develop options and alternatives.
* Evaluate and decide course of action.
* Implement.

All these decision-making steps are intrinsically part of the control cycle. The decisions can now be made on what control to apply to keep the project on course.

11.10 Revision and Correction

The decision-making function will determine what revisions and corrections to implement. This function is to up-date the documents and issue them for execution. The control cycle is now complete.

11.11 The Project Expeditor

The project expeditor or **progress chaser** is a key player in the control cycle, because it is his responsibility to make the project instructions happen. To be effective the expeditor has to adopt a criminal investigator approach, where everyone is under suspicion until proven innocent. When an instruction has been issued, for example, to the shopfloor to manufacture a component, the expeditor would follow up and check:

* Has the instruction been received by the foreman ?

* Has the foreman received all the details; drawings, specifications and planning ?

* Has the material been ordered ? Has it arrived ? Has it been inspected and passed ?

* Has the work started ? Are the men suitably qualified ?

* Compare actual performance with planned. Are they on schedule ?

By asking all these questions the expeditor becomes an invaluable source of progress information for the project manager.

11.12 Project Audit

A project audit is an official examination of a declared system. Audits are not limited to the accounts, they can be applied to any aspect of the project. An audit on the planning and control system could investigate the following:

* Inspect the management plan and project procedures for operating the planning and control function.

* Have the operators the required qualifications ?

* Have the documents been compiled and filed in accordance with the work procedures ?

* Has the control cycle been implemented ?

The first step is to determine the required condition as declared in the project quality plan. The audit is conducted by a combination of interviews and inspection of documents and files to determines if the required condition has been achieved.

The audit closeout meeting will highlight and discuss any observed non-conforming deviations. A list of corrective actions and recommendations will form part of a written report.

11.13 How to Apply Project Control

There are many ways of applying project control, this section has gathered together a number of pointers as a general guide:

* An effective way to achieve commitment is to make the person aware of the cost of any delay to the project.

* When the project involves the repetitive manufacture of components it may be appropriate to change the management style to production management. The production management technique applies effective control not through activity based planning but through earned manhours. Progress is then monitored and controlled using the production line earned manhours S curve.

* Any changes to the plan should be discussed with the foreman first:

   a) To see if they are possible.
   b) To get their input for the planning.
   c) To gain their commitment.

* If your resources are being under utilized remember that assigning more men to the job may actually slow down production. This is because those already working effectively will have to spend time explaining the job to the newcomers.

PROJECT MANAGER   SUB-CONTRACTOR

*   An excuse often used for not feeding progress back to the planner is ''we don't have the time'' or ''we are too busy doing the work''. It is the project manager's responsibility to ensure that all the project members appreciate that data capture is an important aspect of their management function.

*   Short training programmes should be developed to ensure that all the managers appreciate and understand how the information is flowing in the project.

*   Avoid persecution of the responsible parties if there are overruns, otherwise in future the managers will be reluctant to give you any information for fear that it will be held against them. Project control should be seen as a tool to assist everyone reach their objectives, not as a weapon of attack.

*   The process of project tracking and analysis should be seen as a tool for the project manager and not a means of removing responsibility. In fact, by identifying future problems, CPM enforces the project manager's authority to apply timely control to keep the project on course.

*   Failure to co-ordinate and communicate information between departments may lead to a dissipation of company resources and duplication of effort. It will also limit the amount of cross-checking, which is a useful method for identifying discrepancies and future problems.

*   Be flexible, especially during situations where you become a passive recipient. Consider the scheduling problems the planner has while he is waiting for drawings and other deliverables. In this situation flexibility is the only sensible approach.

*   It is the project manager's responsibility to establish priorities and differentiate between what is urgent and what is important. If you allow the workforce to set their own priorities they may leave low paying jobs and jobs they dislike to the end, which could adversely affect the scheduling of the project.

*   Research has shown that workers tend to have a preference for a regular income, which, if not controlled can influence their progress reporting. For example, if workers are paid **piece-rate** and they have just had a good month, but know the work load for the following month will be less, they may be tempted to under claim in the first month to give them a balanced income in the following month. If project progress is based on worker production claims, it may distort the reported status of the project.

* Ensure that responsibility is commensurate with effective authority, otherwise the party with the authority may not be held responsible and this can lead to all sorts of political problems.

11.14 Controlling the Project Participants

The effective control of the project participants is essential for project success. Projects are executed through people, who must be managed. This section will outline a simple method to control the numerous transactions between the project manager and project participants.

Step 1.   Set up a file for each identity on the project, this could be per person, per department, per supplier or per contractor.
Step 2.   When any of these people are contacted, log the conversation and confirm in writing any agreements. Try to set performance targets which can be monitored.
Step 3.   File the minutes of any discussions and keep a copy of all memos.
Step 4.   As a memory prompt, mark in your work diary all future meetings or items to be expedited.

This procedure can be supplemented by developing an Action list.

Action list: The action list is a control sheet which logs all the actions numerically and groups them per responsibility. An action may be any item of work that needs controlling by the project manager himself. The process is as follows:

Step 1.   Open an action file per work item. This could be a person, department, location or item of work.
Step 2.   Sort the action list per work item, which will usually relate to a person.
Step 3.   Initiate control.
Step 4.   Regularly update the list increasing the rev number each time.

The action list lends itself to be set up on a spreadsheet, which will certainly enable quick sorting. Sort on the work item or action number fields. Therefore when talking with the responsible person all work items to be discussed are listed together. How many times have you been talking to someone only the remember an important item after putting the telephone down !! A typical action list structure would be:

Work item	Action no.	Description
John	2	Write progress report.
Painting	24	Repair damaged areas.
Procurement	10	Bolt order status.
Site	15	Has the scaffold been erected.

Comments are usually written on the action list and incorporated in the next update. Keep the old lists as they may carry valuable information, like telephone numbers scribbled down. The action list provides an excellent prompt list, the only thing you have to remember is look at your list.

11.15 Summary

The discussion in this chapter showed that the planning of a project is a pointless exercise unless the execution of those plans are tracked and controlled. It is essential for effective project control that performance is measured while there is still time to take corrective action.

The benefits of project control were outlined, together with the effect of over reporting. The scope of what can be planned and controlled was developed to include all the main topic headings. The planning and control cycle was shown to be a closed loop flow of information starting with the baseline plan through to monitoring, evaluation and control.

The importance of data capture as a control function was shown with respect to its position in the information and control system. A suggested format for data capture was developed to improve reporting by making the reports more quantified and less subjective. The various reporting formats were discussed, this included; the revised barchart, the rolling horizon barchart and the progress trend barchart.

The next step in project control is to use the earned value approach which is a new development towards full integration of cost and time. When this approach is combined with forecasting, the project manager has the best of both worlds. This technique will be developed in the next chapter.

Chapter 12

Earned Value

This chapter continues the project control theme by introducing **earned value** as an integrated planning and control tool. The **earned value** approach is a development of the **Cost / Schedule Control System** (C/SCS) towards full integration of cost and time. When this approach is combined with forecasting, the project manager has the best of both worlds. The performance measuring mechanism should periodically (usually weekly) assess progress and costs in comparable units against a baseline plan. It is essential for effective project control that performance is measured while there is still time to take corrective action.

Although the **earned value** technique was set up initially to track the progress of cost and time, in practice it is often more appropriate to track progress measured as earned manhours and time.

Earned value more than any other planning and control technique covered in this book is shrouded in esoteric terminology, to guide the reader through this new language the first part of this chapter will define all the key words.

12.1 Terminology

This section will explain many of the terms and expressions used in the **earned value** technique. It may be argued that if one wishes to enter the field of project management, then one must speak the language of project management. Consider figure 1 in conjunction with the following terms:-

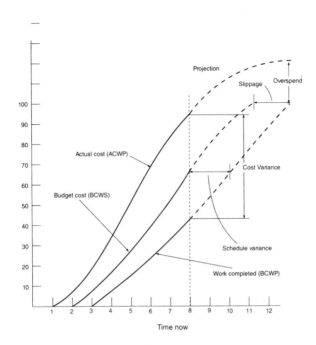

Figure: 1. Cost / schedule integration curve

Timenow: Also called **progress to date** or **progress at week-ending**. These terms are used to inform the planner up to what date the data capture has been recorded and processed.

Budget at Completion (BAC): This is the original cost estimate, budget or quotation, indicating the funds required to complete the work. At the project management level the BAC does not include profit. The reason for this will become clear later when the actual costs are compared with the planned costs. If manhours are tracked in preference to costs, then the BAC terminology would also apply to manhours.

Percentage Complete (PC): The PC is a measure of the activities performance and progress to timenow and is required for the **earned value** calculation. Percentage complete can also be calculated from remaining duration.

Example (1): Some of the following terms are best explained by a worked example. Example (1) is a simple five activity project, the only data required is outline in figure 2.

Activity Number	BAC	1	2	3	4	5	6
001	100	100					
002	400		200	200			
003	1200		400	400	400		
004	600				300	300	
005	200						200
Daily expenditure	2500	100	600	600	700	300	200
BCWS		100	700	1300	2000	2300	2500
Planned PC		4%	28%	52%	80%	92%	100%
ACWP							
Actual PC							
BCWP							

Figure: 2. Earned value example (1)

Remaining Duration (RDU): The remaining duration is the estimated time required to complete the activity from timenow. The production feedback overrides the network logic if the activity has already started, but for work that has not started the original network logic must be assumed to hold.

When progress is recorded as remaining duration only, percentage complete can be calculated if one assumes a mathematical relationship between the two. It is not unreasonable to assume a relationship if there is a linear resource profile. In **example (1)**, if activity 002 (duration 2 days) has a remaining duration of one day it may be assumed to be 50% complete.

Budgeted Cost for Work Scheduled (BCWS): The BCWS may be considered to be the same as the accumulated expenditure **S curve**, which was covered in the Cost Management chapter. This curve forms the basis of the baseline plan by providing a measure of planned work output with respect to time. The BCWS is calculated and plotted from the following equation:

BCWS = (Baseline planned percentage complete) x BAC

The BCWS curve is drawn for **example (1)**

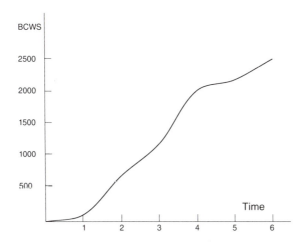

Figure: 3. Example (1), BCWS curve

Budgeted Cost for Work Performed (BCWP): The BCWP which is also called **earned value**, is a measure of achievement or value of the work done. The BCWP is calculated and plotted from the equation:

BCWP   =   PC (actual) x BAC

From **example (1)**, assume timenow is 2 and PC for the whole project is 25%, then:

BCWP   =   25%   x $2500
          = $625

Actual Cost for Work Performed (ACWP): This is the amount payable for the work done to timenow. It is the real cost incurred executing the work to achieve the reported progress. Take care to ensure that both **PC** and **ACWP** are based on the same data. A common mistake is to report progress as the work is performed, but only report costs on receipt of the invoice. This differential cash flow will make the project accounts look deceptively good in the short term.

From **example (1)**, assume ACWP at timenow 2 is $750

Estimate at Completion (EAC): The EAC is a revised estimate of the cost to complete the activity, work package or project, based on current productivity.

The EAC is calculated by extrapolating the performance trend from timenow to the end of the project. This value assumes that the productivity to-date will continue at the same rate to the end of the project.

$$\text{EAC} = \frac{\text{ACWP}}{\text{BCWP}} \times \text{BAC}$$

But $\qquad \text{BCWP} = \text{PC} \times \text{BAC}$

Therefore $\qquad \text{EAC} = \frac{\text{ACWP}}{\text{PC} \times \text{BAC}} \times \text{BAC}$

$$\text{EAC} = \frac{\text{ACWP}}{\text{PC}}$$

From **example (1)**, at timenow 2

$$\text{EAC} = \frac{750}{25} \times 100$$

$$= \$3000$$

Schedule Variance (SV): The Schedule variance calculation is a measure of the time deviation between the actual progress and the planned progress. The interesting feature about this time variance is that it is measured in money units. This is the key to cost and time integration. The variance is reported per activity and rolled up for the project.

$$\text{SV} = \text{BCWP} - \text{BCWS}$$

From **example (1)**,

$$\text{SV} = \$625 - \$700$$

$$= -\$75$$

The sign of the variance will indicate if the project is ahead or behind the planned progress.

Negative variance: $\qquad$ The project is behind the planned progress.

Positive variance: $\qquad$ The project is ahead of planned progress.

Schedule Variance Percentage (SV%): Converting the schedule variance to a percentage will address any distortion caused by the size of the activity.

$$SV\% \quad = \quad SV \ / \ BCWS$$

From **example (1)**,

$$SV\% \quad = \quad -75 \ / \ 700$$

$$= \quad -10.7\%$$

Cost Variance (CV): The cost variance is a measure of the deviation between the **earned value** and the actual cost of doing the work.

$$CV \quad = \quad BCWP - ACWP$$

From **example (1)**,

$$CV \quad = \quad \$625 \quad - \$750$$

$$= \quad -\$75$$

The sign of the variance will indicate if the costs are under or over the estimate.

Negative variance: The cost is higher than the original estimate (BAC).

Positive variance: The cost is lower than the original estimate (BAC).

Cost Variance Percentage (CV%): Converting the CV to a CV% will reduce the distortion caused by the size of the activity.

$$CV\% \quad = \quad CV \ / \ BCWP$$

From **example (1)**,

$$CV\% \quad = \quad -\$75 \ / \ \$625$$

$$= \quad -12\%$$

Threshold Variance: The threshold variances can be used to flag problem areas and thereby assist the decision-making function. The threshold limits may be set as a percentage (say +/- 5%) to give an early indication of an undesirable trend.

The terms outlined here have gained acceptance in the management press and business schools. They are commonly used in technical articles and management texts. Unfortunately many of the planning software packages have invented new terminology for some of the above terms. This new software terminology serves only to confuse, particularly for those users who are struggling to get to grips with a new concept in the first place.

The recommended approach is to relate the above terms to the standard or preferred language. **Open Plan** for example uses code 1 and 2 instead of WBS and OBS, while **Super Project** uses WBS and Account Code.

12.2 Why Use Earned Value ?

The project manager is often responsible for implementing the project's planning and control system. If an **earned value** system is proposed senior management may question why the company needs to introduce yet another management system. The following points can be used to lend support to a proposal.

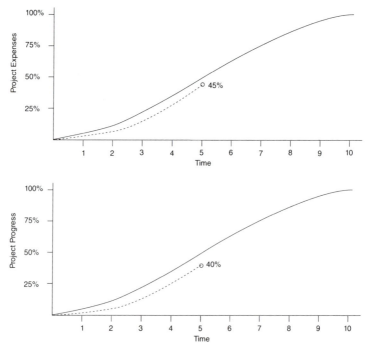

Figure: 4. Example (2), Lack of cost and progress integration

Traditional Reporting: The **earned value** approach to project control overcomes the problem of managers making decisions based on isolated information. Consider **example (2)**, where cost and progress information are being reported separately. From the top graph the accountant would report that the project is underspent, with planned expenditure 50% and actual expenditure 45%. Here the forecast looks good for the project to be completed under budget.

The planner on the other hand would not be so optimistic with planned progress 50% and actual progress 40% complete; the prognosis would predict a project time overrun, but now consider what happens when the two are integrated. The project is 45% spent but has only achieved 40% of the work. The analysis now indicates that not only is the project overspent but is also behind schedule. Thus giving a clear signal to the project manager that he needs to apply control and correct the deviation.

Example (2) clearly shows a need to integrate the project's cost and time information. Based on progress information alone the project manager would have been mislead, believing that the project would meet its objectives without the need for corrective control.

Flag for Project Control: During the project the activities are usually at various stages of completion, some on target, some ahead of plan, some behind plan, some overspent and some underspent. In this situation it is extremely difficult to access the project's overall status visually and it may be argued that a subjective assessment on a complex project is bound to be inaccurate.

This problem can be addressed by using the **earned value** model to roll-up all the activity data and report a bottom line for the project giving an over-all position. From **example (1)**, at timenow 3:

Activity	BAC	BCWS	BCWP	PC	Status
001	100	100	100	100	On time
002	400	400	300	75	Behind
003	1200	800	1080	90	Ahead
Total		1300	1480		

Project status: At timenow 3 the project's overall actual progress is ahead of the planned progress.

The worked example shows that **earned value** provides a management tool which will aggregate individual performances to give an overall picture of the project. If the overall performance is not sufficient, going down a level will highlight the offending activities. Note this technique does not consider the critical path.

12.3 Earned Value Steps

The following steps have been developed as a guideline for the project planner to follow, in order to produce:

* The Earned Value table.
* The integrated cost / schedule graph.

Step 1: Set up an **earned value** table using the following abbreviated field headings:

Activity	BAC	BCWS	PC	BCWP	ACWP	SV	SV%	CV	CV%	EAC

Figure: 5. The Earned value table

Step 2:   Calculate BCWS for the project, draw the curve BCWS against time. This is the project course to steer and forms the backbone of the baseline plan.

Step 3:   Track project to timenow. Record the following data for each activity: percentage complete and ACWP.

Step 4:   Calculate BCWP = BAC x PC, draw BCWP to timenow, then extrapolate (assume progress as originally planned) until the line intersects with BAC. This intersection will give a forecast completion date. This completion date, however, should not be looked at in isolation because it does not consider the logic and timing of the activities.

Step 5:   Draw ACWP to timenow, and extrapolate the line to the new completion date. This will forecast the EAC.

$$EAC = (ACWP / BCWP) \times BAC$$

This equation assumes progress to timenow will continue at the same rate to the end of the project.

Step 6: Calculate the variances SV / SV% / CV / CV% and EAC.

Step 7: Plot variances. Plotting the schedule and cost variances will help to indicate trends in the project. This technique was developed in the project control chapter.

Step 8: Apply Control. The above information will help to indicate if there is a need to apply control, and if so on which activities and by how much.

Using the above steps **example (1)** will be developed at timenow 4. The reported progress was:

Activity	**PC**	**ACWP**
001	100	100
002	100	500
003	75	1100
004	25	200
005	0	0

These figures are transferred on to the Earned Value table.

Activity	BAC	BCWS	PC	BCWP	ACWP	SV	SV%	CV	CV%	EAC
001	$100	$100	100%	$100	$100	0	0	0	0	$100
002	$400	$400	100%	$400	$500	0	0	-100	-25%	$500
003	$1200	$1200	75%	$900	$1000	-300	-25%	-100	-11%	$1333
004	$600	$300	25%	$150	$200	-150	-50%	-50	-33%	$800
005	$200	0	0	0	0	0	0	0	0	$200
Totals	$2500	$2000		$1550	$1800	-450	-22%	-250	-16%	$2933

Figure: 6. The earned value table at timenow 4

Project Accounts: The project manager will need to ensure that the project accounting system will generate costs to timenow. Corporate accounting departments usually base their reports on invoiced costs which may be 4 to 6 weeks behind timenow. When using **earned value** the costs will have to be gathered at the order stage, it is essential to compare like with like. Progress to timenow must be compared with the associated costs (ACWP) to achieve that progress.

Extended site: If costs are being incurred off site, such as stage payments then the progress (PC) must be reported along with the associated cost (ACWP).

Cash flow: The **earned value** technique is not the same as cash flow. The cash flow only looks at the timing of the inflows and outflows of money, it does not consider committed costs or progress of work.

12.4 Client's View of Earned value

So far the **earned value** has only been looked at from the sub-contractor's point of view. This section will change the perspective to focus on the client's position.

* If the sub-contractors are working to a fixed price contract the BCWP and ACWP will always be the same, however, if extra work is priced differently, for example, on day works then the client will need to monitor performance.

* The client can effectively use **earned value** to track the progress on his project in terms of manhours or costs.

*   A client must check that sub-contractors do not over claim:

    a)   If a sub-contractor has claimed 80% of the contract by value but only completed 50% of the work, consider what financial pressures could be exerted. An even worse case is when it is financially viable for the sub-contractor to walk away without finishing the job. The 10% retention may pale into insignificance.

    b)   The sub-contractor's management may not realize their site manager has been over claiming. This could seriously affect the sub-contractor's financial position, which may have a knock-on effect for the project.

*   If the contractor under-claims the client could also be adversely affected because:

    a)   By delaying the claim the sub-contractor could increase income by applying higher escalation rates.

    b)   The client could have made arrangements to meet a Forecast Rate of Invoice (FRI) payment and released high interest earning bonds only to find a lower claim was made. The funds must now be invested on short term savings which pay less interest.

    c)   At year end a late claim could affect the client's fiscal budgeting.

This section clearly shows that **earned value** can provide the client with a powerful management tool.

12.5 Analysing the C/SCS Graph

Once the data has been captured and processed the next step would be to analyze the information being generated by the cost / schedule control system's graph.

Forecasting: When trying to forecast the trends in the project by extrapolating the earned value curves, the following considerations should be made:

a) Will the same performance be maintained.

b) Will the performance improve because of a learning curve effect.

c) Will the performance reduce because of unforeseen problems and rework.

These three situations can be shown graphically.

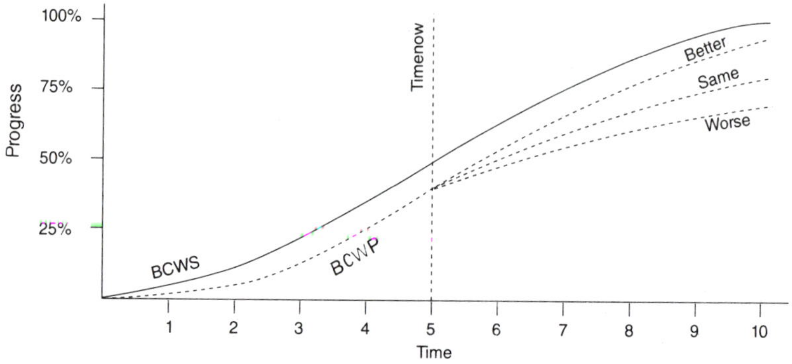

Figure: 7. The different progress extrapolations

There are thirteen different combination of planned BCWS vs actual ACWP and BCWP. These are shown in the table below, along with a description of each situation.

Example	BCWS	ACWP	BCWP
1.	1000	1000	1000
2.	1000	800	800
3.	1000	800	1000
4.	1000	800	1200
5.	1000	1000	800
6.	1000	1000	1200
7.	1000	1200	800
8.	1000	1200	1000
9.	1000	1200	1200
10.	1000	800	600
11.	1000	600	800
12.	1000	1200	1400
13.	1000	1400	1200

Example 1. This is the planned situation, where planned and actual are the same.

Example 2. The project is running late, but the costs are within budget.

Example 3. The project is on time and the costs are under budget.

Example 4. The progress is ahead of planned and the costs are under budget. Retire while you are ahead !

Example 5. The project is running late and the costs are over budget.

Example 6. The progress is ahead of planned and the costs are under budget.

Example 7. The project is running late and the costs are well over budget.

Example 8. The project is on time, but the costs are over budget.

Example 9. The progress is ahead of planned while the costs are on budget.

Example 10.The project is seriously behind and the costs are over budget.

Example 11.The project is behind, but the costs are under budget.

Example 12.The project is well ahead and the costs are under budget.

Example 13.The project is ahead, but the costs are over budget.

Self test: The best way to understand these thirteen different combination is to plot them.

How to Measure Time Deviation: The schedule variance so far has been measured in money units. This section will show a number of methods to translate the variances directly into time units by measuring distances from the **earned value** graph. Three ways of measuring are:

1.   Horizontally (backwards).
2.   Vertically.
3.   Horizontally (forwards).

These will now be discussed:

1.   The time difference between planned and actual is measured horizontally between the intersection of the planned BCWS at timenow (A) and the horizontal projection to BCWP extrapolated (B), see figure 8.

2.   Alternatively the schedule time unit can be measured horizontally from the intersection of BCWP and timenow (C) to the horizontal projection backwards onto the BCWS (D). Note that both of these methods may contain certain inaccurate information when measuring how far behind or ahead of schedule a project is because the actual sequence and timing of the activities is not considered.

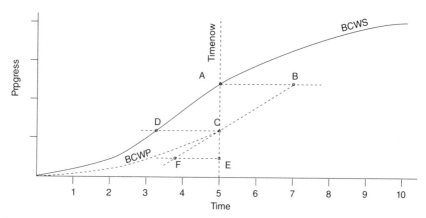

Figure: 8. Earned value / Measuring progress

3.   However, even if the sequence and timing of activities were the same as the baseline plan, converting the schedule variance to time units on the BCWP curve would be more accurate if based on the tangential rate (CF), where (CA) = (EC). The reason for this is that future progress is more likely to occur at the current actual rate of progress rather than the planned BCWS slope.

12.6 Escalation

The cost curves so far developed work well under stable wages and prices, but not during high inflation or deflationary conditions. The problem is due to the different money values assigned. BCWS and BCWP are as per the base date of the project, while ACWP must be in current money values by definition.

To address this problem the planner must either increase BCWS and BCWP by the escalation amount or reduce ACWP by the escalation amount, so as to enable the planner to compare like with like. The value for escalation can be obtained from the contractually agreed index. The figure outlines a revised cost / schedule control system where the ACWP is reduced by the escalation amount, called the deflated cost of work performed (DCWP).

The cost variance (CV) is now broken down into two sub-variances, namely.

Inflation variance   IV   =   DCWP - ACWP
Expenditure variance   EV   =   BCWP - DCWP

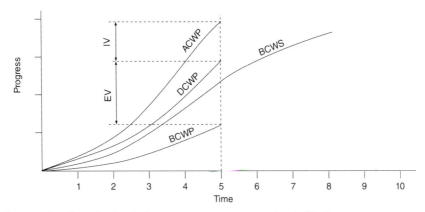

Figure: 9. Cost / schedule progress report under inflation

The managers have no control over the escalation so cannot, realistically, be held responsible for the inflation variance (IV). The expenditure variance (EV), however, is an area where the managers should have control, so by separating out the different costs the situation can be clarified.

12.7 Reporting

The Earned Value output lends itself to effective reporting for the following reasons.

* When reporting to senior management, the preferred presentation should show the whole project graphically. The overall status can be seen at a glance, if more detail is required information can be presented from the lower activity level.

* When reporting to functional management the report should clearly indicate the activities that fall under their responsibility. This information can be separately reported if a responsibility field has been included in the data base.

* The reports can use a Management By Exception (MBE) technique to identify problem areas. The MBE thresholds can be set using any of the following:-

    a)   Threshold variance SV% and CV%. Set upper and lower percentages, for example, -5% to +10%.

b)   Activity float = 0 days, to identify the critical path. Activity float < 5 working days, to identify activities which could go critical in the next week.

*   The sign of the variance should influence the management response. Consider the following situations:

SV (+)   The project is ahead of schedule, move labour off the project if they can be used more effectively elsewhere.

SV (-)   The project is behind schedule, move resources on to the project to increase production.

CV (+)   The project costs are less than budget, if significant amend estimating data base for future projects.

CV (-)   The project costs are greater than budget, try to increase productivity through increased efficiency and effectiveness.

*   Plot trends wherever possible to indicate the direction of the project. Extrapolating trends will give an indication of future events and a quick feedback on recent actions. Even if the variances are negative, but reducing, this will show a positive trend indicating that the project is coming back onto course.

12.8 Summary

The earned value approach was shown to be a development of the cost/schedule control system (C/SCS), towards full integration of cost and time. When this approach is combined with forecasting, the manager has the best of both worlds. It is essential for effective project control that performance is measured while there is still time to take corrective action.

In this chapter we discussed the terminology used before going on to outline the benefits of this control technique. To give a total picture of the earned value concept, both the client's and the contractor's points of view were considered. We also discussed how the earned value model can reflect escalation and inflation, together with its benefit as a reporting structure.

Finally the approach used for tracking time and cost performance in this chapter constitutes the basis of integrated project control. It is not possible to perform effective control without the actual performance being compared against a baseline plan (BCWS). Any project manager who does not integrate time and cost performance will find that he has only part of the performance information, and may well be misled by some of the data.

Chapter 13

Planning for
Project Management

This chapter on planning for project management has been included to widen the scope of the book and briefly outline a number of associated topics which can be included under the umbrella heading of project management planning and control.

The chapter starts with a discussion on the different types of organization structures often used to manage projects, particularly focusing on the different types of matrix structures. This is followed by an outline of a project team structure citing benefits to the individual and the project, together with why some teams win and some lose. As the project manager is the most important member of the team a simple selection criteria is discussed.

The human factor section will consider a number of the well known leadership styles, motivation theories, conflict symptoms and cures, before finishing on a framework for effective delegation. Quality management will be discussed under sub-headings; quality assurance, quality control, quality audit, quality control plan and project quality plan. The main emphasis will be on the application of these techniques.

13.1 Organisation Structures

The management of multi-discipline projects has highlighted a number of shortcomings with the traditional function, line, hierarchy type structure. One of the novel approaches used to address these problems has been the introduction of matrix structures. This section will develop a project organisation continuum featuring functional, matrix and pure project structures.

The type of organisation structure used to manage projects generally falls into one of the three main types:

*   Functional.
*   Matrix
*   Pure project

The working of the structures will be outlined.

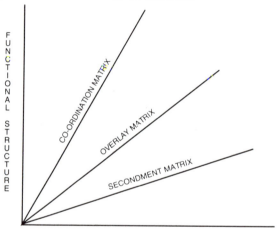

Figure: 1. The project organisational structure continuum

When defining an organisational structure the following terms will be used:

Responsibility: The obligation incurred by individuals in their roles in the formal organisation in order to effectively perform assignments.

Authority: The power granted to individuals (possibly by their position) so that they can make decisions for others to follow. Authority should be commensurate with responsibility.

Accountability: The state of being totally answerable for the satisfactory completion of a specific task. Accountability is the summation of responsibility and authority.

Delegation: To assign responsibility and authority to subordinates at lower levels of the organisation.

13.1.1 Functional Organisation Structure

The traditional organisation structure is based on the sub-division of product lines or disciplines into separate departments, together with a vertical hierarchy. The figure outlines a typical structure with a number of functional departments reporting to the general manager.

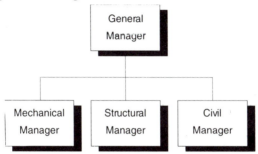

Figure: 2. Functional organisation structure

Functional organisation structure **advantages**:

1.   A high degree of flexibility of staff can be achieved, because people in the department can be assigned to the project, then immediately re-assigned to other work. Switching back and forth between projects is easily achieved.

2.   Functional departments provide a home for technical expertise and continuity of development.

3.   The functional department provides the normal career path for advancement and promotion.

4.   Functional department's work is simpler to estimate and apply budgetary control.

5.   Lines of communication are well established.

6.   A quick reaction time to problems within the department is possible.

7.   Some employees prefer a more consistent work routine.

Functional organisation structure **disadvantages**:

1.   The client is not always the main focus of concern, particularly when the scope has moved to another department. The client may well feel like a football being passed from one department to another.

2.   No single point of responsibility as the project scope moves from one department to another, this can lead to co-ordinating chaos.

3.   Departmental work may take precedence over project work.

4.   The department may myopically focus only on their scope of work in preference to a holistic approach.

5.   No formal line of communication between the people within the different departments. The formal line of communication is established at department manager level, this will lengthen the lines of communication and slow down the response time.

6.   The motivation for people assigned to the project can be weak if the work is not perceived to be in the mainstream.

The functional organisation structure does offer excellent facilities within its own department, but where a multi-discipline scope calls for interaction with other departments the system is found lacking. To address this problem consider the matrix structure.

13.1.2 Matrix Organisation Structures

The topology of the matrix structure has the same format as a mathematical matrix, in this case the vertical lines represent the functional responsibility and authority, while the horizontal lines represent the project line of responsibility and authority. Thus giving the matrix structure its unique appearance.

Where the lines of interest intersect, this represents people to people contact. The point to notice here is that it is at an operational level, the people who make the product. Thus providing shorter lines of communication.

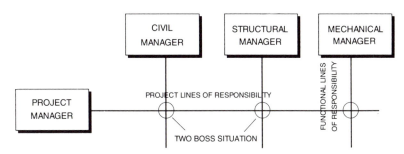

Figure: 3. Matrix organisation structure

The matrix structure is considered by many practitioners to be the natural project organisation structure, because it simply formalises the informal links. On multi-discipline projects people need to communicate at the operational level to perform the tasks.

The matrix structure is a temporary structure created to respond to the needs of the project where people from the functional departments are assigned to the project on a full-time or part-time basis. Thus the matrix structure is initially superimposed on the existing functional structure.

Within this matrix structure there are a number of variants caused mainly by the distribution of power. The three different types shown here are:

* Co-ordination matrix.
* Overlay matrix.
* Secondment matrix.

Co-ordination matrix: This is the nearest to the traditional functional hierarchy where the project manager (more likely called project co-ordinator or progress chaser) co-ordinates the resources across functional departments. The co-ordinator may come from the department that initiated the project. Although the project co-ordinator is generally in a junior position with little formal power, as titular head of the project he may well be held responsible for the project meeting its objectives.

The project co-ordinator can, however, compensate for his lack of formal power by;

* Offering the co-ordinating facilities as a service to the other departments.

*   Having a senior mentor who the functional managers would respect.

Despite the many short comings this arrangement may have, it does address project co-ordination between departments and is therefore a step in the right direction.

Overlay matrix: Also called **balanced matrix**. This is the commonest type of matrix structure, where the project manager through a project office would assign resources from the functional departments to make the product. The project manager would be on the same level of seniority as the other functional managers. This could put the project manager in a difficult position, because he may now be deemed to have sufficient seniority to be held responsible for the project, but at the same time does not have formal authority over the other managers who **own** the resources.

The onus is on the project manager to practice an appropriate leadership style towards the other functional managers, which would certainly include negotiation to address the trade-off between who controls the what, when, who and how.

Secondment matrix: This is the nearest type of organisation structure to the pure project where the project manager has a wide range of powers over the whole project.

Although the project manager would usually be senior to the functional managers, he would still need to negotiate with them for the use of their resources. During the secondment the functional personnel would formally report to the project manager.

The project office would develop an information and control system tailored to the needs of the project, together with procedures and work instructions. This ability to either modify existing systems or development new systems from scratch is a fundamental requirement for high-tec projects.

Although the functional personnel will return to their department after tneir involvement in the project, to help gain commitment and respect from the seconded staff, it is in the project manager's interest to ensure their continuing employment after the project has been arranged. To recap and combine the three matric structures, their **advantages** would include:

1.   The project has a single point of responsibility, the project manager.

2.   The project can draw on the entire resources of the company.

3.   When the seconded personnel have completed their assignment they can return to their functional department, thus relieving anxiety about continuing employment.

4.   Rapid response to client needs.

5.   The corporate link will ensure consistency with company policies, strategies and procedures.

6.   When several projects are operating concurrently, the matrix structure allows a time-share of expertise, which leads to a higher degree of resource utilisation.

7.   The matrix structure can be tailored to the needs of the project with respect to; job descriptions, procedures and work instructions.

8.   The needs of the project and functional departments can be addressed simultaneously by negotiation and trade-off. The project is mainly concerned with, what and when (scope and planning), while the functional department is concerned with, who and how (resources and technical).

The **disadvantages** with the matrix structure include:

1.   With functional and pure projects it is clear who has the power to make decisions, however, with the matrix structure the power may be balanced between departments. If this causes doubt and confusion the productivity of the project may suffer.

2. The sharing of scarce resources could lead to inter-departmental conflict.

3. After a secondment for a few years personnel may find they either do not have a functional department to return to, or their position has been re-appointed.

4. In the matrix structure the project manager controls the administration decisions, while the functional managers control the technical decisions, this division of power and responsibility could lead to an overly complex situation.

5. Where the project and functional lines of influence cross there exists a two boss situation which is a recipe for conflict.

6. The corporate employees' career path is usually within the functional department. Therefore, while working on projects he may miss-out on functional promotion.

7. Where project and functional reporting is required, this double reporting may lead to additional work load and therefore additional costs.

8. The functional departments are unlikely to give up their best personnel to the project.

13.1.3 Pure Project Organisation Structure

The pure project organisation structure is similar in shape to the functional organisational structure except it is dedicated to one project. It has autonomy from the rest of the company, as a self contained unit with its own technical staff and administration. This type of structure is typical of large projects like Concorde, NASA and offshore projects.

The **advantages** with the pure project structure include:

1. The project manager has full line authority over the project.

2. All members of the workforce report directly to the project manager. There are no functional department heads whose permission must be sought.

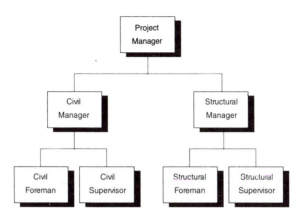

Figure: 4. Pure project structure

3.   The lines of communication are shorter then the multi-disciplined functional route.

4.   If there are a series of similar projects, the team of skilled experts can be kept together.

5.   Because the project team tends to have a strong separate identity, this encourages a high level of communication between members. Motivation is high and task orientated.

6.   With centralized authority decisions are made quickly.

7.   With the one boss situation the lines of communication, responsibility and authority are clear and undisputed.

8.   Pure project presents a simple structure which is easy to understand, implement and operate.

9.   There is a holistic approach to the project.

The **disadvantages** with the pure project structure include:

1.   If the parent company has a number of projects running concurrently, with pure project structures this could lead to duplication of effort in many areas.

2.   To ensure access to technical know-how and skills there may be a propensity to stockpile equipment and personnel. This may lead to resources staying on the project longer than required.

3.   If the project divorces itself from the functional departments and other projects, this could sever the cross flow of ideas and information on new technology.

4.   The project cannot offer continuity of employment, this may encourage the company to use sub-contractors. If a detailed closeout report is not generated by the sub-contractors the company would lose valuable experience.

This completes the discussion on the different types of project structures, we now move on to decide which one to select.

Organisation Structure Selection: Selecting the right organisation structure is essentially a balancing act between addressing the scope needs, the project needs and the client needs. The client may request or instruct the contractor to use a certain type of structure.

The choice can be further complicated when a structure appropriate for one company may be a burden for another, the project could therefore evolve into many different structures running concurrently. The project manager is often selected from a functional department, but which one ?

*   The department that initiated the project.
*   The department with the largest part of the project.
*   The department with the initial phase of the project.
*   The department with the least work on at the time.

The selection is often influenced in favour of the department with the appropriate technical background. This structure would be called **lead technical**. When the project requires input from a number of different departments the matrix structure offers a real solution to the functional division of responsibility and authority.

If the project is a large capital project which will run for a few years, setting up a pure project structure may be the most expedient and appropriate decision.

13.2 Project Teams

This section on project teams will outline the purpose of project teams, the benefit to the individual and the project before explaining why some teams win while others lose. The growth of new technology and increased complexity of projects has certainly generated a need for multi-discipline teams to work closely together. A team may be defined as a number of individuals all working together to achieve a common task or goal.

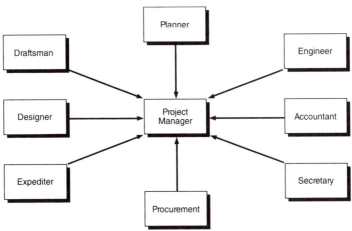

Figure: 5. Project team structure

Teamwork should bring individuals together in such a way that they increase their effectiveness without losing their individuality, for example, an orchestra works on this basis. When individuals work together they can be more effective than working alone, this ability to bounce ideas off each other and constructively assist other team members leads to greater output, this concept is called **team synergy**.

13.2.1 Purpose of Project Teams

Why should project teams be encouraged ? Consider the following reasons:

1. For the improved distribution of work. To bring together a set of skills, talents, responsibilities and allocate to them their respective disciplines.

2.   For the management and control of work. To allow the work of individual team members to be organised and controlled by other team members.

3.   For problem solving and decision-making. To bring together a set of skills, talents and responsibilities so that the solution to any problem will have all available capacities applied to it.

4.   For testing and ratifying decisions. To test the validity of a decision taken outside the group, or to ratify such decisions.

5.   For the information processing and lines of communication, to pass on decisions or information to those who need to know.

6.   For information and collection of ideas. To data capture ideas, information and suggestions.

7.   For co-ordination and liaison. To co-ordinate problems and tasks between functional departments or divisions.

8.   For increased commitment and involvement from the team members. To set up an environment for individuals to participate in the plans and activities of a company.

9.   For negotiation and conflict resolution. To resolve disputes and arguments between managerial levels.

10.   For inquest and inquiries into past performance on company projects to improve the project estimating data base.

With these benefits in mind let us now consider the benefit to the individual.

13.2.2 The Individual's Purpose for Team Membership

Why should an individual wish to be part of a project team, consider the following points:

1. It is a means of satisfying an individual's social or affiliation needs, to belong to something or be part of a group.

2. It is a means of establishing self-esteem. People like to introduce themselves as Joe Bloggs from Eurobuilders Ltd. This way they are defining themselves in terms of their relationship to others, as a member of a team or company.

3. It is a means of gaining support to carry out their particular goals. It also allows one to bounce ideas off other team members who can offer support, constructive criticism and alternate suggestions.

4. Share risk with other team members.

5. The team provides a psychological home for the individual.

The above outlines why some people prefer to work in groups.

13.2.3 Benefits of Teams

In the past, corporations have been preoccupied with the individual, any attempt to list the qualities of a good manager would demonstrate abilities which are mutually exclusive to any individual:

1. He must be **highly intelligent** but not **too cleaver**.

2. He must be **forceful** but also **sensitive** to people's feelings.

3. He must be **dynamic** but also **patient**.

4. He must be a **fluent communicator** but also a **good listener**.

5. He must be **decisive** but also **reflective**.

6. He must be an **expert** on a wide range of different fields.

And if a manager is found with the above attributes, a paragon of mutually compatible characteristics, what happens if he;

*   Steps under a bus.
*   Goes to live in another country.
*   Takes up a better position with a competitor.

But if no individual can combine all these qualities, a team of individuals certainly could for the following reasons:

1.   It is not the individual but the team that is instrumental in sustaining and enduring management success.

2.   A team can **renew** and regenerate itself through new recruitment as individual teams members leave.

3.   A team can also build up a store of shared and collectively owned experiences, information and judgement which can be passed on to new team members.

4.   Many people are **more successful** working within a team than working alone.

5.   Team **synergy** generates more output than the sum of the individual inputs.

6.   The team can offer a wide range of technical support.

Having established the need for a team we move on to determine the appropriate size of the team.

13.2.4 Team Size

The appropriate team size depends on a number of factors:

1.   How many people are required to process all the data generated by the project.

2.   What variety of technical expertise is required by the project.

3.   What is the appropriate level of conflict in a team ? Mathematically, the odds of conflict increase with the number of people in the team. However, if the number of people is too small, the team is likely to be dominated by one strong member.

The ideal team size depends very much on its application. Teams tend to grow in size until some magic number is reached when they sub-divide, the experts recommend between five and ten people. Sporting teams provide us with some guidelines, consider a rugby team which consists of fifteen players. This number is slightly higher than recommended and sure enough there is sub-division into a pack of eight people and seven backs, with a scrum half linking the two groups.

13.2.5 Why Teams Win

Research has shown that some or all of the following items were present in a successful team:

1.   The team leader had an appropriate management style for the project and other team members.

2.   At least one member of the team generated innovative ideas as a means to solve problems.

3.   There was a spread of mental abilities.

4.   There was a spread of personalities which gave the team a balanced appearance.

The person in the chair or team leader will be successful if he gains respect from the other team members. Generally he does not need to dominate the proceedings but should know how to pull matters together. In practice **Belbin** p.93 found the leader always works closely with the talented members of the team.

Creativity: The inclusion of a good ideas man was found to be a necessary contribution for a successful team. Creativity was considered to be a most important input. Another feature of the winning team was that they had a wider range of team roles types on which to draw than unsuccessful teams. A broad base of team roles also helps to reduce the friction caused by similar personalities competing for the same position.

Flexibility: Successful teams exhibit flexibility where members were able to move around in the team to find the best match between people and jobs. They also realise that if they did not have a balanced distribution of team roles they would have to appoint members to play those missing roles. A successful team then should have an effective leader, be innovative, creative and flexible with a broad spread of personalities.

13.2.6 Why Teams Fail

The main virtue of analysing a badly composed team is that it furnishes information on what to avoid.

Mental ability: **Belbin** found that the single factor evident in all poor teams was low mental ability. If this is compared with the innovation and creativity of winning teams, then it would imply that poor teams were not able to take advantage of opportunities or were poor at problem solving. Large companies address this problem by simply recruiting graduates.

Negative selection: The failure of companies to produce teams which have an adequate proportion of managers with good mental ability must surely not be due to any conscious search for such people, but rather the unintended by-product of negative selection. Negative selection refers to the recruitment process designed to filter out the type of people the company needs. Consider the company which is looking for a good manager to reverse their present decline, but will not increase the current salary package offered. This low salary is unintentionally designed to actually exclude the sort of manager the company needs.

13.2.7 Profile of a Project Manager

The selection of the project manager is one of the key appointments influencing project success. This section will discuss whether the project manager should be a generalist or specialist. The project manager should be a **generalist**:

* As a manager moves up the corporate ladder he will be concerned more and more with people, costs and co-ordinating multi-disciplines and less with technical issues. In time this will make him more of a generalist.

* It may not be desirable to have the technical expert leading the team, as he could suppress innovation from the other team members, particularly in his area of expertise.

*   Effective project management requires many non-technical skills such as: human resource management, team building, financial accounting, negotiation, integration and co-ordination.

Now for the other side of the discussion. The project manager should be a technical **specialist**:

*   Companies prefer their managers to be experts in the field of the project, mainly as it enables the managers to confirm technical decisions themselves based on past experience rather than be advised to accept by other team members. This view is supported by the fact that most project management positions advertised require the managers to be technically competent in field of the project.

*   If the project manager knows and understands the technical issues of the project he will be in a better position to apply judgement and forecast problems relating to the planning and control of the project.

*   Team selection can be based on both human compatibility and technical ability. The technical ability he would be able to verify.

*   He can be effectively involved up-front at the estimating and quotation stage of the project.

*   He will be able to gain respect from the team by demonstrating not only good management but also technical expertise.

*   The company can use the lead-technical co-ordinating matrix approach, where the project manager comes from the department that has the most work on the project.

It would seem from commercial feedback that initially to embark on a career in project management one needs experience in the field of the project, but once established one may find oneself becoming more of a generalist in project management.

13.3 Human Factors

The implementation of the project planning and control techniques is through people, therefore to effectively implement the system one must gain support and commitment from the project team. Many projects fail to reach their optimum level of performance, not because of any lack of equipment or systems, but purely because the human factors were not addressed. This section will discuss leadership styles in the context of decision-making and introduce two popular leadership theories; **situational leadership** and **action centred leadership**.

13.3.1 Leadership

For a manager to be effective and successful he must not only demonstrate good administrative skills and technical know how but also practice an appropriate style of leadership. The leadership style used can profoundly affect employee morale and productivity so that the success of an organisation may be directly dependent on good leadership.

Leadership bridge: Leadership is seen as forming the bridge between the objectives of the organisation and the goals of the individual.

Leadership styles: Leadership styles may be considered as a continuum from autocratic to democratic. The leadership style used by the manager may depend on the type of decision required, the pressures prevalent at the time and the type of people he is working with. The continuum of leadership styles relating to decision-making may be conveniently sub-divided into a number of categories as shown below:

The six stages from autocratic to democratic are:

1.   The manager solves the problem or makes the decision himself, using information available to him at the time. There is no communication with the team.

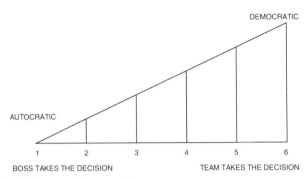

Figure: 6. Decision-making continuum

2. The manager obtains the necessary information from his subordinates then decides on the solution to the problem himself.

3. The manager shares the problem with relevant subordinates individually, gathering their ideas and suggestions. Then he makes the decision himself.

4. The manger shares the problem with his subordinates in a group. Then makes the decision himself.

5. The manager shares the problem with his subordinates as a group. Then together they make the decision.

6. The manager gives the problem to the team and lets them make the decisions themselves. This is the laissez-faire approach or policy of non-interference.

The following questions can be used as a guide to select the appropriate leadership style.

*   Is one decision likely to be better than another? If not, go for number 1.

*   Does the leader know enough to take the decision on his own ? If not avoid number 1.

*   Is the problem clear and structured ? If not use numbers 4 or 5.

*   Must the subordinates accept the decision ? If not then numbers 1 and 2 are possibilities.

* Will the subordinates accept the managers' decision ? If not then number 5 is preferable.

* Do subordinates share the manager's goals for the organisation ? If not then number 5 is risky.

* Are subordinates likely to conflict with each other ? If yes then number 4 is better than 5.

This relationship between leadership and decision-making is fundamental to effective project management.

13.3.2 Situational Leadership

The concept and terms of situational leadership were developed by **Paul Hersey**, and are now generally accepted as a practical, easy to understand and apply approach to managing and motivation people. **Blanchard** p.46 sees situational leadership as a combination of directive and supportive behaviours.

Directive behaviour: Involves the issuing of instructions to the team members: what to do, how to do it, where to do it, when to do it together with close supervision and control of their performance.

Supportive behaviour: Involves listening to people, providing support and encouragement for their efforts together with facilitating their involvement in problem-solving and decision-making. The foundation of situational leadership is based on the development levels a person goes through in the working environment. The model looks particularly at the competence and commitment of the individual.

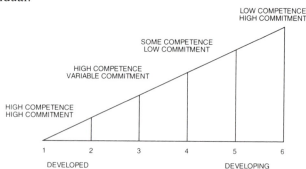

Figure: 7. Competence and commitment continuum Blanchard p.50

Leadership styles appropriate for the various development levels according to **Blanchard** p.56 are:

Directing is an autocratic leadership style appropriate for use with people who lack competence but are enthusiastic and committed to their work. They need direction and supervision to get them started. The leader should provide specific instructions usually through one way communication and close supervision of task accomplishment.

Coaching is appropriate for use with people who have some competence but lack commitment. They need direction and supervision as they are still relatively inexperienced. They also need support and praise to build their self-esteem together with involvement in decision-making to restore their commitment. The manager should encourage two way communication to develop the ideas and suggestions the subordinates make. Meanwhile the leader continues to direct and closely supervises task accomplishment, but does explain decisions, solicits suggestions and supports progress.

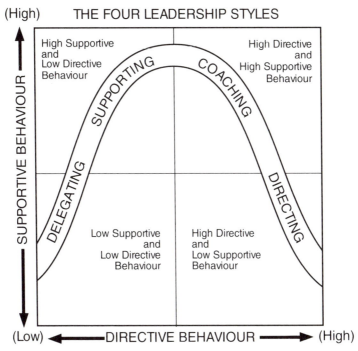

(High)   THE FOUR LEADERSHIP STYLES

High Supportive and Low Directive Behaviour

High Directive and High Supportive Behaviour

Low Supportive and Low Directive Behaviour

High Directive and Low Supportive Behaviour

SUPPORTING

COACHING

DELEGATING

DIRECTING

SUPPORTIVE BEHAVIOUR

(Low) ◄━━━━DIRECTIVE BEHAVIOUR ━━━► (High)

Figure: 8. Situational leadership

Supporting style is appropriate for use with people who have competence but lack confidence or motivation. They do not need much direction because they have high ability, but support is necessary to bolster their confidence and motivation. The leader facilitates and supports the subordinates' efforts towards task accomplishment and shares responsibilities for decision-making. Supporting also builds up their confidence and motivates them to take risks while supporting their progress.

Delegating style is appropriate for people who have both competence and commitment. They are able and willing to work on a project by themselves with little supervision or support. The leader turns over responsibility for decision-making and problem solving to the subordinates.

Fill the gap: Leaders need to fill the gap between what people can do on their own and what is required by the project.

Consider this example on a sailing yacht. The navigator reports to the skipper that the latest weather forecast has issued a gale warning. As skipper how do you respond ?

Skipper to crew:

Directing: ''I want you to put one reef in the main and change the head sail to the storm jib''.

Coaching: ''The navigator says we are in for a bit of a blow, I think you should put one reef in the main and change the set the storm jib''.

Supporting: ''The navigator says we are in for a blow what do you suggest?''

Delegating: ''A gale is forecast''.

The manager should gradually increase the competence and confidence of his team so that he needs to spend less time on supervision styles and more time on delegating.

13.3.3 Action Centred Leadership

Action centred leadership, developed by **John Adair** for leadership training at Sandhurst, is now being applied to the commercial environment.

Figure: 9. Action centred leadership

The three intersecting circles indicate the three basic needs; the individual's need, the team's need and the task's need, with areas of common interest shown overlapping.

Action centred leadership neatly combines the motivation theories for the individual with the team building theories for the group. Consider a situation where an individual has a personal problem at home, this would be expressed in terms of **Maslow's** hierarchy of needs (see motivation section) and would probably preoccupy his mind in preference to the team's need and the task's need until it has been addressed. Only when the individual's problem has been solved can he apply himself effectively through the team to perform the task.

13.4 Motivation

The term motivation is often misunderstood and misused in a managerial context. Motivation is an inner force that causes or induces someone to do something. The manager's task is to influence the work situation in such a way as to encourage the individual to motivate himself to achieve the project's goals.

Commitment: When we assess a person's ability to complete a job successfully it can be sub-divided into calibre and commitment.

Performance = Function (calibre x commitment)

Calibre: Calibre is the term used to describe the personal qualities and ability a person brings to the job. These are qualities of skill (welding or carpentry) that enable a person to perform a task, and give him the capacity to cope with the demands of the job. A person's level of calibre is associated with their innate ability and the amount of training and experience they have acquired.

The performance of an individual, however, also depends on his willingness and drive to complete the task, in other words their commitment. Unlike calibre, commitment is not a fixed commodity. It may change quite frequently in response to conditions and situations the individual encounters.

To this extent, the manager must use an appropriate style of leadership to control the working environment in such a manner that the workforce will be committed to the task and so motivate themselves to achieve the objectives of the project. Therefore to achieve maximum output from the workforce the manager must address both calibre and commitment.

13.4.1 Hierarchy of Needs

The corner stone of motivation theory is **Maslow's** hierarchy of needs, which was first published in 1960. Maslow stated that motivation is an unconscious attempt on behalf of the individual to satisfy certain inner needs. He expressed this in the form of a hierarchy:

Figure: 10. Maslow's hierarchy of needs

The hierarchy illustrates a priority of needs. Maslow indicated that one is always striving to achieve the higher order needs, but this can only be achieved once the lower order needs have been satisfied.

1. The **physiological** needs refer to the needs of the body to survive, the most fundamental need of all. If one was to be deprived of air to breath or food to eat, one would become totally preoccupied trying to acquire these lower order needs in preference to any other need.

2. The **Security** needs refer to not only the obvious immediate concern for continuity of job, income and protection from accident and physical danger, but also, according to one's personality and character, freedom from disapproval, risk of failure and unfair criticism which may be seen as psychologically damaging.

    When one has reached a level of economic security that satisfies, one will only want to ensure that they stay there. But when the security needs are reasonably well satisfied one is unlikely to be motivated towards activities aimed at increasing security still further. A fundamental point about the hierarchy of needs is that a satisfied need does not motivate. Once hunger is satisfied one is no longer motivated to seek more food.

3. The **social** needs refer to the need to associate with other people, one needs to be accepted by others and belong to a team or group.

4. The **self-esteem** need is related to a person's **ego** needs, which drives the person to feel wanted and important within their own working group. This need for recognition, prestige and status is a higher order need.

5. **Self-actualisation** relates to a person's own self fulfilment. This category of need includes creativity, achievement, competence and productivity. This is the highest of all the needs.

Maslow's hierarchy of needs has established itself as one of the classical management theories.

13.4.2 Motivation Cycle

The motivation cycle outlines the dynamic and changeable nature of motivation. When a need becomes unsatisfied it creates within the individual a kind of tension, which in turn creates a driving force or impetus towards certain activities or behaviour.

This behaviour will be aimed at satisfying the need. When the need is satisfied the tension is relieved. The cycle now starts all over again with respect to a different need, which has to be satisfied, by a goal requiring a certain behaviour.

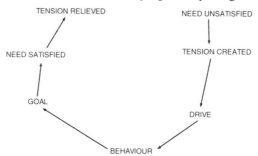

Figure: 11. Motivation cycle

13.4.3 Managing for Motivation

The first step towards managing people is to effectively understand what internal forces are influencing their commitment. This will be a function of their personality profile and psychological needs. These basic functions are at the root of personal motivation. Two of the popular theories which will be discussed here are:

* McGregor's theory X, theory Y.
* Herzberg's motivation and hygiene factors.

McGregor in his **Theory X, Theory Y** outlined how management often worked under a particular set of assumptions.

Theory X assumed that the average man has:

a) An inherent dislike of work and will avoid it if he can.

b) People must be coerced, controlled, directed and threatened in order to get any work out of them.

c) People actually prefer to be directed and actively avoid responsibility.

d) People have relatively little ambition and are primarily concerned with their own security.

Theory Y on the other hand takes a completely different view of human nature, it assumes that people will:

a)   Naturally expend physical and mental effort at work as they do for recreation or leisure.

b)   The worker is capable of exercising self-direction and self-control in order to meet objectives which he is committed to.

c)   His commitment is directly related to the rewards.

d)   He will actively seek responsibility, and will want to use his creativity, imagination and ingenuity.

McGregor's contention was that theory Y represented a more accurate profile of human nature. He felt the limits were managements ingenuity in discovering how to realise the potential of their human resources.

McGregor also observed the self-fulfilling prophesy, where a manager who assumes his people are lazy and unco-operative often ended up with just that, McGregor found the converse was also true. Managers' assumptions about their people tend to condition the way they approach their own role and the reaction they receive.

As a result of these observations McGregor suggested that the essential task of management is to create opportunities, release human potential, remove obstacles, encouraging growth and provide guidance. He referred to this as **management by objectives**.

13.4.4 Herzberg's Motivation and Hygiene Theory

Herzberg's theory was designed to improve our understanding of working people, what factors determine job satisfaction and what determines job dissatisfaction. Here the term motivation indicates factors which increase one's commitment for the job, while hygiene factors will cause a sense of grievance leading to job dissatisfaction and hence a reduction of motivation and commitment.

A hygiene factor can be likened to a sewer, when it fails it becomes extremely important to people in the vicinity that it should be repaired as quickly as possible !!!! However, once repaired the sewer now loses importance to those people concerned, and improving its efficiency still further is of little interest.

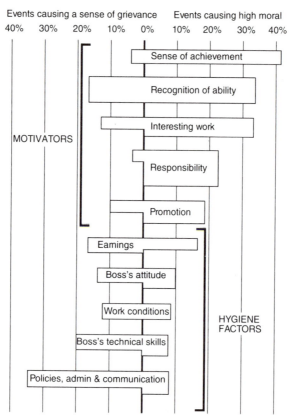

Figure: 12. Herzberg's motivation and hygiene theory

The x-axis indicates the frequency with which the factor was reported as causing high morale or causing a sense of grievance. The factors are listed vertically, sorted by high morale, while the depth (y-axis) of each box indicates the time the feeling lasted.

Analysis indicates some interesting findings:

* Earnings, although a motivator for a short while were mostly reported as a hygiene factor. This means if the employees are paid above average, they will be motivated for a short period of time, until the new salary becomes the norm. If, however, they are paid less than their colleagues they will become dissatisfied.

*   Once the working conditions are at an acceptable level, improving them further will not necessarily stimulate additional effort or commitment.

*   On the positive side there can be no substitute for factors like opportunity to gain a sense of achievement, recognition of ability, more interesting work, greater responsibility and opportunities for promotion.

The motivation theories outlined have the benefit of being mutually supportive. Herzberg's motivators for example relate closely with Maslow's hierarchy of needs.

13.5 Conflict

This section will discuss the causes, symptoms and solutions of conflict. Before going into the causes of conflict the project manager should be aware of the wider theatre of the working environment and the ecology. Ecology is the study of the relationship between a working environment and an individual's behaviour and attitudes. The understanding of ecology is necessary to understand employees behaviour. We are all affected by the environment we work in, for example:

1.   Small groups are easier to participate in than larger groups.
2.   Noise tends to impair performance on complicated tasks.
3.   Variety relieves monotony, provides stimulation and contributes to improved performance.
4.   Seating arrangements tend to affect interaction with other people.
5.   Open-plan offices are popular and improve communications, certainly suitable for routine work.

The use of ecology as an environmental control can have a large impact on the individual's commitment and motivation. It should be seen as the project manager's responsibility to influence the environment to match his employees working preferences. Thus addressing the individual's needs which in turn will help achieve the project team's needs and the needs of the project task.

Where the **causes of conflict** may be associated with a deep rooted psychological problem an employee has, this would be better addressed by a psychologist. For the project manager, however, it is important to recognise the symptoms of conflict so that problem areas can be identified and corrective action taken. Some of the symptoms of conflict may be expressed as follows:

1. Poor communication laterally and vertically. Decisions taken on incomplete information. Two levels in the same company are moving in different directions on the same problem.
2. Inter-group hostility and jealousy expressed as "they never tell us anything" or "they expect us to know by intuition".
3. Inter-personal friction affects the relationships between individuals where it can deteriorate to icy formality or argument. Problems seem to focused on people and personalities.
4. Escalation of arbitration by senior management.
5. Proliferation of rules and regulations. It becomes more and more difficult to do anything without riding roughshod over somebody's regulations.
6. Low morale expressed as frustration and inefficiency.

The project manager should be on the constant lookout for these types of symptoms.

13.5.1 Control of Conflict

When symptoms have been identified which cannot be addressed by rearranging the ecology to create an amenable working synergy, then consider the following:

1. **Arbitration**: Conduct arbitration at a low level. This solution is useful when the conflict is apparent and specific, but not very useful in episodic or continual conflict. Agree on an arbitrator at the outset of the project, because later when there is conflict the parties will each nominate a person sympathetic to their own view.

2. **Rules and regulations**: Strive to compile rules, regulations and procedures by negotiation. This approach is useful when the conflict is recurrent and predictable, but should not be regarded as a permanent solution.

3. **Confrontation**: A technique much favoured by those who believe in openness. This strategy will be effective, if the issue can be clearly defined and is not a symptom of more underlying differences. Confrontation and inter-group meetings can do a lot to increase understanding of people's views, but they cannot be a complete substitute from the ecological point of view.

4. **Negotiation**: An interesting variation on confrontation is an approach called role negotiation, where conflicting parties negotiate and trade items of behaviour, e.g. I will stop doing X if you stop doing Y. This method goes a long way to reduce the pains of conflict, particularly between individuals, although it may leave the underlying problem untouched.

5. **Separation**: If interaction increases the depth of the sentiments, separation should cool them down. This solution will work if the true cause of the conflict is two incompatible individuals, incompatible in personality, or more often with relative status inappropriate to the situation. To separate the individuals, transferring one to another department may be a successful strategy. This will allow both parties to be productive in different areas.

6. **Neglect**: To ignore conflict is appropriate if the cause is trivial.

7. **Co-ordination device**: A position is created in the company between the conflicting parties. This eliminates the contact and so the conflict. There are, however, additional administration costs for the company. This device is not an effective solution for episodic or occasional conflict, but useful where the conflicting pressures are continuous.

The larger the company, the greater the potential for conflict. Conflict is a great diverter of energies. Better management of differences could have a significant impact on productivity as well as making organisations more pleasurable places to live and work in.

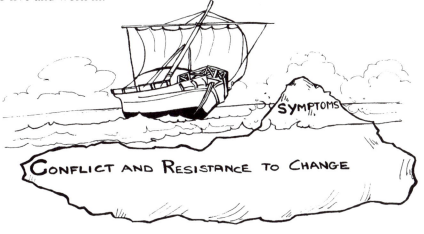

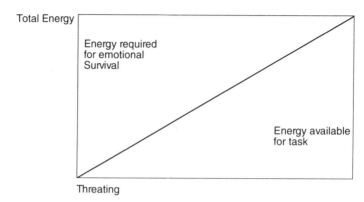

Figure: 13. Team energy continuum

This concludes the section on conflict, the next section will discuss delegation.

13.6 Delegation of Authority

Skilful delegation is the key to effective project management. Through delegation the project manager can improve:

* Project team efficiency.
* Develop employee ability.
* Contribute to the growth of the company.

Feedback from commerce and industry suggests, however, that delegation is not a widely practised technique and that project managers are held back by performing trifling tasks themselves. The project managers become over-worked, overtaxed, and at the same time miss the opportunities to encourage initiative and motivate growth among their employees. Delegation has three basic elements:

1.   Assign a function, duty or task to an employee.
2.   Allocate sufficient authority so that the employee can command the resources necessary to accomplish the assignment.
3.   Gain commitment from the employee for the satisfactory completion of the task.

The employee must know that he will be held accountable for the work delegated. Note: under performance may indicate that further training of the employee is required.

It should always be remembered that delegating work will not reduce the project manager's ultimate authority and responsibility for the task, this is not transferable. However, although it is unreasonable to imply that the manager should be responsible for the actions of a shopfloor worker, it does mean the manager is responsible for setting up the system to ensure that the shopfloor worker does his job correctly.

13.6.1 Method of Delegation

There are three basic methods of dividing and delegating work to the team members.

1 **Incremental**: The limits of the employees authority to make changes are defined in terms of specific position, locations, numbers or time periods.

2. **Sequential**: The limits of the employees authority to perform a duty or task are defined in accordance with the sequence of the actions, from beginning to end, that are required to complete the job. For example, a manager may be given the authority for the complete hiring sequence for the London branch which involves recruitment, screening and selection of all new employees.

3. **Functional**: Functional delegation occurs when there is a need for highly developed knowledge and skills. It typically grants authority over activities to a specific individual with particular expertise in a well defined area of operation. It usually involves authority over **how** and sometimes **when**, but rarely over the **who, where,** or **what**.

The method of delegation may include one or all of the above, once the method has been decided the next section will outline a number of implementation steps.

13.6.2 Steps in Delegation:

The following list is a managerial guide to delegate a task and authority to a subordinate.

1. Accept the need to delegate.

2. Develop a detailed plan for delegation.

3. Obtain the supervisor's approval for the delegation plan.

4. Establish a climate of mutual confidence and trust.

5. Select the function, duties and tasks to be delegated and assigned.

6. Establish clear lines of authority and responsibility and ensure that they are understood by all.

7. Adopt a constructive attitude, demonstrate patience when a subordinate makes a mistakes. (Saint !)

8. Monitor performance and provide frequent feedback.

9. Reward effective delegation.

The crunch comes when the subordinate makes a poor decision, how does one react ? Try not to reverse the decision without discussing it with him first, otherwise he is unlikely to make another decision. Skilful delegation is the key to effective management. Through delegation the manager can improve team efficiency, develop employee ability and contribute to the growth of the company.

13.7 Quality Management

Product quality is a powerful tool many businesses use to guarantee their survival and continuing existence in today's competitive market, especially when price is not always the deciding factor.

With projects becoming larger, more complex and using new technology, the need to assure the product will meet stringent requirements is the focus of quality management. These requirements may be set not only by the client, but also insurance companies, governmental laws and regulations, and national and international standards.

This section will discuss quality management under the following headings: quality circles, quality audit, quality costs and project quality plan. Products are made to satisfy a client's need, which is often expressed as part of the specification, but the technical specification can not always guarantee that the client's need will be met. Therefore the specification is supplemented by a quality system tailored to the objectives of the project.

Quality assurance: Quality assurance is a global term used to incorporate the quality policy, quality management and quality control functions which combine to assure the client that the product will be consistently manufactured to the required condition.

Quality control: Quality control defines the method of inspection, in-process inspection and final inspection to determine if the product has met the required condition.

The required condition is laid down in the scope of work, specifications and the project quality plan. Where a non-conformance has been identified, an audit can be used to gather more information before corrective action is authorised. In some cases the corrective action may call for quality awareness training.

13.7.1 Quality Circles

Quality circles are a management concept the Americans set up for Toyota after the Second World War. The basic structure is outlined below:

* **Objectives**: To improve communication between all parties, particularly between production and management. To identify and solve problems.

* **Organisation**: The quality circle consists of a selected leader and eight to ten people from one work area.

* **Membership**: Participation is entirely voluntary.

* **Scope of interest**: The quality circle selects its own problems. Initially the quality circle is encouraged to select problems from its immediate area. Problems are not restricted to quality, they can include productivity, costs, safety, morale and the working environment.

* **Meetings**: Usually one hour per week, held during working hours.

* **Rewards**: Usually no financial benefit, satisfaction is deemed to be achieved through solving problems and observing the implementation of their solutions.

The quality circle approach is becoming more pervasive as the benefits are recognised.

13.7.2 Quality Audit

When a non-conformance is reported or suspected the quality audit provides the project manager with an excellent source of information. An audit is essentially an inspection of a declared system to ensure it is operating correctly. Although an audit is synonymous with accounts, the application can be applied to any part of the project management system.

The audit may be motivated by the client to inspect (say) the project manager's project quality plan, or pre-qualify a supplier or sub-contractor. The procedure would be as follows:

1.   The client advised that he wishes to conduct an audit and establishes a date and venue for a pre-audit meeting.

2.   At the pre-audit meeting the scope of the audit is discussed, who will conduct the audit, when and where and also the involvement from the contractors side.

3.   The audit is carried out by a series of interviews, inspections and evaluations.

4.   A closeout meeting is held between the client and contractor, where the preliminary results of the audit are announced together with any non-conforming findings.

5.   A formal report is presented to the client by the auditors.

6.   Corrective actions are carried out and re-inspected.

The **benefits** of an audit are:

*   It provides a wealth of information.

*   The data collected is actionable.

*   The approach is objective.

*   The auditor should be an independent expert with no personal agenda.

The **disadvantages** of an audit are:

* There may be an unintentional bias on the part of the auditor.

* The auditor's experience may be unique and provide misleading evidence.

* An audit can only be carried out infrequently due to its complexity and costs.

* The results may be too detailed, not seeing the wood for the trees.

Where audits try to quantify subjective items like quality of service a weighting may help to improve the accuracy of response.

Worse than expected	as expected	Better than expected
-5	0	+5

The quality audit is a powerful management tool which is gaining popularity as its benefits are becoming known.

13.7.3 Quality Costs

The implementation of quality management is generally felt to be expensive, it is, but the cost of failure without it could be even more expensive. This section will list a number of expense items under the four main headings:

* Prevention costs.
* Appraisal costs.
* Failure costs / internal.
* Failure costs / external.

Prevention costs: Prevention costs are those expenses associated with steps taken to make sure the product will be made to the required condition.

* Quality planning.
* Quality auditing.
* Assuring vendor and sub-contractor's quality.

* Reviewing and verifying designs.
* In process control engineering.
* Design and development of quality measurement and test equipment.
* Quality training.
* Acquisition analysis and reporting quality data.
* Quality improvement programs.
* Product recall and liability insurance.
* Planning of product recall.

Appraisal costs: Appraisal costs relate to expenses incurred while checking and inspecting the work to confirm that it has achieved the required condition.

* Design appraisal.
* Receiving inspection.
* Inspection and NDT testing.
* Inspection and test equipment.
* Materials consumed during inspection and testing.
* Analysis and reporting of test and inspection results.
* Field performance testing.
* Approval and endorsements.
* Stock evaluations.
* Record storage.

Internal failure costs: These costs relate to expenses incurred within the company, many of them are influenced by efficiency.

* Scrap and waste material.
* Replacement, rework or repair.
* Reinspection and retesting.
* Defect diagnosis.
* Downtime.
* Downgrading.

External failure costs: These costs again relate to efficiency, but this time they are motivated by the client.

* Complaints.
* Warranty claims.
* Products rejected and returned.
* Concessions.

* Loss of sales.
* Recall costs.
* Product liability.

This list seems frighteningly long, considering all these items may have a cost associated with them. The criteria for success is that the increase in prevention costs should be less than the fall in failure costs as shown in the diagram.

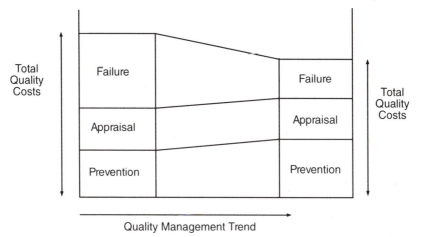

Figure: 14. Quality costs

The main problem with this diagram is that people have a natural propensity to cover up their mistakes, therefore the figures for the cost of rework may never be accurately known.

13.7.4 Project Quality Plan

The project quality plan is a detailed document explaining how the company will assure that the product will be made to the client's requirements. The sub-headings from ISO 9000 can be used to structure the document:

1. Management responsibility.
2. Quality system.
3. Contract review.
4. Design control.
5. Document control.
6. Purchasing.

7. Purchaser supplied product.
8. Product identification and traceability.
9. Process control.
10. Inspection and testing.
11. Inspection, measuring and test equipment.
12. Inspection and test status.
13. Control of non-conforming product.
14. Corrective action.
15. Handling, storage, packaging and delivery.
16. Quality records.
17. Internal quality audits.
18. Training.
19. Servicing.
20. Statistical techniques.

These headings form the basis of most quality systems, therefore to use the same headings must be a step in the right direct.

Quality control plan: The quality control plan integrates planning and quality, by identifying the sequence of the main work items and the performance requirement, together with the inspection requirements. This document was developed in the project control chapter (p. 264).

13.8 Summary

This chapter on planning for project management has broadened the scope of project planning to consider a number of other important related topics.

The different types of organisation structures used on projects were discussed, with particular attention focusing on the three types of matrix structures. The benefits of project teams were outlined together with why some teams win and some fail. The selection of the project manager was discussed using technical background as the selection criteria.

Human factors were discussed around the different leadership styles and their effect on decision-making. The principal motivation theories were outlined together with how to approach conflict and methods of delegation. The quality management system was discussed using the following sub-headings; quality circles, quality audit, quality costs and project quality plan.

Chapter 14

Project Computing

A revolution is taking place in the field of information processing, up until recently all data processing was performed by either large mainframe computers or by hand. Now with the introduction of powerful but inexpensive micro-computer hardware and computer software, offering a full information and control system, there is a dramatic shift towards the project office processing all the project information.

This chapter is based on the author's book: **Project Managers Guide to Computers**, where the key points have been extracted to give the reader a brief outline of the history of computing as it relates to project management, before developing a framework for computer software and computer hardware selection.

A feasibility study format is discussed before outlining a number of implementation and training methods. The chapter finishes with a worked example on **Timeline and Super Project**.

It must be stressed that using project management software will help the project manager to plan and control his project, but only if he understands and can apply the principles and techniques of project management. The software will not tell him what decisions to make or how they should be implemented, but if implemented effectively it will release him from processing large amounts of data manually. This should leave the project manager with more time and accurate information to manage his project effectively.

14.1 History of Project Management Computing

The history of PC based project management computing dates back to 1983 with the launch of the **Harvard Project Manager** software package. Although this may be an isolated event it does reflect the general development of a broad range of management software taking place at the time. To fully appreciation the overall picture there are two other prerequisites to consider, computer facilities and project management techniques. The key dates for computer facilities and project management techniques are:

1920's   Development of the Gantt chart.

1950's   Development of PERT and CPM.

1977   Launch of Apple 11.

1979   Launch of VisiCalc, Lotus came a little later.

1981   Launch of the IBM PC.

1983   Launch of Harvard Project Manager software.

Although this is a very simplified analysis, having ignored many other important developments that were required to support the above, like the mass production of cheap micro chips (see **Palfreman** and **Swade**), it does highlight the key dates for project management.

The sequence of dates indicates that the project management techniques were developed first, followed by hardware and software. The situation has changed recently where the computer facilities are now leading the development of the management techniques. The limiting factor now is project management education and training, this more than any other factor is holding back the successful implementation of the latest project management technology.

14.2 Project Management Techniques

The development of project management techniques can be dated back to Henry Gantt's barchart and the development of PERT and CPM in the late 1950's. These developments have already been discussed in the text. Initially the processing was done laboriously by hand, then by mainframe computers using punch card input, both were not very satisfactory and may well have held back further development at the time.

It was not until the introduction of the PC that the real potential of project management techniques were realised. With the IBM PC becoming the market standard the software houses produced a comprehensive range of business software.

14.3 Computer Hardware

Although mainframe and mini computers have been around for many years the real step forward came with the launch of the personal computer, initially the Apple 11 in 1977, but more importantly the IBM PC in 1981. When the Apple 11 was introduced many businessmen felt this was a computer hacker's fad, having started life in Steve Job's back garage. The IBM PC, on the other hand, was from a professional company which essentially endorsed the PC as a business product.

There were also a number of other vendors besides Apple pioneering the market; Radioshack, Commodore, Siemens, Tandy and Sinclair to name a few. With each vendor offering different operating systems requiring specially written software the question of compatibility became a major issue. In spite of all the confusion, the computer companies were experiencing very respectable market growth. The real boom though started when IBM entered the market. Up to that time IBM had taken a back seat, but not for long. In 1981 they launched the IBM PC and immediately set the market standard. IBM addressed the confused market with a simple advert:

No manager was ever sacked for choosing an IBM PC.

Hardware components: To assist computer hardware selection a few of the basic components will be identified. The basic configuration of a micro computer system consists of:

1. A central processing unit (CPU).
2. A memory (RAM).
3. A visual display unit (VDU).
4. A keyboard and mouse.
5. Mass storage (Hard-drive).
6. A printer / plotter.

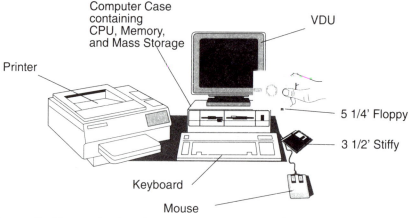

Figure: 1. Computer hardware

1. The CPU is essentially the brains of the computer and gives a pointer to the processing power.

2. The **random access memory** (RAM) is the computer's active memory, this determines how much data it can handle at any one time. RAM memory should not be confused with hard disk storage, as RAM is volatile and is lost when the computer is switched off. There has been rapid growth in this area, 1 MB RAM is now common. (MB = mega byte or one million bytes)

3. The **visual display unit** (VDU) has developed from black and white to high definition colour, now used extensively for detailed graphics.

4. The **keyboard** has maintained the typewriter format, but an additional feature is the **mouse** for software control.

5.   The mass storage devices include the **hard drive** which is permanently fitted to the computer with storage ranging from 20 MB to 160 MB. The disk drive uses a 5 1/4 inch floppy (360 KB or 1.2 MB) or a 3 1/2 inch stiffy (720 KB or 1.4 MB) (KB = kilo bytes or one thousand bytes)

6.   The **printer** facility has developed from the golf ball and daisy wheel printers to be replaced by the dot matrix as the market standard with enhanced presentation from ink jets and laser printers. Colour printers are the latest enhancement.

14.4 Computer Software

Computer software provides the written commands and instructions to control the hardware and process the data. There are a number of software levels; the machine code, the operating system and the application software to name the most obvious. When referring to software today we are usually referring to the high level language type application software, for example, Wordperfect and Lotus.

DOS: All computers have an operating system such as DOS (Disk Operating System). This controls a number of devices, which include the disk drives, the keyboard, the mouse, the screen and the printer.

Word processor: A word processing package can be used to write letters and reports.

Spreadsheets: A spreadsheet has a mathematical capability, which makes it ideal for generating accounting reports and estimating.

Graphics: Business graphic software offers presentations like pie chart, barcharts and graphs which can be incorporated in reports or made into presentation slides.

Data base: The relational data base offers selection of data, sorting and ordering functions to manage large volumes of data.

Project management planning: The planning packages are by far the most complex software in the project managers software portfolio. It uses a combination of the above packages to make full use of the CPM techniques.

ONE COMPUTER

MANY
DISCIPLINES

14.5 Feasibility Study

As projects have become larger and more complex in nature the support systems used to plan and control these projects must become more sophisticated to reflect these changes. This section will outline a simple framework for a feasibility study.

The decision to implement a computer system will not only commit the company financially, but will also change the information systems. This implementation should, therefore, not be taken lightly, as history shows some companies have experienced difficulties during the transition from manual to computerised systems. The feasibility study should quantify the need and recommend a direction and a solution. The feasibility study can be split up into a number of operations:

1. Appoint feasibility study team.
2. Identify design constraints.
3. Define the present system's information flow.
4. Evaluate the hardware and software facilities available.
5. Preliminary design of proposed system.
6. Prepare the cost-benefit analysis.
7. Present the feasibility study.
8. Accept or reject the feasibility study's recommendations.

A plan of action should be drawn up for each phase of the system development, which clearly indicates:

a)   What is required.
b)   When it should be completed.
c)   Who is responsible.
d)   What resources are required.
e)   The budget.

Companies often opt for the step-by-step approach, where the initial use is to computerise the present manual system. Although this may not be fully utilising the capacity of the computer system it is still a positive step in the right direction. During this time many of the problems associated with operating a new computer system can be ironed out, offering a debugged base to work from.

14.6 Vendor Selection

The computer supplier or vendor should play a very important part in the selection of computer hardware and software. The vendor is not simply the supplier of a product, but can also be the key to effectively utilising the software and hardware facilities purchased. The function of the vendor can vary from salesman to consultant depending on the nature of the product and the ability of the vendor. The experts recommend the buyer to select the vendor before considering the product.

Many of the basic application packages such as: Wordperfect, Lotus and Harvard Graphics, can be bought off the shelf and may not require any vendor support as public training is generally available. But the more complicated packages such as: dBase and Project Planning software (Artemis, Open Plan and Super Project to name a few) do need vendor support. What should you expect from the vendor ? This may be answered under the following headings:

Expert hot line: This is a telephone service where problems can be discussed, some vendors even offer a modem link. Also establish the vendor's response time when called out.

Training: The training should cover a continuum of courses presented by trainers who regularly use the package.

Vendor stability: Will the vendor be in business next year when you may need them ?

Cost of service: What is included in the one year warranty, what is not and how much will it cost ?

As the facilities have become more complicated it is important to ensure that the well chosen hardware will support the equally well chosen software. Again the vendor's assistance here is invaluable. The vendor must confirm that their product is compatible with the other systems, in some cases they may even have to change components or programmes to make it work.

14.7 Computer Hardware Selection

Once the vendor has been selected the next step is to select the hardware. The most common type is called the IBM compatible, this means the computer should run any software which has been written for the IBM computer. The experts advise, however, that there are varying degrees of compatibility. The purchaser should therefore request the hardware vendor to ensure that all the planned software will be compatible with their machine.

For the layman, computer quality is difficult to differentiate. When choosing a car, for example, one usually differentiates by product name, selecting a Rolls Royce in preference to a Ford. Computers have the same range of qualities, but the manufactures and component suppliers have yet to become household names.

The size or power of the computer depends on the CPU, the more powerful the more expensive. The two main types of CPU on the market today are called the 386 and 486. The main difference to the layman being the speed of calculation.

Printers: The basic printer is the dot matrix type, the 9 pin head is ideal for draft copies and internal correspondence. A wide carriage of 132 characters which can use A3 size paper is very useful when printing out wide spreadsheets.

For letters and correspondence where presentation is important it is preferable to use an ink jet or laser printer. The key to success is printer compatibility, if one machine goes down can you use the others ?

14.8 Computer Software Selection

The feasibility study should determine the data capture, data processing and information reporting. The software selection should match not only the information system's requirements, but also the company's capability. If in doubt consider the market standard software as a first step.

Word processor: The word processor market is currently led by Wordperfect and Multi-Mate.

Spreadsheet: Lotus is definitely the market standard for spreadsheets, but also consider Quatro which currently offers more facilities and if nothing else, will emulate Lotus.

Graphics: For simple business graphics, Harvard Graphics is the market standard.

Data base: The data base market is dominated by dBase.

Planning: Planning software is still a developing market, with many players jostling for position. Although most of the packages offer excellent facilities it is suggested that you look to the vendor first to see what can be supported locally. Although a wide range of software packages will be used on a project, the intention here is to focus particularly on the software used for planning.

Project planning software can be broadly separated by the cost of the package. Although it is tempting to associate higher prices with richer functions and better quality, some of the lower priced software can offer similar capabilities. In general though, the higher priced programs are able to manage larger projects, define constraints in greater detail and with more precision and will produce more flexible reports. On the other hand, the cheaper programs are easier to use, have better designed screens, are more interactive and process the data much faster.

Most of the lower budget packages keep the project in RAM, thus offering high speed calculations. The more expensive programs, however, have to go back and forth to the hard disk for task data and algorithms, which tends to make them slower although they are able to offer more features and handle larger amounts of data by using this mainframe thinking.

The most important functional difference between the two ends of the market is the size of the project each can handle. Because they can process larger projects, the higher priced programs are also more capable of managing multiple project calculations. They usually keep project scheduling independent, but share and level resources across projects. By contrast, the cheaper programs usually append multiple projects into an overall project in order to share resources. By becoming a sub-project, one should be aware that the projects can lose their individual identity.

Some of the higher priced programs began life as a mainframe product and although they can now run on a PC they have kept the mainframe look and feel. They would use a command driven language rather than a menu driven interface. As a result, although offering more flexible command language driven programs, the implementation period will take longer and may need special training courses for the operators and programmers. The programs specially written for PC's, on the other hand, use sophisticated user interfaces and eye-catching menus. The programs are more user friendly with plenty of help facilities which makes them easier to learn and operate.

The higher priced programs tend to handle the project cost requirements more effectively, offering more cost fields, earned value schedule cost integration and a wider range of management reports. Reporting is another area of difference with the higher priced programs offering full report writers, which let the user generate almost any kind of management report. While the low budget packages usually have a restricted number of report formats available with limited customisation.

Local Area Networks (LAN's) Most project management programs claim to support LAN's but it is the weakest form of support, allowing read-only multiple file access. To address the project management needs, true LAN support is required, to enable the various departments to regularly access updated schedules as well as tracking multiple projects. The first step towards finding the right software package is to first consider your requirements. This can be quantified under the following headings:

    (1).   Time analysis.
    (2).   Resource analysis.
    (3).   Cost management.
    (4).   Report writing.
    (5).   General items.

Taking each of these headings in turn a selection matrix can be compiled to adjudicate the various packages. The selection matrix consists of a column of software attributes together with a column for each software package under consideration.

Attributes	Package 1	Package 2	Package 3
Item 1	--------	--------	--------
Item 2	--------	--------	--------

Tick the items that are important to your project needs and try to weight them. (A simple way to initially weight the features is to give one tick if it is important and two ticks if it is very important). When you have completed this process add the ticks to see which packages gives the highest score. This process should be repeated, refining the selection criteria each time.

14.9 Implementation

The implementation phase converts ideas into reality. This stage can have the greatest influence on the success of a new system. Implementation can start at any time during the feasibility study, certainly the training of operators and programmers should start as early as possible to allow them time to progress up the learning curve. There are a number of implementation strategies, **Cleland** and **King** cite four main methods;

Operating a pilot system: A pilot system is essentially a small version of the planned system. It is used on a small project alongside the manual system. This way if there are problems it should not effect production, but more importantly it offers the opportunity to carry out a heuristic development process to progressively iron out all the teething troubles.

Running parallel systems: Parallel systems are when the computer and manual processing are run at the same time. This effectively doubles the work load, but if there are problems with the new system then the manual method is always available as a backup. This method would be preferable for a company who could not risk having a system down for an unknown period of time, e.g. emergency services and hospitals.

Phase-in / phase-out: This method uses a slice by slice approach, computerising a little bit at a time, getting each section up and running before moving on to the next part. This method has the advantage of allowing the project manager to make the implementation slowly and keep control of the changes so that if there are any problems, he will only have to address a small area of the information flow rather than the whole system.

Cut off method: The cut off or big bang approach is to change from a manual system to a computerised system over night. The advantage here is that the extra cost of running parallel systems is removed and the new system is up and running quicker, but of course one does run the risk of the new system failing with all the associated costs. Only use this method if you are confident the new system will work first time without any significant debugging. The London stock exchange used this method. Although they were very confident and had spent years planning the new system, the news for months after the "big bang" was of interrupted service.

In reality implementation tends to be most effectively done by combining all the different methods and using the one that is most appropriate to the company at the time.

14.10 Training

The education and training of the people who will run your system is absolutely essential for both its smooth and efficient operation and also to ensure a return on the investment.

With the introduction of a new system the first step is to establish who is going to operate it. This will usually consist of people already working for the company, plus additional people from outside if required. To quantify the requirements use a **skills training matrix**. The skills training matrix will document the present skill status, the required skill position, and what training or employment is needed to get from A to B.

Name		Skill X	Skill Y
	Present	A	
Chris	Training	x	
	Required	B	
	Present		A
Sandra	Training		x
	Required		B

Figure: 2. Training matrix

Although the skills matrix may suggest that certain skills should be employed from outside, the employment agencies advise that there is a general shortage of experienced computer personnel, so in-house training may be the only real option. Late training of personnel has been identified by **Clelend** and **King** as one of the main problems limiting the initial effectiveness of project management software. It takes time for an operator to advance up the learning curve, so the sooner training starts the better.

14.11 Project Planning Software

This section will illustrate how a planning software package can be used to process a simple project. The software packages selected without prejudice are **Timeline and Super Project** and the project used is appendix 4 (see appendix 4 for the manual working of the calculations). The intention here is to show a few of the typical computer screen inputs and outputs, CPM processing and reporting.

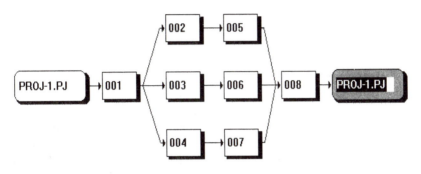

Figure: 3. Super Project. Network diagram

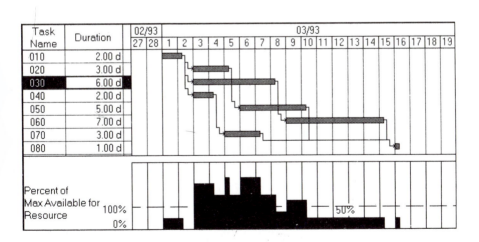

Figure: 4. Timeline. Linked barchart and Resource Histogram

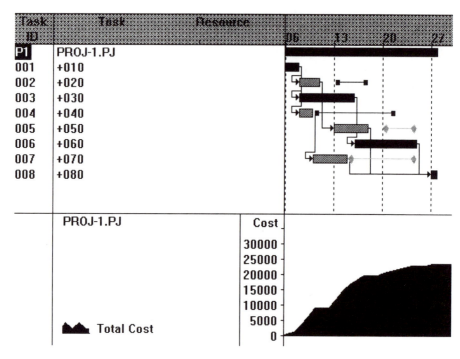

Figure: 5. Super Project. Scheduled barchart and cost curve

14.12 Benefits of Using Project Management Software

As project manager you may have to substantiate a proposal requesting the purchase and implementation of project management software. Senior management may see your proposal as yet another information system, here are a list of benefits to support your proposal:

*   Project management software offers fast calculations. This can be demonstrated on a spreadsheet where any number changes are processed almost immediately, however, by hand the calculations would take much longer.

*   The calculations are always correct, the accuracy of the output is directly dependent on the accuracy of the data input. Validation of date entry is also possible, which will reduce human errors.

*   Editing is very quick once the data base has been established.

*   The application packages offer a well thought out information struc-
     ture which, if used, will help standardise methods and enforce a
     disciplined approach.

*   The software has the capacity to process large projects with 10000 +
     activities.

*   Select and sort functions enable the operator to present the informa-
     tion in a structured format.

*   Management by exception and variance reports are easily obtained,
     e.g. where float = zero, this will highlight the activities on the critical
     path.

*   Once the data base has been established, **what-if** analysis can be
     performed quickly.

*   The project data base can be linked to the corporate data base.

*   The software can offer centralised or distributed reporting which is
     flexible to suit the organization structure.

*   Better quality reporting, the documents and graphics can be custo-
     mised to facilitate dissemination of information within the project
     team.   Most packages offer a large number of standardised and
     customised reports.

*   Quicker calculation can lead to a shorter reporting period which gives
     greater control and more accurate trend analysis.   It will also be
     quicker to respond to a changing situation.

*   Reports can be structured by the Work Breakdown Structure (WBS)
     or Organisation Breakdown Structure (OBS).

*   The software will release the manager from processing large amounts
     of data manually, which should give him time to concentrate on
     managing the project and the people involved on it.

*   It is relatively simple to make back-ups and safe copies of the project
     data.   This addresses the need for disaster recovery.

*   Managers can type their own reports and faxes.

There are, however, a number of **disadvantages** which include:

* There will be additional costs associated with education and training, hardware and software procurement and loss of production while implementing the new system.

* The additional cost of maintenance and up-grading.

* The organization may need to be restructured.

* The new system may cause a resistance to change which could affect company morale and productivity.

* If the computer goes down this could stop the company's operation, especially if effective back-up systems have not been established.

* If data safety precautions are not taken it is possible to lose vast amounts of data.

14.13 Summary

This chapter introduced the reader to computerised project management, starting with a brief history lesson to establish the sequence of developments and indicate that the PC was introduced in the late 1970's.

The selection of computer hardware and software was discussed along the lines of; vendor support, basic components, market standards and software package attributes.

The implementation phase was reported to have the greatest influence on the successful operation of the new system. Lack of effective training was cited as the main cause of system under performance.

A simple planning example was developed using **Super Project** and **Timeline** to outline a number of the computer input and output screens. The chapter finished with a list of benefits which could be used to support planning software implementation.

Appendix 1

Appendix 1 will develop four network diagram exercises with model answers. The purpose of an activity network is to graphically present the project's tasks and activities in a logical sequence. Drawing the network diagram on paper is one of the first steps of the Critical Path Method (CPM).

Question No.1 Draw the following network diagram.

This exercise is based on something we do everyday, go to work. The first activity is to get up (activity A), after which we get dressed (activity B) and then have breakfast (activity C) before driving to work (activity D).

Draw the network yourself before looking at the solution.

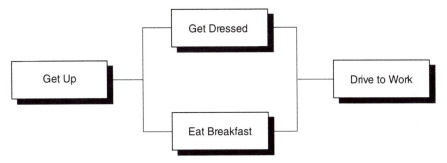

The network diagram shows the logical relationship between the activities. On inspection this would imply that the person can get dressed and have breakfast at the same time. This is obviously not the case (for most of us), but logically they can both start after the person has got up, the limitation here is the resource. The network diagram may also be described using letters or numbers to identify and code the activities.

Activity A is a start activity,
When A is finished B can start,
C can start when A is finished,
When both B and C are finished, D can start,
D is a finish activity.

Solution No.1 Using letters to identify activities.

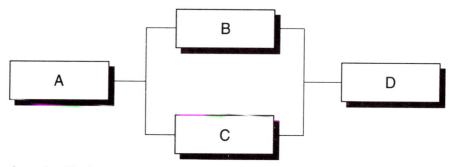

Question No.2 Draw the following network diagram, this time using numbers to code the activities.

Activity 010 is a start activity,
020 and 030 can start when 010 is finished,
When 020 is finished 040 can start,
When 040 and 030 are finished, 050 can start,
050 is a finish activity.

Draw the network now before reading on: To take the network diagram a step further we will focus on the logical relationships between the activities. Taking the above information a logic table is developed which looks at the activity **before** and **after** a logical relationship. Note: all the logical relationships in these examples, unless otherwise stated, will be a finish-to-start (FS) type.

Before Activity	After Activity
Start............................010	
010...............................020	
010...............................030	
020...............................040	
040...............................050	
030...............................050	
050...............................Finish	

Solution No.2

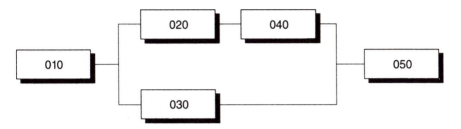

Question No.3 The third question uses the **before** and **after** activity data, this time slightly more difficult.

Before Activity	After Activity
Start.............................100	
100.............................200	
100.............................400	
100.............................600	
200.............................300	
400.............................500	
600.............................700	
300.............................800	
500.............................800	
700.............................800	
800.............................Finish	

Draw the network now before looking at the solution.

Solution No.3

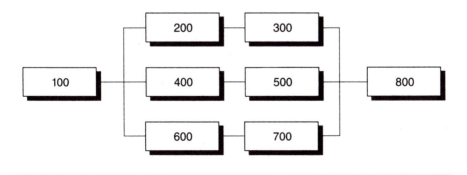

Question No.4 The last question in this section uses the terms commonly found in project planning software, namely **preceding** for before the constraint and **succeeding** for after the constraint.

Preceding Activity	Succeeding Activity
Start	1000
1000	2000
1000	4000
1000	6000
2000	3000
4000	5000
2000	5000
6000	7000
3000	8000
5000	8000
7000	8000
8000	Finish

Try the exercise now before looking at the solution.

Solution No.4

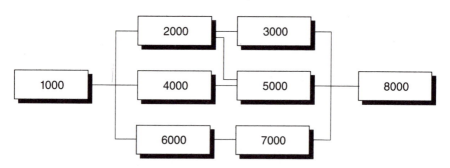

These exercises have introduced a number of network diagram terminologies and techniques. Starting with simple expressions up to the planning software buzz words. The next step is to add time durations to the activities, this will be developed in the following appendices.

Appendix 2

Appendix 2 will develop the network diagram and CPM analysis. Please note: the solution is detailed for the beginner, if this is too simple move on to appendix 4 where this project will be developed further.

The project data is given in the form of a logic table and an activity table.

Logic Table		Activity Table	
Preceding Activity	**Succeeding Activity**	**Activity**	**Duration**
Start	010	010	2
010	020	020	3
010	030	030	6
010	040	040	2
020	050	050	5
030	060	060	7
040	070	070	3
050	080	080	1
060	080		
070	080		
080	Finish		

Activity information will be shown in a box as below:

ES	EF
\ 000	
F	DU
LS	LF

ES = Early Start EF = Early Finish

000 = Activity Number

F = Float DU = Duration

LS = Late Start LF = Late Finish

The logical relationships between the activities are shown as lines between the boxes, for example, from the logic table 010 precedes the constraint while activity 030 succeeds the constraint. The lines are always drawn horizontally or vertically, leaving and entering from the side of the box. The start of the project is from the left side of the page, moving right and downwards.

CPM steps: Each step of the CPM analysis will be explained.

Step 1. Draw the network diagram. From the logic table, look at the first four lines.

Preceding Activity	Succeeding Activity
Start	010
010	020
010	030
010	040

Activity 010 is drawn first, because this is the start activity, the other three follow, finish-to-start FS.

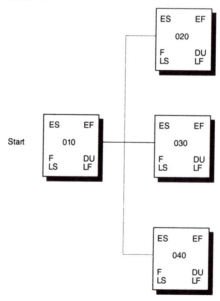

Step 2. The next three lines from the logic table show:

Preceding Activity	Succeeding Activity
020	050
030	060
040	070

This means that activity 050 follows 020, 060 follows 030 and 070 follows 040.

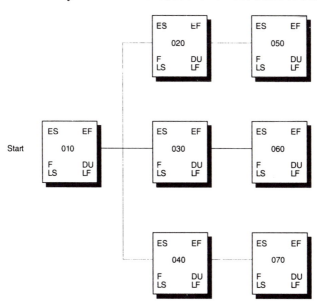

Step 3. The last four lines of the logic table show:

Preceding Activity	Succeeding Activity
050	080
060	080
070	080
080	Finish

This means activities 050, 060 and 070 must be completed before 080 can start and activity 080 is the last activity of the project.

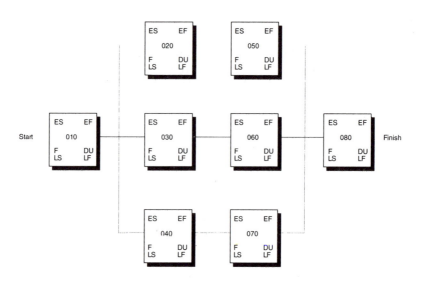

The network diagram showing the logical relationships is now complete. The network diagram on its own is important because it shows the sequence of work, besides Critical Path Method this is also a key input document for the Quality Control Plan.

Step 4. The next step is to transfer the activity durations from the activity table to the activity boxes in the position marked **du**.

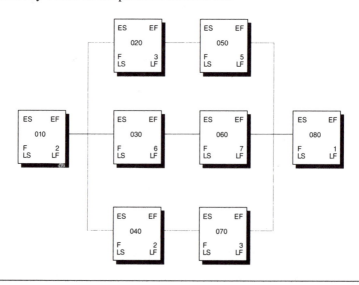

Step 5. We now perform the **forward pass** to determine the early start (ES) and early finish (EF) of each activity. Activity 010 starts on day 1 or in calender notation say 1st March. The activity has a duration of 2 days, so it will finish on day 2 or 2nd March. The equation is: $EF = ES + duration - 1$.

Step 6. If the EF of 010 is 2nd March, then the ES of 020, 030 and 040 is the following day 3rd March. Calculate the EF for 020, 030 and 040.

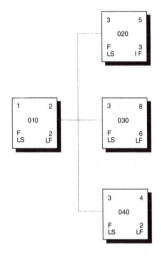

Step 7. Calculate ES and EF for activities 050, 060 and 070.

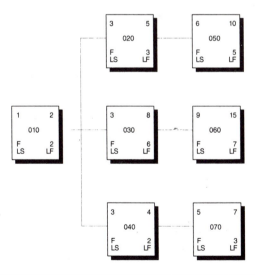

Step 8. We now have an interesting situation, when there are many activities leading into one, select the highest EF value to give the ES for the following activity. This means activity 080 cannot start until all the preceding activities have finished.

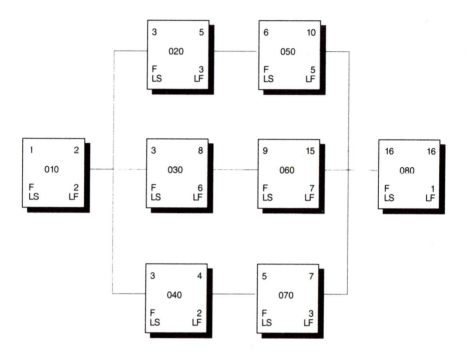

Step 9. The EF of activity 080 is a key date, as this indicates the earliest date it is possible to complete the project, in this case 16th March.

Step 10. We now perform a **backward pass** to determine the LS and LF of each activity. Starting with activity 080 set the LF to be the same as its EF (16th March), then work backwards to find the late start for each activity. The equations is:

$$LS = LF - Du + 1$$

Note: On the backward pass where there are many activities leading into one, select the lowest number or date. This ensures that all the preceding activities have finished before the succeeding activities start.

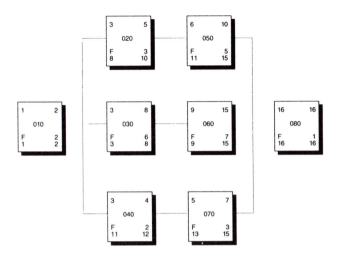

Step 11. The next process is to calculate the activity float. Use the following equation: **Float = LS - ES**

Float = 1 - 1 = 0 (Activity 010)

Using this equation the float for all the activities can be calculated.

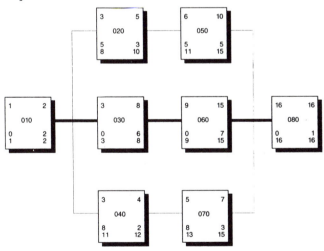

The critical path by definition links all the activities with zero float. If any of these activities are delayed the end date of the project will be extended. In this case the following activities have zero float, 010, 030, 060 and 080. It is normal practice to highlight the critical path in heavy print, double lines or red ink.

Appendix 3

Does a project start on day zero or day one, practitioners will argue either way. This example will take the same data as appendix 2, but start on day zero. Although this is not used by the computer software it does offer a simpler calculation to determine Early Start (ES) and Early Finish (EF). Whichever method is used the scheduling information will be the same.

This method assumes an activity is executed from the start of the day to the end of the day. For example, a two day activity will start on day zero and finish at the end of day two, with the following activity also starting at the end of day two.

To help understanding, follow the calculation on the calendar barchart, where both time scales are shown.

$$EF = ES + Duration$$
$$ES_{020} = EF_{010}$$

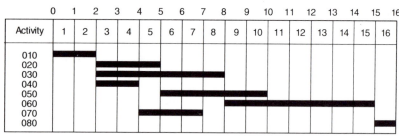

Consider activity 010, $EF = 0 + 2$
$$= 2$$

Activity 020 start on day 2, therefore $EF = 2 + 3$
$$= 5$$

The benefit here over the over the appendix 2 method is that there is no (-1) in the calculation. However it should be noted that the ES figures do not correspond directly to a date.

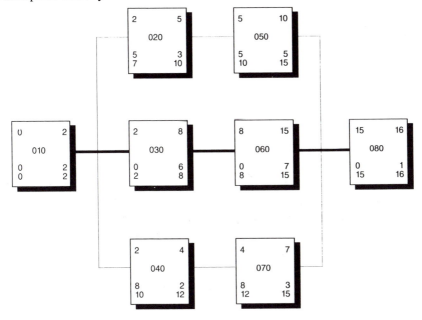

Appendix 4

This example is a continuation from appendices 2 and 3 which developed the network diagram and the activities; start dates, the finish dates and float. Here the CPM model will be developed further, to include; project acceleration or crashing, resource management, the expenditure S curve, the cash flow statement and the revised barchart.

To calculate the above, additional activity information is required together with data capture at timenow 4 and 8.

Activity Number	Normal Time	Resources per day	Total Normal Cost $	Crash Time	Total Crash Cost $	Additional Crash Cost per day
	A		B	C	D	[D-B]/[A-C]
010	2	2	100	1	200	100
020	3	3	150	2	200	50
030	6	3	60	3	120	20
040	2	2	100	2	100	-
050	5	3	50	4	60	10
060	7	2	210	4	255	15
070	3	3	90	2	145	55
080	1	2	50	1	50	-

Step 1. Appendices 2 and 3 analysed the network to give completion day 16. Consider the situation where the client requests the contractor to advise the cost implication to complete in 10 days.

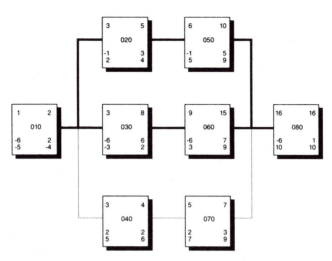

The network diagram is first re-analysed by setting the LF of activity 080 to 10 days or 10th March and then performing a **backward pass** to calculate the new LS, LF and float for all the activities. The negative float will indicate which activities need to be crashed and by how much. A priority list is then established with least cost to crash, first. After crashing an activity the network should be reprocessed to see if any other paths have gone critical.

Priority list: Critical activities only.

Activity	Cost to crash	Priority
060	15	1
030	20	2
010	100	3

Crash by	Cost	(days x activity no.)
3 days	$ 45	(3 x 060)
4 days	$ 65	(3 x 060) + (1 x 030)
5 days	$ 85	(3 x 060) + (2 x 030)
6 days	$ 115	(3 x 060) + (3 X 030) + (1 x 050)

Note here how the network arm (020, 050) also goes critical when the target completion date is reduced to 10 days. For this example, the client decides not to crash the project.

Step 2. The information from the forward pass, backward pass and float calculations (see appendix 2) are usually presented in a tabular format.

Activity Number	Duration (days)	Early Start	Early Finish	Late Start	Late Start	Float (days)
010	2	1 Mar	2 Mar	1 Mar	2 Mar	0
020	3	3 Mar	5 Mar	8 Mar	10 Mar	5
030	6	3 Mar	8 Mar	3 Mar	8 Mar	0
040	2	3 Mar	4 Mar	11 Mar	12 Mar	8
050	5	6 Mar	10 Mar	11 Mar	15 Mar	5
060	7	9 Mar	15 Mar	9 Mar	15 Mar	0
070	3	5 Mar	7 Mar	13 Mar	15 Mar	8
080	1	16 Mar	16 Mar	16 Mar	16 Mar	0

Step 3. The data can now be used to produce a graphical barchart. For this example the barchart will be ordered by activity number, however, in industry it is common to order by Early Start (ES).

Early Starting Barchart (Showing Resources)

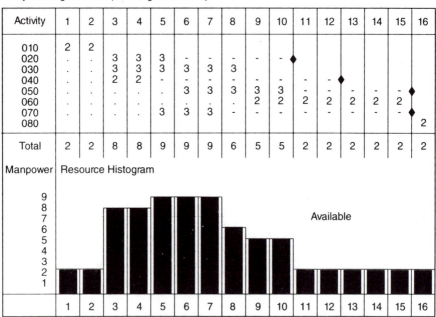

The barchart is further enhanced by including the number of resources required per day which are summed daily to give the resource histogram. The resource histogram indicates the number of men required per day. For this example the company only has seven men available, this means there will be an overload on days 3,4,5,6 and 7th March.

Step 4. Resource overload is initially addressed by moving activities within their float. Try moving activities 040 and 070 to their LS.

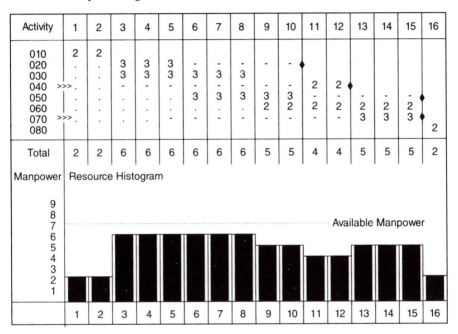

Activity	1	2	3	4	5	6	7	8	9	10	11	12	13	14	15	16
010	2	2														
020	.	.	3	3	3	-	-	-	-	.	♦					
030		.	3	3	3	3	3	3								
040	>>>.	.	-	-	-	-	-	-	-	-	2	2 ♦				
050	.	.		.	.	3	3	3	3	3	-	-	-	-	- ♦	
060	.	.	.	.	.	.	.	.	2	2	2	2	2	2	2 ♦	
070	>>>.	.	.	.	-	-	-	-	-	-	-	-	3	3	3 ♦	
080																2
Total	2	2	6	6	6	6	6	6	5	5	4	4	5	5	5	2

A second way to smooth the resources is to move 040 to 6th March, 050 to 8th March and 070 to 13th March.

Activity	1	2	3	4	5	6	7	8	9	10	11	12	13	14	15	16
010	2	2														
020	.	.	3	3	3	-	-	-	-	.	♦					
030		.	3	3	3	3	3	3								
040	>>>	.	-	-	-	2	2	-	-	-	-	- ♦				
050	>>>	.	..	.	.	-	-	3	3	3	3	3	-	-	- ♦	
060	.	.	.	.	.	.	.	.	2	2	2	2	2	2	2	
070	>>>	.	.	.	-	-	-	-	-	-	-	-	3	3	3 ♦	
080																2
Total	2	2	6	6	6	5	5	6	5	5	5	5	5	5	5	2

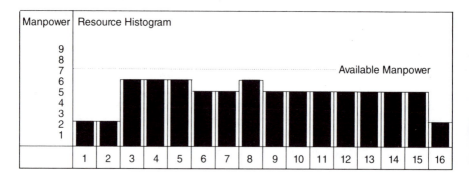

A third way to smooth the resources would be to move 020 and 050 to their LS.

Activity	1	2	3	4	5	6	7	8	9	10	11	12	13	14	15	16
010	2	2														
020	>>>	.	-	-	-	-	-	3	3	3 ♦						
030		.	3	3	3	3	3	3								
040		.	2	2	-	-	-	-	-	-	-	- ♦				
050	>>>	.	.	.	.	-	-	-	-	-	3	3	3	3	3 ♦	
060		.	.	.	.	.	.	.	2	2	2	2	2	2	2	
070		.	.	.	3	3	3	-	-	-	-	-	-	- ♦		
080																2
Total	2	2	5	5	6	6	6	6	5	5	5	5	5	5	5	2

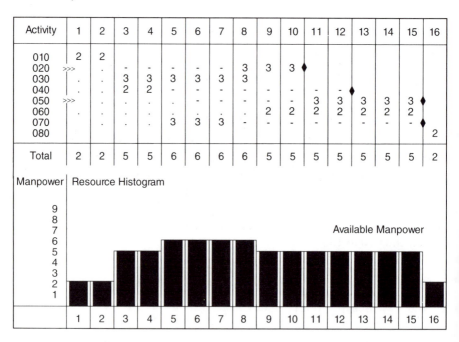

Mathematically there may be many ways to smooth the resources as shown here. Note: care must be taken not to change the activity logic, for instance if 020 has been moved, then 050 must also be moved because of their Finish-to-Start relationship.

Step 5. If the company resources were to be reduced further to (say) 5 men, then moving activities within their float would not be sufficient, other methods need to be considered:

* **Split the activity**: This option is not always feasible.

* **Time-limited smoothing**: Here the end date of the project cannot be exceeded, where the resources are overloaded more men must be applied.

* **Resource-limited smoothing**: Here the maximum number of a resource is stipulated, in this case it is 5 men. To achieve this lower resource level it will be necessary to move an activity on the critical path, thus extending the end date of the project.

Step 6. The next step is to consider the cash flow. This will be influenced by the timing of the costs, for this example the two extremes, ES and LS will be considered.

The cost per day is assumed to be linear over the activity, the expenses are shown in the bars. The expenses are calculated per day by adding vertically, then accumulated from left to right.

Early Start Barchart, showing expenses.

Activity	1	2	3	4	5	6	7	8	9	10	11	12	13	14	15	16
010	50	50														
020	.	.	50	50	50	-	-	-	-	-						
030	.	.	10	10	10	10	10	10								
040	.	.	50	50	-	-	-	-	-	-	-	-				
050	.	.	.	.	.	10	10	10	10	10	-	-	-	-	-	
060	.	.	.	.	.	.	.	.	30	30	30	30	30	30	30	
070	.	.	.	.	30	30	30	-	-	-	-	-	-	-	-	
080	.	.	.	.	.	.	.	.	.	.	.	.	.	.	.	50
Total	50	50	110	110	90	50	50	20	40	40	30	30	30	30	30	50
Running Total	50	100	210	320	410	460	510	530	570	610	640	670	700	730	760	810

Late Start Barchart, showing expenses.

Activity	1	2	3	4	5	6	7	8	9	10	11	12	13	14	15	16
010	50	50														
020	.	.	-	-	-	-	-	50	50	50 ◆						
030	.	.	10	10	10	10	10	10								
040	.	.	-	-	-	-	-	-	-	-	50	50 ◆				
050	.	.	.	.	.	-	-	-	-	-	10	10	10	10	10 ◆	
060	.	.	.	.	.	.	.	.	30	30	30	30	30	30	30	
070	.	.	.	.	-	-	-	-	-	-	-	-	30	30	30 ◆	
080	.	.	.	.	.	.	.	.	.	.	.	.	.	.	.	50
Total	50	50	10	10	10	10	10	60	80	80	90	90	70	70	70	50
Running Total	50	100	110	120	130	140	150	210	290	370	460	550	620	690	760	810

The two expense curves can now be plotted cost against time. The expense curve, also called the Budgeted Cost for Work Scheduled (BCWS) is the link between the CPM and the budget.

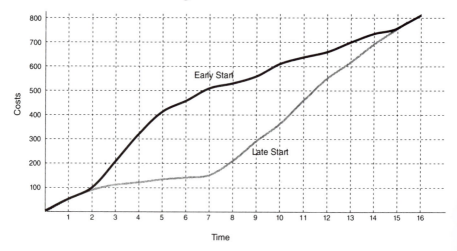

This double curve between ES and LS is often called the **banana curve** because of its shape. The important feature though is to appreciate the affect scheduling has on the cash flow.

Step 7. This step will show how the **cash flow statement** is linked with the scheduled barchart. Using the following information a cash flow statement will be developed for every time period (for this example make every four time units or days equal to one period), also assume you are considering the cash flow from the contractor's perspective.

* For period 1 the brought forward amount is zero.

* Income is calculated at costs plus 30% as they occur on the ES barchart. The client takes 1 period to pay and a completion bonus of $200 will be paid with the final invoice.

Time units	0-4	5-8	9-12	13-16	17-20
Periods	1	2	3	4	5
Costs Income (times 1.3) Bonus	320	210 416	140 273	140 182	182 200

* Cost of sales:

[1] Overheads are $50 per period.

[2] Activity costs from the ES barchart (assume costs are split 50:50 between labour and materials). The labour costs are paid in the period they occur.

Time units	0-4	5-8	9-12	13-16	17-20
Periods	1	2	3	4	5
Total costs	320	210	140	140	
Labour costs	160	105	70	70	

[3] The material supplier gives 1 period to pay, therefore the cash flow is moved forward 1 period.

Time units	0-4	5-8	9-12	13-16	17-20
Periods	1	2	3	4	5
Total costs	320	210	140	140	
Material costs	0	160	105	70	70

[4]   If the closing statement is negative the funds can be borrowed @ 10% per period, these bank charges are then levied in the following period. Round up 0.5 and above if necessary.

Cash Flow Statement

Time units	0-4	5-8	9-12	13-16	17-20
Brought forward Income Completion bonus	0 0	(210) 416	(130) 273	(95) 182	(113) 182 200
Total funds available [A]	0	206	143	87	269
Expenses Overheads [1] Labour [2] Materials [3] Interest [4]	 50 160 0 0	 50 105 160 21	 50 70 105 13	 50 70 70 10	 0 0 70 11
Total payments [B]	210	336	238	200	81
Closing amount [A-B]	(210)	(130)	(95)	(113)	188

From the cash flow statement it is obvious that the project will require up-front financing, but will, however, go positive during the last period.

Step 8. The above calculations form the main part of the **baseline plan**, once this information is available the project can be executed.

Using the data capture at **timenow 4** the revised barcharts can be drawn in conjunction with the network diagram (p. 359).

Activity Number	Actual Start	Actual Finish	Percentage Complete	Remaining Duration
010	1 Mar	2 Mar	100 %	-
020	2 Mar	4 Mar	100 %	-
030	3 Mar	-	-	5
040	4 Mar	-	50 %	-

The analysis at timenow 4 shows that activity 010 has started and finished as planned, but activity 020 started and finished 1 day early. Because activity 020 and 050 have a FS relationship, 050 should also be able to start 1 day early assuming resources are available. Activity 030 started on time but is going to be finished 1 day late, this will have a knock-on affect and delay 060 and 070 by 1 day. Activity 040 started 1 day late and is estimated to finish 1 day late, this will delay 070 by 1 day. Finally the last activity 080 will be delayed one day because 060 is forecast to finish 1 day late.

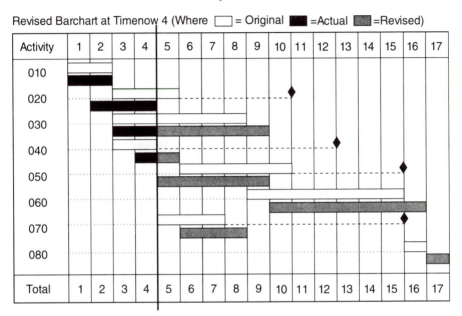

Revised Barchart at Timenow 4 (Where ☐ = Original ■ =Actual ▨ =Revised)

Date capture at **timenow 8**:

Activity Number	Actual Start	Actual Finish	Percentage Complete	Remaining Duration
010	1 Mar	2 Mar	100 %	-
020	2 Mar	4 Mar	100 %	-
030	3 Mar	7 Mar	100%	-
040	4 Mar	6 Mar	100%	-
050	5 Mar	-	-	1
060	8 Mar	-	-	5
070	7 Mar	-	50 %	-
080	-	-	-	-

Revised Barchart at Timenow 8 (Where ☐ = Original ■ =Actual ■ =Revised)

Activity	1	2	3	4	5	6	7	8	9	10	11	12	13	14	15	16

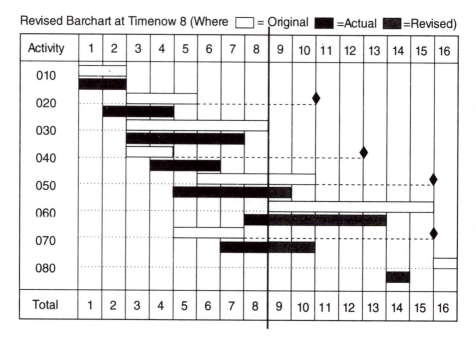

Total	1	2	3	4	5	6	7	8	9	10	11	12	13	14	15	16

The analysis shows activities 030 and 040 are now finished, 050 and 060 have remaining durations of 1 and 5 days respectively, 070 is 50% complete which can be mathematically transposed to a remaining duration of 1.5 or round up to 2 days. Because 060 has now finished early 080 can also finish 1 day early, on day 14 if the resources are available.

Appendix 5

Cash flow exercise: In this appendix you are required to prepare a cash flow statement for the months January to June, using the following information.

1. Brought forward for January $5000.

2. Sale price forecast for units @ $20 each. The client pays for sales 1 month after delivery. The sales forecast in units:

Nov	Dec	Jan	Feb	Mar	Apr	May	Jun	Jul	Aug	Sep
100	120	130	140	100	110	110	120	150	130	100

3. Cost of sales: The imported units cost $10 each and are ordered 2 months ahead of the sale date. They arrive just-in-time (JIT) for the sale.

[1]   A payment of 10% is required on order.
[2]   A payment of 50% is required on receipt.
[3]   The remaining 40% of the cost price is paid a month after delivery.
[4]   Monthly loan payments of (20% of funds available) are made; round up 0.5 and above.

Cash Flow Statement

	JAN	FEB	MAR	APR	MAY	JUN
Brought forward	5000	4690	4502	4672	4268	4034
Sales	2400	2600	2800	2000	2200	2200
Total funds available [A]	7400	7290	7302	6672	6468	6234
Cost of sales [1]	100	110	110	120	150	130
[2]	650	700	500	550	550	600
[3]	480	520	560	400	440	440
[4]	1480	1458	1460	1334	1294	1247
Total payments [B]	2710	2788	2630	2404	2434	2417
Closing amount [A-B]	4690	4502	4672	4268	4034	3817

Appendix 6

Cash flow exercise: Stocking and destocking. This appendix will consider the cash flow within a manufacturing environment as the output increases or decreases. The cash flow proformas are printed as a self test for the reader, with the solution following. The student is requested to work out the cash flow himself before looking at the solution.

Consider a company manufacturing computerised machines. If the sales were 5 units per month selling @ $10000 each and the costs were; overheads $5000 per month, raw materials $5000 each unit and a manufacturing labour @ $1000 per unit, then the cash flow be:

Self Test (Sales 5 units per month)

	JAN	FEB	MAR	APR	MAY	JUN
Sales	50000					
Supplier	25000					
Labour	5000					
Overheads	5000					
	15000					

Solution (Sales 5 units per month)

	JAN	FEB	MAR	APR	MAY	JUN
Sales	50000	50000	50000	50000	50000	50000
Supplier	25000	25000	25000	25000	25000	25000
Labour	5000	5000	5000	5000	5000	5000
Overheads	5000	5000	5000	5000	5000	5000
	15000	15000	15000	15000	15000	15000

This indicates a profit of $15000 per month. Consider now what would happen if the sales were to drop from 5 to 4 units per month ?

Assume:

1.   The client takes three months to pay.
2.   The suppliers give two months credit.
3.   The manufacturing labour is paid in the month of manufacture.
4.   Overheads are paid in the month of use.

Self Test (Sales reduce from 5 to 4 units per month)

	JAN	FEB	MAR	APR	MAY	JUN
Sales	50000					
Supplier	25000					
Labour	4000					
Overheads	5000					
	16000					

Solution (Sales reduce from 5 to 4 units per month)

	JAN	FEB	MAR	APR	MAY	JUN
Sales	50000	50000	50000	40000	40000	40000
Supplier	25000	25000	20000	20000	20000	20000
Labour	4000	4000	4000	4000	4000	4000
Overheads	5000	5000	5000	5000	5000	5000
	16000	16000	21000	11000	11000	11000

Surprise ! the profit in the short term actually increases, this phenomena is due to the differential credit periods. The global situation is actually a little more complicated, when **destocking** is consider. In this case the company's stock includes raw material and finished goods to meet the following month's manufacturing and sales. Therefore, when the sales reduce, the company is over stocked with both raw materials and finished goods.

The finished goods stock is used to cover the current month's sales. With 5 units in stock and a reduced sales of 4 units, this leaves 1 unit available to roll forward a month. Therefore this month the company need only make 3 units, to bring the finished goods stock up to 4. In the following month the old stock will be used up and 4 manufactured units will be required.

The raw material stock is purchased to meet the following month's production. With the reduced sales, only 3 of the 5 available components were used, leaving 2 in stock. Therefore only 2 more components are required to bring the raw material stock up to 4. With the excess stock being used up, the following month will require 4 raw material components.

	JAN	FEB	MAR	APR	MAY	JUN
Sales Supplier Labour Overheads	50000 25000 3000 5000	50000 25000 4000 5000	50000 10000 4000 5000	40000 20000 4000 5000	40000 20000 4000 5000	40000 20000 4000 5000
	17000	16000	31000	11000	11000	11000

The first 3 months have actually produced a windfall, the cash flow has been more than when the sales were higher at 5 units. Thus, the immediate affect of a drop in business is to make the company flush with cash. Consider now what happens when there is an increase in production, called **stocking**.

1.   Sales increase from 5 to 8 units per month.

2.   The company now experiences de-stocking in reverse. Both the finished good stock and buffer stock of raw material will need to be increased. This means in the first month the company will have to manufacture an additional 3 units for this month plus the eight for next month (8+3), this will increase the labour costs to $11000. In addition there is the raw material buffer stock of 5 components which requires 11 for manufacture plus a further 3 components (8+3+3) making the delivery in the first month 14 units.

3.   With this additional work one might expect the overheads to increase, in this case by $1000 to $6000 per month.

Self Test (Sales increase from 5 to 8 units per month)

	JAN	FEB	MAR	APR	MAY	JUN
Sales Supplier Labour Overheads	50000 25000 11000 6000					
	8000					

Solution (Sales increase from 5 to 8 units per month)

	JAN	FEB	MAR	APR	MAY	JUN
Sales	50000	50000	50000	80000	80000	80000
Supplier	25000	25000	70000	40000	40000	40000
Labour	11000	8000	8000	8000	8000	8000
Overheads	6000	6000	6000	6000	6000	6000
	8000	11000	(34000)	26000	26000	26000

The cash flow statement now indicates a reduced cash flow in the short term, which in this case actually goes negative $ (34000) in third month, March. This will have to be financed. In the fourth month, April the new steady state is reached with an increased profit margin of $26000.

This exercise clearly indicates the difference between profit and cash flow and how a business can run into cash flow problems as the sales increase because of the increased stock and working capital. This condition is known as **over-trading**. Once the transition period is over the company will of course reach a higher level of profit, the problem is getting there. Using the same costs as above calculate the change in monthly cash flow for the following conditions.

a)   Sales reduce from 6 to 4 units per month.
b)   Sales increase from 6 to 9 units per month.

Solution (Sales reduce from 6 to 4 units per month)

	JAN	FEB	MAR	APR	MAY	JUN
Sales	60000	60000	60000	40000	40000	40000
Supplier	30000	30000	0	20000	20000	20000
Labour	2000	4000	4000	4000	4000	4000
Overheads	5000	5000	5000	5000	5000	5000
	23000	21000	51000	11000	11000	11000

Solution (Sales increase from 6 to 9 units per month)

	JAN	FEB	MAR	APR	MAY	JUN
Sales	60000	60000	60000	90000	90000	90000
Supplier	30000	30000	75000	45000	45000	45000
Labour	12000	9000	9000	9000	9000	9000
Overheads	6000	6000	6000	6000	6000	6000
	12000	15000	(30000)	30000	30000	30000

Appendix 7

This appendix will develop a number of financial selection criteria models. Consider the purchase of a machine for $25000 with the following cash flow:

Cash flow Timing Years	Project Cash flow $
0	(25000)
1	5000
2	7000
3	13000
4	16000

The solutions will be presented under the following headings:

*   The payback period.
*   The return on investment.
*   The net present value (NPV) at 15%.
*   The internal rate of return (IRR).

The payback period: If the project starts with a capital outlay of $25000, the payback period is the time to recover this initial outlay from the cash flow. In this case it will take 3 years.

Cash flow Timing Years	Project Cash flow $	Cash flow Balance $
0	(25000)	(25000)
1	5000	(20000)
2	7000	(13000)
3	13000	0

Return on investment: The return on investment is determined from the following expression:

$$\text{Annual profit} = \frac{\text{Total gain - Total outlay}}{\text{Number of years invested}}$$

The total gain is the same as the total cash flow during the life of the project; $5000 + 7000 + 13000 + 16000 = \$41000$. The total outlay is the same as the initial investment = ($25000). The number of years of the investment is 4.

Profit = $16000 over 4 years

$$\text{Annual profit} = \frac{41000 - 25000}{4} = 4000$$

The annual return on investment is the annual profit expressed as a percentage of the initial investment.

$$\text{Annual return on investment} = \frac{\$4000}{\$25000} \times \frac{100}{1} = 16\%$$

Net present value (NPV): Using the proforma below, transfer the discount factor at 15% from the discount factor table, then multiply the cash flow by the discount factor and summate the present values.

Cash flow Timing Years	Discount Factor (15%)	Project Cash flow $	Present Value
0		(25000)	
1		5000	
2		7000	
3		13000	
4		16000	
		NPV	

Solution:

Cash flow Timing Years	Discount Factor (15%)	Project Cash flow $	Present Value
0	1	(25000)	(25000)
1	0.8696	5000	4348
2	0.7561	7000	5293
3	0.6575	13000	8548
4	0.5718	16000	9149
		NPV	$2338

Internal rate of return (IRR): The IRR value is the same as the discount factor when the NPV is zero. The IRR figure is found by varying the discount factor until the NPV is zero. The first guess is often a stab in the dark, but it will indicate which way to go. If the NPV is positive increase the discount factor and if the NPV is negative decrease the discount factor.

Solution: The discount factor is increased in 1% steps until the NPV value goes negative. The IRR, therefore, lies between 18% and 19%.

Cash flow Timing Years	Discount Factor (16%)	Project Cash flow $	Present Value
0	1	(25000)	(25000)
1	0.8621	5000	4311
2	0.7432	7000	5202
3	0.6407	13000	8329
4	0.5523	16000	8837
		NPV	$1679

Cash flow Timing Years	Discount Factor (17%)	Project Cash flow $	Present Value
0	1	(25000)	(25000)
1	0.8547	5000	4274
2	0.7305	7000	5114
3	0.6244	13000	8117
4	0.5337	16000	8539
		NPV	$1044

Cash flow Timing Years	Discount Factor (18%)	Project Cash flow $	Present Value
0	1	(25000)	(25000)
1	0.8475	5000	4238
2	0.7182	7000	5027
3	0.6086	13000	7912
4	0.5158	16000	8253
		NPV	$430

Cash flow Timing Years	Discount Factor (19%)	Project Cash flow $	Present Value
0	1	(25000)	(25000)
1	0.8403	5000	4202
2	0.7062	7000	4943
3	0.5934	13000	7714
4	0.4987	16000	7979
		NPV	($162)

Appendix 8

Earned value exercise: From the scope of work and information given, perform the following calculations:

a) Draw a three level WBS and analyse the CPM.
b) Draw an ES barchart and resource histogram.
c) Track the project at timenow 4 and 8.

Project Information: The scope of work for this project includes the construction of a house, the outbuildings and landscaping the garden. The main house can be sub-divided in the main trades: civil, carpenters/plumber and electrical/painters. The outbuildings consist of a garage and greenhouse, while the landscaping includes the grounds and fencing. The civil work can be further sub-divided into: foundations, walls and roof. The carpenters and plumbers also includes the door/windows and bic's. The electrical and painters also includes the internal finishes. **Activity Table**

Activity	Description	Duration	Resources	Costs(BAC)
010	Garage	3	2	9000
020	Greenhouse	2	2	2000
030	Foundations	1	3	1000
040	Walls	3	4	12000
050	Roof	5	2	10000
060	Doors	3	2	6000
070	Plumbing	2	2	4000
080	Bic's	3	1	6000
090	Wiring	4	1	8000
100	Finishes	2	2	4000
110	Painting	2	6	6000
120	Driveway	2	3	8000
130	Garden	4	2	8000
140	Fence	4	2	4000
			Total	$88000

Logic Table

Preceding Activity	Succeeding Activity	Preceding Activity	Succeeding Activity
Start	030	Start	120
030	040	120	040
120	010	120	140
040	070	040	060
040	050	070	100
060	090	050	090
050	080	010	020
020	110	100	110
090	110	080	110
140	130	110	Finish
130	Finish		

Work Breakdown Structure:

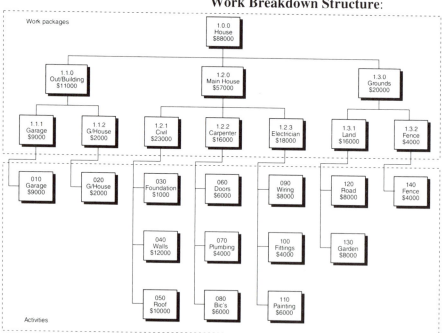

Note: The numbering system for the WBS cells and the activities has been kept different. This will allow both numbering systems to operate linked and autonomous. One or more activities can be linked to a work package, this gives the planner more flexibility when developing the logic.

The network diagram:

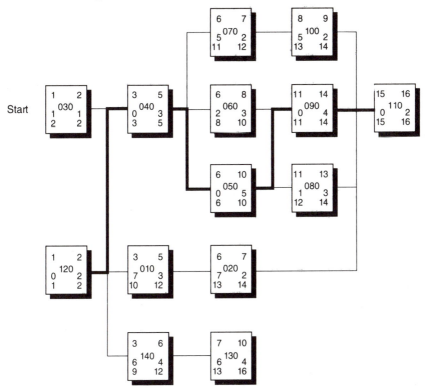

Activity Table: The activity table collates the data in the network diagram and presents it a preferred format.

Activity	Description	Early Start	Early Finish	Late Start	Late Finish	Float
010	Garage	3 Mar	5 Mar	10 Mar	12 Mar	7
020	Green house	6 Mar	7 Mar	13 Mar	14 Mar	7
030	Foundations	1 Mar	1 Mar	2 Mar	2 Mar	1
040	Walls	3 Mar	5 Mar	3 Mar	5 Mar	0
050	Roof	6 Mar	10 Mar	6 Mar	10 Mar	0
060	Doors	6 Mar	8 Mar	8 Mar	10 Mar	2
070	Plumbing	6 Mar	7 Mar	11 Mar	12 Mar	5
080	BIC's	11 Mar	13 Mar	12 Mar	14 Mar	1
090	Electrical	11 Mar	14 Mar	11 Mar	14 Mar	0
100	Fittings	8 Mar	9 Mar	13 Mar	14 Mar	5
110	Paintings	15 Mar	16 Mar	15 Mar	16 Mar	0
120	Road	1 Mar	2 Mar	1 Mar	2 Mar	0
130	Garden	7 Mar	10 Mar	13 Mar	16 Mar	6
140	Fence	3 Mar	6 Mar	9 Mar	12 Mar	6

Early Start Barchart and Resource Histogram: The early start barchart offers yet another preferred presentation format, which indicates the link with the resource histogram.

Early Start Barchart (Showing Resources)

Activity	1	2	3	4	5	6	7	8	9	10	11	12	13	14	15	16
010	.	.	2	2	2	-	-	-	-	-	-	-	.	.	.	.
020	.	.	.	.	.	2	2	-	-	-	-	-	-	-	.	.
030	3	-	.	.	.	.	.	.	.	.	.	.	.	.	.	.
040	.	.	4	4	4	.	.	.	.	.	.	.	.	.	.	.
050	.	.	.	.	.	2	2	2	2	2	.	.	.	.	.	.
060	.	.	.	.	.	2	2	2	-	-	.	.	.	.	.	.
070	.	.	.	.	.	2	2	-	-	-	-	-	.	.	.	.
080	.	.	.	.	.	.	.	.	.	.	1	1	1	-	.	.
090	.	.	.	.	.	.	.	.	.	.	1	1	1	1	.	.
100	.	.	.	.	.	.	2	2	-	-	-	-	-	-	.	.
110	.	.	.	.	.	.	.	.	.	.	.	.	.	.	6	6
120	3	3	.	.	.	.	.	.	.	.	.	.	.	.	.	.
130	.	.	.	.	.	.	2	2	2	2	-	-	.	-	-	-
140	.	.	2	2	2	2	.-	-	-	-	-	-	.	.	.	.
	6	3	8	8	8	10	10	8	6	4	2	2	2	1	6	6

The resource histogram indicates the resource requirements per day. For the purpose of this exercise the available resources are assumed to be sufficient.

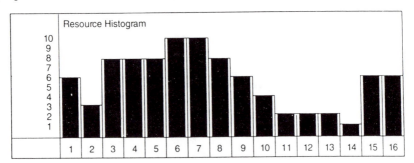

The Expenditure Barchart and Expense Curves: The expenditure barchart assumes a linear cash flow for the activities. By summing the daily expenses and accumulating them will provide the basis for cost control. The BCWS is the integration of cost and time which forms the baseline plan to track the project's performance against. Draw the early start barchart showing expenses (as p. 363) to give the BCWS.

Equations: The following equations will be used in the earned value analysis.

Earned value $\quad$ BCWP = PC * BAC

Scheduled variance   SV   = BCWP - BCWS
Scheduled variance %   SV%   = SV / BCWS
Cost variance   CV   = BCWP - ACWP
Cost variance %   CV%   = CV / BCWP
Estimate at completion EAC   = (ACWP / BCWP) * BAC

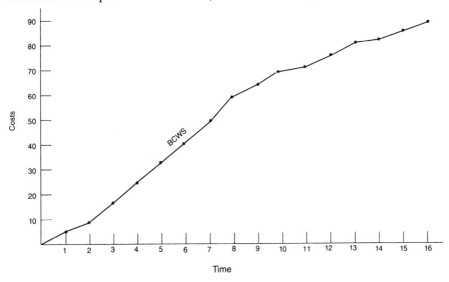

Data Capture at Timenow 4: The project has now started and the progress information is presented in the following format.

Activity Number	Actual Costs	Actual Start	Actual Finish	Percentage Complete	Remaining Duration
010	8000	3 Mar	-	66.6 %	-
030	0	1 Mar	2 Mar	100 %	-
040	3500	4 Mar	-	33.3%	-
120	7000	2 Mar	3 Mar	100%	-
130	1000	-	-	-	-
140	0	4 Mar	-	25%	-

Earned Value Table at Timenow 4: The earned value table provides a simple format to compare the baseline plan with the progress. The partly completed proforma should be completed as a self test.

Activity	BAC	BCWS	PC	BCWP	ACWP	SV	SV%	CV	CV%	EAC
010	9000		66.6%		8000					
020	2000		0		0					
030	1000		100%		0					
040	12000		33.3%		3500					
050	10000		0		0					
060	6000		0		0					
070	4000		0		0					
080	6000		0		0					
090	8000		0		0					
100	4000		0		0					
110	6000		0		0					
120	8000		100%		7000					
130	8000		0		1000					
140	4000		25%		0					
Totals	88000				19500					

Activity	BAC	BCWS	PC	BCWP	ACWP	SV	SV%	CV	CV%	EAC
010	9000	6000	66.6%	6000	8000	0	0	(2000)	(33.3%)	12000
020	2000	0	0	0	0	0	0	0	0	2000
030	1000	1000	100%	1000	0	0	0	1000	100%	1000
040	12000	8000	33.3%	4000	3500	(4000)	(50%)	500	12.5%	10500
050	10000	0	0	0	0	0	0	0	0	10000
060	6000	0	0	0	0	0	0	0	0	6000
070	4000	0	0	0	0	0	0	0	0	4000
080	6000	0	0	0	0	0	0	0	0	6000
090	8000	0	0	0	0	0	0	0	0	8000
100	4000	0	0	0	0	0	0	0	0	4000
110	6000	0	0	0	0	0	0	0	0	6000
120	8000	8000	100%	8000	7000	0	0	1000	12.5%	7000
130	8000	0	0	0	1000	0	0	(1000)	(100%)	8000
140	4000	2000	25%	1000	0	(1000)	(50%)	1000	100%	4000
Totals	88000	25000	22.7%	20000	19500	(5000)	(20%)	500	2.5%	88500

The Revised barchart at Timenow 4: The revised barchart and the Earned Value table, contain complementary information. When calculating the Revised barchart it is important to follow the activity logic through to completion.

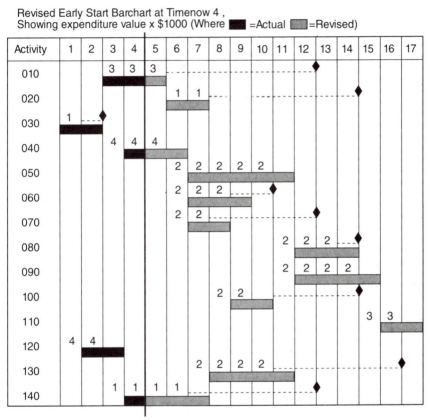

Revised Early Start Barchart at Timenow 4,
Showing expenditure value x $1000 (Where ■=Actual ▨=Revised)

Project Analysis at Timenow 4: The variance figures indicates that overall the project is late, but slightly under budget. The figures may be distorted, however, because activity 130 costs have been reported, although there appears to be no progress. This is a flag highlighting data that is conflicting and therefore needs checking.

Activity 040 is on the critical path and is one day late. The knock-on effect can be seen on the revised barchart. If this activity were crashed by 1 day this will bring the project's schedule back on course. The activity is under budget so there should be funds to cover any additional expenditure.

Data Capture at Timenow 8: The project has now progressed to Timenow 8.

Activity Number	Actual Costs	Actual Start	Actual Finish	Percentage Complete	Remaining Duration
010	11000	3 Mar	6 Mar	100 %	-
020	2000	7 Mar	8 Mar	100 %	-
030	2000	1 Mar	2 Mar	100 %	-
040	11500	4 Mar	6 Mar	100 %	-
050	7000	7 Mar	(crash)	50 %	2
060	4000	7 Mar	-	66.6 %	-
070	2500	8 Mar	-	50 %	-
100	1500	8 Mar	-	50 %	-
120	7000	2 Mar	3 Mar	100 %	-
130	1000	8 Mar	-	25 %	-
140	3500	4 Mar	7 Mar	100 %	-

The Earned Value Table at Timenow 8:

Activity	BAC	BCWS	PC	BCWP	ACWP	SV	SV%	CV	CV%	EAC
010	9000	9000	100%	9000	11000	0	0	(2000)	(22.2%)	11000
020	2000	2000	100%	2000	2000	0	0	0	0	2000
030	1000	1000	100%	1000	2000	0	0	(1000)	(100%)	2000
040	12000	12000	100%	12000	11500	0	0	500	(4.2%)	11500
050	10000	6000	50%	5000	7000	(1000)	(16.6%)	(2000)	(40%)	14000
060	6000	6000	66.6%	4000	4000	(2000)	(33.3%)	0	0	6000
070	4000	4000	50%	2000	2500	(2000)	(50%)	(500)	(25%)	5000
080	6000	0	0	0	0	0	0	0	0	6000
090	8000	0	0	0	0	0	0	0	0	8000
100	4000	2000	50%	2000	1500	0	0	500	25%	3000
110	6000	0	0	0	0	0	0	0	0	6000
120	8000	8000	100%	8000	7000	0	0	1000	12.5%	7000
130	8000	4000	25%	2000	3000	(2000)	(50%)	(1000)	(50%)	12000
140	4000	4000	100%	4000	3500	0	0	500	12.5%	3500
Totals	88000	58000	58%	51000	55000	(7000)	(12%)	(4000)	(7.8%)	97000

The Revised Barchart at Timenow 8:

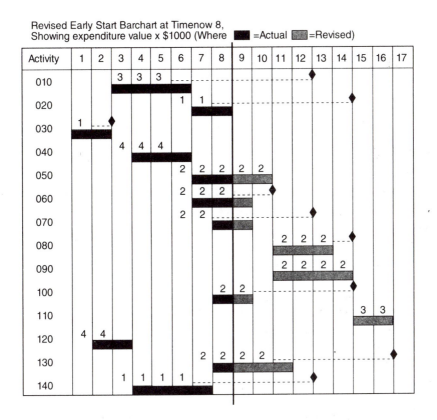

Revised Early Start Barchart at Timenow 8, Showing expenditure value x $1000 (Where ■=Actual ▨=Revised)

Project Analysis at Timenow 8: From the schedule and cost variances, overall the project is still late, but now the budget is over spent. The trends indicate SV% improving from (20%) to (12%), but CV% deteriorating from 2.5% to (7.8%). This is a flag to check productivity on activities 010, 050, 070 and 130. They are either under performing, the estimate was optimistic, or there are special circumstances.

Although the SV is negative the revised barchart indicates that the project will finish on time. The discrepancy is caused by activities with float running late. The negative cost variance indicates a need to apply control on activities 050, 070 and 130, to bring the project in on budget.

Bibliography

Adair J. Effective Leadership, Pan, 1988, ISBN 0-330-30230-2.

Begg D. Economics, McGraw-Hill, 1984, ISBN 0-07-084146-2

Belbin R. Management Teams, Heinemann, 1986, ISBN 0-434-90127-X.

Bergen S.A. Project Management, Basil Blackwell, 1986, ISBN 0-631-14706-3.

Blake R. & Mouton J. The Managerial Grid 111, Gulf, 1987, ISBN 0-87201-470-3.

Blanchard K. Leadership and the One Minute Manager, Fontana, 1985, ISBN 0-00-637080-2.

Cleland D. & King W. Systems Analysis and Project Management, McGraw-Hill, 1975.

Fellows R., Langford D. & Newcombe R. Urry S. Construction management in practice, Construction press, 1983, ISBN 0-582-30522-5.

Kerzner H. Project Management A Systems Approach to Planning, Scheduling, and Controlling, Van Nostrand Reinhold, 1984, ISBN 0-442-24879-2.

Knight A. & Silk D. Managing Information, McGraw Hill, 1990, ISBN 0-07-707086.

Levine H. Project Management Using Microcomputers. Osborne McGraw-Hill. 1986. ISBN 0-07-881221-6

Lock D. Project Management, Gower, 1988, ISBN 0-566-02818-2.

Lockyer K. Production Management, 1983, Pitman, ISBN 0-273-01771-3.

Meredith J. & Samuel J. Project Management A Managerial Approach, 1989, John Wiley, ISBN 0-471-50534-X.

Nolan V. Teamwork, Sphere, 1987, ISBN 0-7221-6411-4.

Palfreman J. & Swade D. The Dream Machine, BBC Books, 1991, ISBN 0-563-36221-9.

Schonberger R. & Knod E. Operational Management, Business publications, 1988, ISBN 0-256-05834-2.

Turner R., Anderson E., Grude K. & Haug T. Goal Directed Project Management, Kogan Page, 1984, ISBN 1-85091-734-5.

Wild R. Production and Operations Management, Holt, Rinehart and Winston, 1984. ISBN 0-03-910480-X.

Index

Forthcoming Titles
by Rory Burke

Project Manager's Guide to Computing

Featuring; Software selection, Hardware selection, Feasibility study, Training and Implementation.

Project Manager's Guide to Human Factors and Teambuilding

Featuring; Teambuilding, Organisation structures, Leadership, Motivation, Conflict, Delegation and Resistance to change.

Project Accounts

Featuring; Estimating, Financial feasibility, Cost codes, Cash flow, Discounted cash flow, Sources of finance, Escalation, Cost planning, Cost control, Cost reporting and Computer applications.